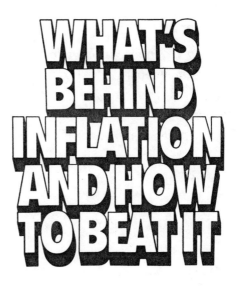
WHAT'S BEHIND INFLATION AND HOW TO BEAT IT

Also by George Jackson Eder

*Comparison of American Legislation on Bills of Exchange and
    Promissory Notes*
Current Trends in Argentine Trade
Taxation in Colombia
Inflation and Development in Latin America

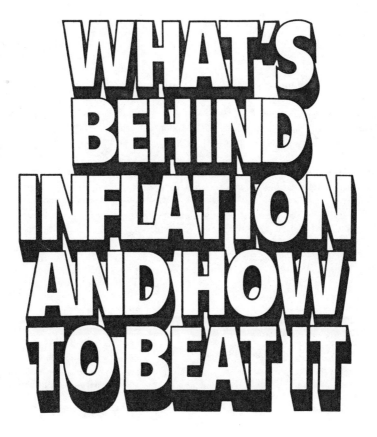

WHAT'S BEHIND INFLATION AND HOW TO BEAT IT

George Jackson Eder

Prentice-Hall, Inc., Englewood Cliffs, N.J.

The author expresses appreciation for permission to reprint excerpts or quotations from the following works:

Kemmerer on Money, by Edwin Walter Kemmerer. London: Routledge, 1934. Reprinted by permission of Routledge & Kegan Paul, Ltd., London, and John C. Winston Co., Philadelphia.

General Theory of Employment, Interest and Money, by John Maynard Keynes. London: Macmillan, 1936. Reprinted by permission of Harcourt Brace Jovanovich, Inc., New York, and Macmillan, London and Basingstroke.

The Collected Essays, Journalism and Letters of George Orwell. New York: Harcourt, Brace & World, Inc., 1968. Reprinted by permission of Harcourt Brace Jovanovich, Inc., New York.

The Age of Inflation, by Jacques Rueff, translated by A.H. Meeus and F.G. Clarke. Chicago: Regnery, 1963. Reprinted by permission of Editions Payot, Paris, and Regnery/Gateway, Inc., South Bend.

Economics of the Free Society, by Wilhelm Röpke, translated by P. M. Boarman. Chicago: Regnery, 1963. Reprinted by permission of Regnery/Gateway, Inc., South Bend.

What's Behind Inflation and How to Beat It
by George Jackson Eder
Copyright © 1979 by George Jackson Eder

Prentice-Hall International, Inc., London
Prentice-Hall of Australia, Pty. Ltd., Sydney
Prentice-Hall of Canada, Ltd., Toronto
Prentice-Hall of India Private Ltd., New Delhi
Prentice-Hall of Japan, Inc., Tokyo
Prentice-Hall of Southeast Asia Pte. Ltd., Singapore
Whitehall Books Limited, Wellington, New Zealand
10 9 8 7 6 5 4 3 2

Library of Congress Cataloging in Publication Data

Eder, George Jackson
　　What's behind inflation and how to beat it.

　　Includes index.
　　1. Inflation (Finance)　　2. Inflation (Finance)—
United States.　　I. Title.
HG229.E39　　332.4'1'0973　　79-13519
ISBN 0-13-952143-7

To the memory of M.G.E.

And swiche a blisse is ther betwix hem two
That save the joye that lasteth evermo
Ther is non lyke that any creature
Hath seyn or shal while that the world may dure.

Chaucer, "Man of Lawes Tale"

Contents

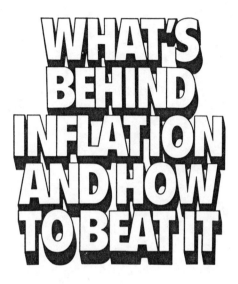

1. What to Do About Inflation

If to do were as easy as to know what were good to do, chapels had been churches and poor men's cottages princes' palaces. *The Merchant of Venice,* Act I, Scene ii

The whole purpose of this book is to explain what ought to be done about inflation—what you should do to protect yourself, and what the government should do to stop inflation.

And so Chapter 17—"How Can You Protect Yourself?"—describes the various investment media that can be used as a hedge against inflation, and points out the advantages and dangers of each. It mentions briefly the *total* hedge against inflation devised by Hugo Stinnes at the time of Germany's trillion-to-one inflationary catastrophe in 1923. But, as this approach is not within reach of most of us, the chapter discusses in greater detail the various investments that are open to all of us, whether as a hedge against further inflation or as a means of maximizing one's income so long as inflation persists.

Corporate and tax-exempt bonds are cited as providing a maximum return, although with no protection against the continuing decline in the purchasing power of the dollar. Likewise discussed are "convertible" bonds that one can exchange at any time for a fixed number of shares of common stock, thus providing a two-way hedge; bonds payable in Swiss francs (or German marks or Japanese yen); investments in common stocks, with their potentialities and risks; mutual funds, pointing out the advantages of "closed-end" funds as against the usual mutual funds; investments in gold, whether in gold bars or coins or "futures," or gold mine shares in South Africa or Canada; the purchase of commodity futures, diamonds, works of art or antiques; the possibilities in real estate, whether purchased as "income property" or for your own use and enjoyment.

In each case, the advantages and dangers are outlined. For there can be no perfect hedge or ideal investment so long as inflation continues uncontrolled.

1

So we come to an even more important subject—what must be done to stop inflation. Which means what the government must do, for there is little that we as individuals can do to put a stop to the inflationary spiral, which has been caused almost in its entirety—95 percent of it, as this book will show—by government spending financed by "printing-press money," whether in the shape of currency or of printed government IOUs which are bought by the Federal Reserve System or by private banks and thus added to the "money supply."

But, as it does not suffice to show what the government *should* do to stop inflation without at the same time showing how it *can* do it, as a practical political matter, that phase of the book is divided into two parts—Chapter 15, which tells what *must* be done, and Chapter 16, which tells *how it can be done.*

The figures—and the facts

It will be impossible, however, to understand fully the conclusions in those three "bottom-line" chapters—how you can protect yourself and what the government should and can do—unless you have a sufficient grasp of certain basic facts of economics bearing on the subject of inflation. And, incidentally, one function of this book is to expose with factual data the fallacies of Keynesian economics that have brought inflation and disaster to this country and to many other countries of the world—the false theories that high interest rates will attract investment and curb inflation; that stopping inflation means increased unemployment; that recession and unemployment can be cured by greater government expenditures while at the same time reducing taxes; and other egregious errors that are accepted as truisms by the majority of economics professors in this country and in England. But not in Germany, Japan, France and Switzerland—countries that have managed their economies so wisely that their currencies are the soundest in the world.

Nor will it be possible to understand the three "bottom-line" chapters unless you grasp the magnitude of our present dilemma and realize that all you may have read—all that the government has told you and that the newspapers have printed—with respect to government spending and the deficits in our balance of trade is false and misleading.

Did you know, for example, that the deficits of the Postal System, of Amtrak, and of seven "off-budget" agencies and 560 "government-sponsored" enterprises are not included in the budget, so that the total deficit in the proposed 1979–80 budget will not be $29 billion, but at least $60 billion? And that this figure represents only those outlays that will actually be expended in that year, while the President is asking Congress for authority to spend $630 billion, which will mean a deficit of $127 billion? And that even this figure does not include the losses of 567 nonbudgetary agencies nor losses on government-guarantied loans? As the administration's concept of a "lean" and "austere" budget contemplates expenditures of $630 billion, do you recall when President Johnson insisted that his first budget must be trimmed to under $100 billion—and that was in wartime—because he was convinced that to exceed that figure would mean political disaster?

Were you aware that the debt ceiling, which by law is *"permanently established"* at $400 billion, has been raised again and again until the present *"temporary"* legal limit now stands at $830 billion, while the *actual* debt, according to the 1979–80 budget, will be $899 billion, not counting government guaranties nor some $130 billion of obligations not included in the budget? And that this is only the tip of the iceberg, because the government has accumulated $9 trillion of concealed liabilities which are omitted from the admitted amount of our public debt and for which no funding provisions are included in the annual budgets. *Nine trillion dollars*—nearly double the value of everything we have in the United States: land, buildings, personal property, everything, whether owned by the government or by corporations or individuals!

Did you know, too, that, with the explosion in welfare costs that began with President Johnson's "Great Society" and is continuing apace, welfare is now the largest item in the federal budget, and that the 1979–80 budget calls for welfare appropriations of over $190 billion—nearly 40 percent greater than our total budget for national defense?

You could not have known this if you have relied on the government press releases or on the 88-page "Budget in Brief" that was handed out to the press. And even if you have delved through the four volumes and 2,205 pages of the 1980 Annual Budget, Budget Appendix, and Special Analysis, and the 306-page Economic Report of the President, you could not be sure of arriving at the true totals because the facts are concealed in such a way that only a highly knowledgeable staff of auditors could possibly separate truth from fiction. For example, a substantial chunk of United States foreign aid is hidden in the budget of the Department of Transportation. And, by another piece of budgetary legerdemain, foreign-aid outlays in the 1980 budget are shown at $6 billion, while the actual budget authority for foreign aid will total nearly $22 billion!

Did you realize that, because of a 1978 change in the method of computation, the official balance of payments figures show deficits of $15.3 billion and $16.0 billion (est.) in 1977 and 1978, while the true deficits, based on actual receipts and expenditures, were $21 billion and

$24.6 billion? And is it mere coincidence, or is it cause and effect, that federal government expenditures overseas in those two years were $21.2 billion and $26.7 billion respectively?

And, speaking of international trade and the balance of international payments, would you like to own stock in a department store where the manager reported to the stockholders, as sales, the merchandise that the manager and his family took from the shelves for their own use and never paid for? And when he also reported as sales the goods he gave away to friends free of charge, or on credit accounts that he never collected or could ever hope to collect?

Yet this is exactly what happens when the government figures for the balance of trade, and for the balance of international payments, include among the exports the shipments to American bases overseas, commissaries and personnel abroad, as well as to American diplomatic, consular and other officials in some 140 countries of the world, plus $22 billion of U.S. aid (1980 budget) which is either given away or "sold" to underdeveloped nations on credits at ridiculously low interest rates, and which can only be collected out of the proceeds of future loans or grants. And the $22 to $25 billion a year deficit in our balance of payments accounts for the fact that the gold and foreign exchange reserves that should stand behind the American dollar are now at a *minus* figure of at least $275 billion and perhaps double that amount. And the dollar, which was once worth four German marks, is now worth less than two German marks, with comparable depreciation in terms of Swiss francs, Japanese yen and other solid currencies, as well as in the purchasing power of the dollar at home and abroad.

How other countries have licked inflation

But this book would be fulfilling only half of its mission if it confined itself to revealing and denouncing these facts that the government has concealed from the general view through its accounting practices.

Much more important from the viewpoint of fighting our present inflation is to see how other countries—in seventeen instances in the course of the present century—have succeeded in licking inflation and paving the way for an economic recovery that can only be described as phenomenal. You will thus be made aware of the anti-inflationary methods employed by the great "monetary stabilizers" of the past—men such as Professor Edwin Kemmerer of Princeton and Drs. Hjalmar Schacht and Ludwig Erhard in Germany. And in each case you will see that inflation was stopped, not gradually and over a long period of time, but practically overnight, and that the process was in each case hailed as a "miracle."

Although, as one of the "miracle workers" has himself declared, the accomplishment was in fact no miracle but was precisely what was to have been expected as a consequence of the measures taken, and the only real miracle was that the governments in each of those cases had the foresight and the courage to take those steps that had to be taken—meaning the establishment of a free-market economy and the *total* elimination of government deficit spending at home and abroad—in the face of almost irresistible social and political pressure for price controls and increased government welfare expenditures.

In the one case where I was called upon to stop inflation in one South American country, although it is true that I was hailed as a "miracle worker" (*milagrero*), I must disclaim any credit for the accomplishment, for all I did was to follow in the footsteps of Dr. Schacht, whom I had met, and of my favorite personal mentor, Dr. Kemmerer. The only "miracle" was that I was able to persuade a revolutionary Marxist government to reverse practically everything it had done during the preceding four years in office.

Anti-inflationary measures in the United States
From the methods employed in the successful anti-inflationary programs in those seventeen instances and the analysis of what is now happening in the sound-money nations of Germany, Switzerland and Japan, contrasted with the disastrously Keynesian-oriented economies of Great Britain and elsewhere, as well as from the preliminary discussion of the economics of money and prices, it is made clear that the administration program to control inflation—the unworkable price and wage "standards," the counterproductive high interest rates, and the arrangements to borrow some $30 billion in marks, francs and yen that our balance of payments makes it impossible to repay—is doomed to failure. And that inflation in this country will not be overcome until we ditch the advice of those Keynesian economists who have led this country—and England and Latin America and much of the rest of the world—down the path of limitless government spending and inflation without end. And until we follow the old-fashioned economics of Drs. Kemmerer, Schacht, Erhard et al.

So you will see that you must read the first fourteen chapters in order to understand Chapters 15, 16 and 17, which tell you what you really want to know—what the government must and can do to stop inflation, and what you can do to protect yourself in the meanwhile.

And I must admit that you may find the following four chapters on economics rather heavy going, even though I have tried to follow the precept of St. Augustine, who, over fifteen hundred years ago, wrote that if one truly understands a subject, he should be able to explain it in terms so simple that it can be understood by anyone.

But if you prefer to avoid the tedium of economics altogether, then I advise you to begin with Chapters 6, 7 and 8, skip to Chapter 11 and continue to the end of the book. You may then be tempted to go back and see what you have been missing, in which event I feel sure you will have a much more complete grasp of *What's Behind Inflation and How to Beat It.*

2. The Curse of Paper Money

> Of all the instruments of mischief that the Devil ever invented, nothing was ever equal to paper money.
>
> William Cobbett, *The Curse of Paper Money* (1833)

Inflation!

Look back at the headlines from early 1973 right through to the present time: a group of militant housewives marching on Washington to protest the rising cost of meat and other foods, while their husbands had received pay raises of 20 to 50 percent over the previous three years; Congress, labor and pressure groups calling for more rigorous price controls and rollbacks, while demanding higher wages and excoriating President Nixon for attempting to cut back on welfare costs. The President announcing Phase 4 of price controls, while at the same time his closest economic adviser admitted that price controls were inequitable and that the administration goal was to go back to "that old-time religion—and balance the budget!" President Ford pinning "WIN" buttons on the lapels of his staff as the solution to the problem of inflation, while his Treasury Secretary turned the button upside down and read it: "No Immediate Miracle!"

And now President Carter waging an anti-inflation campaign coupled with an energy plan that he called the "Moral Equivalent of War" while one commentator pointed out that, although the President roared like a lion, his slogan spells "MEOW!" And the President's election campaign promised everything to everyone, with the result that he has given the nation its first $600 billion budget and the highest rate of inflation since President Truman.

It doesn't make sense, does it? No, of course it doesn't! Yet these are all sensible people, and President Nixon's and President Ford's advisers were at least as sensible as the pre-Nixon economists whose advice got us into this inflationary mess in the first place. While President Carter's economic advisers have not yet shown that they are capable of coming up with a more workable solution than their predecessors.

The money illusion

Why, then, do sensible people—the housewives, congressmen, labor leaders, the administration, the economists, the press—propose senseless, ineffective solutions? *Why?* It is the Money Illusion—the illusion that prices are going up. Whereas in reality it is the value of money that is going down. The problem is not one of *rising prices,* but of *debasement of the currency.*

Do you remember when Franklin Roosevelt changed the dollar price of gold from $20.67 an ounce to $35 an ounce—in other words, changed the intrinsic value of the dollar from 1/20 of an ounce of gold to 1/35 of an ounce? And after President Nixon raised the official price of gold to $42.2222 an ounce, dropping the dollar's value to less than 1/40 of an ounce of gold, and after Presidents Ford and Carter auctioned off part of our gold reserves for $165 to $240 an ounce, is it any wonder that our money will buy less than it used to? As Irving Fisher used to say, a big lump of gold will buy more than a small lump of gold. But the value of the dollar in terms of gold is not the sole factor in the situation, as we shall see later on in this discussion.

As long ago as 1928, Professor Irving Fisher of Yale, whom the economic historian Joseph Schumpeter characterized as the greatest of American economists, wrote a book under the title of *The Money Illusion.* In it Fisher described his visit to Germany in the year 1922, at a time when the German mark had dropped to 1/50 of its former value. No one he met—bankers, businessmen, housewives, economists—*no one* seemed to be conscious of the fact that the value of the mark had been dropping at a vertiginous rate. Everyone spoke of the unconscionable rise in prices. They blamed it on the United States.

It was easy enough for Americans and other foreigners to see that the mark *was* being depreciated—you could get 200 marks for $1.00 instead of 4 marks. But to the Germans, a mark was a mark was a mark. Businessmen figured their costs in marks and sold their goods at what they thought was a profit. They failed to realize that the marks they got for their goods were worth only a fiftieth of the marks that they had paid for them. It was not until the mark began to drop to a *millionth* and finally to a *trillionth* part of its former value that they began to realize that a mark itself was no longer a mark.

I had the same experience traveling in France, Belgium and Italy in 1923. Again and again, waiting in line to exchange my traveler's checks for francs or lire, others in the line would angrily accost me, accusing the United States of monopolizing world trade, of buying up all the goods in all the markets of the world and making prices go up in every other country, while at the same time raising the price of the dollar so that no one could buy anything in the United States.

Bank tellers glared at me, reflecting the views of their customers. No one seemed to be able to comprehend my explanation in French or improvised Italian that the dollar was the same as it had always been—that it was the lira and the franc that were worth a fraction of their former values. But to them, a franc was a franc was a franc. It was the dollar whose price we selfish Americans insisted on raising.

And conversely, the press in the United States is now complaining of "the rising yen," when it is not the yen that has risen but the dollar that has fallen.

Economics—new and old

Here it is appropriate to say a few words about economics—the "dismal science" or, more to the point, to use St. Paul's words to Timothy, "science falsely so-called."

For although it dresses itself up in mathematical symbols that would seem to ensure some degree of scientific exactitude to its conclusions, it is not a science but a series of philosophical speculations, some of them valid but few of them subject to proof except on the basis of assumptions as tenuous as the conclusions are positive. One of England's leading economists defines economics as "a branch of ethics striving to become a science."

When Adam Smith wrote *An Inquiry into the Nature and Causes of the Wealth of Nations* in 1776, the subject he taught at the University of Glasgow was "Moral Philosophy." And it is still known as Moral Philosophy in Glasgow University today, with no pretensions that the subject is a science in any proper sense of the word.

But, like other branches of philosophy, its study over the years has led to many conclusions that have stood the test of time, as well as to other conclusions that time has proved fallacious, ridiculous.

And, as in other philosophical and moral questions, the advocates of each passing theory have been just as intemperate and intolerant in supporting their ideas as their opponents have been in attacking them.

For nearly two hundred years, the ideas of Adam Smith and his predecessors had been refined, polished, improved—new ideas added and old ones discarded—until at last a body of economic thought had been built up that had stood the test of time and was, in general, widely accepted except by such iconoclasts as Henry George and Karl Marx and their respective disciples.

This was the old economics—the classical economics formulated by Adam Smith (1723–90), John Stuart Mill (1806–73), Alfred Marshall (1842–1924) and Irving Fisher (1867–1947), to mention only a few of the outstanding economists in this country and in England.

And then, in 1936, John Maynard Keynes abandoned the classical concepts he had laid down in his two-volume *Treatise on Money,* and published *The General Theory of Employment, Interest and Money,* which revolutionized economic thinking throughout the world, and particularly in England, the United States, Scandinavia and Latin America—"The New Economics."

More of the New Economics anon. But, as the subject of this essay is inflation, we had better start with a definition of that term—not a "scientific" definition so abstruse as to be practically incomprehensible, but a popular definition that will suit our purpose.

Inflation defined

The word "inflation" is an apt one, well chosen and graphic. When we think of a rubber balloon inflated bigger and bigger, it gives a pretty good picture of prices rising higher and higher. And that is what inflation is. Not that all prices rise simultaneously or in the same degree. Some prices—the price of polyester fiber and of long-distance telephone service or computer time, for example—actually go down dramatically while other prices are rising. But the general price level—the total cost of all the things and services that people buy—goes up sharply and rapidly.

Rapidly—that is the key word. No one is concerned with the fact that some six hundred years ago one could buy a cow for a shilling, or that two loaves of bread could be had for a farthing. It is when meat prices go up from a dollar and a half to two dollars in a few months, and when we can remember that not so long ago the same cut of beef cost a dollar, that people start to complain, demanding that something be done to stop the inflation.

Inflation, then, may be defined as an increase in the general price level for goods and services occurring over a relatively brief period of time.

Past inflation since 1776

The analogy of the rubber balloon does not work so well on the down side. When a balloon is inflated to the bursting point, it deflates completely—to zero. Prices never do.

It is true that in the past, up to World War II, prices have generally fallen after an inflationary boom to nearly the preinflation level. For example, taking the 1910–14 level as par—100 on the wholesale price index—prices rose from a little below par just before the American Revolution to well over 200 during the Revolutionary War, then slumped again to below 100 right after the war; they rose again to over 180 during the War of 1812, then dropped to well below 100 in the 1830s and 1840s; up again to nearly 200 in the Civil War, then down to far below 100 at the turn of the century; up again to over 200 in World War I, and down below 100 in 1932.

But after World War II and the Korean and Vietnam wars, there has been no return to prewar levels, *nor is there any likelihood that we shall ever see 1910–14 price levels again.* You must remember that the dollar is no longer the same dollar that it was in pre-Roosevelt days. It is officially worth 11.367 grains of gold and not 23.22 grains, a drop of 51 percent. And at auction only a fraction of that value. Yet that is only a small part of the story as we shall see.

Furthermore, it would be an unmitigated disaster if the price level did drop to its pre-World War I level—a tragedy that would make the 1929–32 depression look like prosperity. But that's another story.

Kinds of inflation

The second thing we must remember in defining inflation is that there are two kinds, defined by economists according to their origin. There is *wage-push* or *cost-push* inflation—in other words, an inflation caused by wages and other costs going up faster than the increase in labor's productivity.

It is easy to see that if the farmer has to pay higher wages and higher prices for fertilizer, farm equipment and other costs, and if wages and other expenses in the processing plants, transportation industry and grocery stores all go up at the same time, food prices for the consumer are bound to be higher.

And no one is really to blame. There's not a thing the government or anyone else can do about it. There's no use blaming labor for wanting higher wages. Aren't most of us getting higher wages or salaries or income than we did five years, ten years ago? On the average, the food chains make a profit of only half a cent on each dollar of sales and food takes only about a sixth of our income today compared with one quarter of our income a generation ago.

Would we want to go back to our 1969 or 1974 income levels? If not, can we really complain if the cost of living is higher than it used to be? Especially as this kind of inflation—the wage-push kind—is nearly always gradual and never reaches the extremes that the other kind of inflation sometimes attains.

The other kind of inflation is what economists call *demand-pull* inflation, often described as too many dollars chasing too few goods—too much money to spend and no increase, or very little increase, in the quantity of goods or services to spend it on. Or sometimes—as in the case of the Arab embargo on oil—a decrease in the quantity of goods available and no diminution in the demand.

In part, of course, demand-pull inflation stems from wage increases—wage earners have more money to spend and they spend it. It is a spiral and, in economics, all spirals are vicious, whether up or down.

But that part of the pressure behind a demand-pull inflation is really just wage-push inflation looked at from another angle. And, in general, this kind of demand-pull inflation also works so gradually and to such a limited extent that it seldom poses a major problem—at least no problem that cannot be solved by the steady increase in production efficiency in farms, mines and factories, attributable to capital investment and innovation, features that have characterized the American economy for two hundred years and show no sign of abating.

It is when the demand-pull inflation is the result of government spending, and deficit budgets financed with printing-press money, that it can come with such extreme rapidity that it totally disrupts a nation's economy.

But one kind of inflation begets another. Higher prices caused by government deficit financing mean that labor naturally demands higher wages to meet the rise in the cost of living, which then gives us a dose of wage-push inflation. And higher wages upset the government budget—and so on, in the vicious spiral that we are suffering from today.

Which came first—the chicken or the egg? In this case, as we shall see, the original sin can be traced to the government. This country's dynamic economy can take wage-push pressures in its stride so long as the government does not throw its monkey wrench into the machinery.

3. The Classical Theory of Money

Popular familiarity with money . . . makes everyone a monetary expert . . . without being handicapped by any knowledge of the elementary principles of economics or the facts of economic history.

Edwin Walter Kemmerer (1934)

This chapter is intended to refresh your memory in the event that you have forgotten your college economics or, if you had the misfortune of being indoctrinated exclusively in Keynesian economics, to give you what the late Professor Kemmerer called the elementary principles of economics and the facts of economic history.

In the first place, as demand-pull inflation has to do with the quantity of money that is chasing a given quantity of goods, this is a good place to mention the quantity theory of money—the theory that the quantity of money affects its value and hence its purchasing power in exchange for goods and services. I shan't try to explain the theory in full, as economists are still battling over the question of what it means and what it doesn't mean—the struggle between the "monetarists" and the "structuralists" and the "fiscalists"—i.e., those who emphasize the money supply, or the nation's economic structure, or the government budget, as the key factor in the economy.

"Equation of Exchange"

Irving Fisher used what is known as the "Equation of Exchange" to illustrate the meaning of the quantity theory of money. He modestly disclaimed credit for its invention, which can be traced back to the astronomer, Simon Newcomb, a professor of mathematics at Annapolis and Johns Hopkins. But Professor Fisher certainly deserves credit for its general acceptance, and no one today doubts its validity, although some economists question its utility.

The equation, as formulated by Fisher, is simple, and as significant, as Einstein's $E = mc^2$—viz. $MV = PT$.

In this equation, M stands for the quantity of money in circulation; V the velocity or efficiency of monetary circulation, the number of times a dollar can turn over in any given period and perform its job.

This side of the equation, money times velocity, is bound to equal T—the number of transactions, i.e., the quantity of goods and services bought and sold—multiplied by P, the general price level. That is a truism. It cannot be otherwise.

The equation, as I say, is accepted by all economists, although it is sometimes refined by using the sign ⇌, meaning "equivalent to," instead of the = sign, meaning "equal to." More important, most economists use $M_1 V_1$ which includes the total amount in the checking accounts in the nation's banks, as checks are far more important than cash in the purchase of goods and services. Currency in circulation, plus commercial bank deposits, gives us what is generally known as the "Money Supply"—a useful term that we shall use again and again.

There has been considerable debate as to what other forms of substitute currency should be included, and the International Monetary Fund uses savings bank deposits as "quasi-money." It would seem to me that, in this country at least, if we are going to include the savings bank deposits as "quasi-money," we should also include charge accounts, installment sales and credit cards—some $280 billion of such money, compared with some $1,300 billion of all other kinds of money and quasi-money. The Federal Reserve System uses M_1, M_2, M_3, and M_5, corresponding to five different definitions of the money supply—refinements that we need not go into in this book. Actually, with automatic transfers from savings to checking accounts and other innovations, M_3 gives a truer picture of the "monetary aggregates" than M_1, and the Fed is on the verge of abandoning that conventional measure.

All in all, it is evident that a far larger amount of the nation's business is carried on with checks and other forms of currency substitutes than with currency itself, but this is not to say that Professor Fisher was unaware of that fact. He simply thought it more sensible to use M to indicate all forms of money and money substitutes, rather than complicate the equation by writing $MV + M_1 V_1 + M_2 V_2$, etc. $= PT$.

The importance of the money equation—and let us stick to the simple form—is that if M, the volume of money in circulation, is increased, then either V, the velocity of circulation, will be diminished, or else the quantity of goods and services sold (T), or the price at which they are sold (P), must increase. Simple arithmetic: M times V $=$ P times T.

Now, experience has shown that the velocity of money varies very little or very slowly from one period to another. It used to be considered axiomatic that V always remained practically constant, but in recent years this has not proved true. And nowadays, with the increasing use of credit cards and computerized debits and credits in one's bank accounts for the payment of bills, and other money substitutes, a given quantity of money in circulation can perform a great deal more work than in the past. But, in any event, V is *relatively* constant and is not greatly or quickly affected by changes in the money supply.

Now, T—the number of transactions, or the quantity of goods and services bought and sold—is another factor in the equation that, aside from seasonal trends, varies gradually, following the long-term trend of an almost constant increase in the gross national product and the rising demand for goods and services as the American people become more and more affluent.

Thus, an increase in M—say, adding \$50 or \$100 billion to the present \$360 billion money supply (M_1), as the government does with its deficit financing—will not automatically increase T, the volume of goods and services. It would not induce even the most philoprogenitive hen to lay two eggs a day instead of one, nor would fishermen net any more fish from the sea, nor the mines and factories produce any more goods as a direct and immediate consequence of an increase in M.

That leaves only P as the one volatile, easily movable factor in the money equation when M is increased. And, as a matter of fact, it has been proved again and again in every country of the world that when the government prints more paper money, or the banks greatly expand their credit lines, it is P—the general price level for goods and services—that goes up almost immediately as a consequence.

That, in short, is what inflation is all about.

The fuel of inflation

The great engine of inflation, or perhaps I should say the fuel for the inflationary motor, is printing-press money. And for that, the government and the government alone is to blame.

Bank credit and other forms of credit expand and contract to meet the rising and falling demands of the nation's business. When T, the number of transactions, increases, the volume of bank credit, charge accounts, credit card debits will expand commensurately. And if bank and commercial credits increase at the same rate as T, there is no pressure on P, the price level.

True, there have been occasions in our history when bank and other credit has expanded unduly and given us a temporary dose of the inflationary virus.

In the 1914–20 period, when all Europe was suffering from paper money inflation, we underwent a period of credit inflation generated by the creation of the Federal Reserve System. That expansion made it possible for American industry to supply the Allied powers with the war matériel they needed, and later to equip our own troops. But it also led to the crash of 1920–21 when sugar plummeted from over 23 cents a pound down to below 5 cents a pound in less than six months, and kept on going down to less than 2 cents, far below the cost of production. Other primary products followed suit.

But on the whole the only source of unlimited money expansion in the United States is the federal government borrowing from the banks and the Federal Reserve System. For the government, unlike individuals and corporations, can continue spending beyond its means indefinitely—at the expense of the whole economy.

The different kinds of money

When money is gold or silver—or tin, as it once was in Bolivia and in ancient Britain—there is no way in which a government can create more money except through the slow process of buying or mining the precious metal and minting it into coins. But gold, silver and tin are bulky, and even though the United States was on a fixed gold standard from 1837 until 1933, comparatively little business was transacted in actual gold.

Instead, there were gold certificates, each note certifying to the fact that there was deposited in the Treasury of the United States $10—or whatever the denomination of the note was—in gold, payable to the bearer on demand. Only the Federal Reserve System can legally hold gold certificates today—like warehouse receipts for the gold stored at Fort Knox.

That kind of paper money was a convenience and not inflationary—it was as good as gold. Or at least its inflationary impact was limited, for it is true that the Act of 1863 which first authorized the gold certificates did provide that they could be issued up to 20 percent in excess of the amount of gold deposited in the Treasury. We shall come to bank notes later—paper money not issued by the Treasury, but by the banks.

Aside from gold coins and gold certificates, we have always had subsidiary currency—silver, nickel and copper—and in this country silver has always been a subsidiary currency despite the efforts of the "silver bloc" states in the nineteenth century to make it a primary currency along with gold, at a fixed ratio of sixteen ounces of silver for one of gold. That proved an impossible dream—the value of gold and the value of silver fluctuate independently according to the worldwide supply and demand for each metal, regardless of what the government may decree. And when, under President Lyndon Johnson, the value of the dollar was so debased that the silver content in the one-dollar coins was worth more than the face value, silver was withdrawn from circulation, first by those who could melt the silver coins down or hoard them, and second by the government.

That gave us a vivid demonstration of Gresham's law—bad money drives out good (Sir Thomas Gresham, 1519–79). The "bad money"—the steadily depreciating paper dollar—drove out the "good money"—the sterling silver coins we used to have. Now our "silver" currency is fake—a sandwich of nickel and copper—and those red-rimmed coins will always be a reminder of the utter debasement of our money. Our copper coins may also someday become extinct if the dollar sinks much lower in value.

In any event there is a limit to the amount of coins that the public is willing to accept—some 10 percent of the total currency circulation of nearly $100 billion. So that subsidiary currency has never become a major instrument of inflation in this country.

Elsewhere in the world, the excess coinage of silver did in fact break up the very successful pre-World War I European Monetary Union when certain countries found they could make quite a profit by minting silver money that, under the rules of the EMU, had to be accepted at par in every other country of the Union. The EMU was a splendid arrangement that made it possible to travel between France and Italy, Belgium, Switzerland, etc., without worrying about foreign exchange or foreign money.

Certain of the European countries may be on the verge of reviving this system. In 1979 six of the nine Common Market nations (Belgium, Denmark, France, Luxembourg, the Netherlands and West Germany) established the European Monetary System, creating the "ecu"—the European Currency Unit—as the unit of account, with the six local currencies allowed to fluctuate within 2¼ percent from the centrally fixed foreign exchange rate. The remaining Common Market countries (England, Ireland, Italy) may join the system at a later date and, eventually, one might hope that the ecu will be minted as an actual monetary unit and not merely an abstract accounting concept. In which event, it might then circulate as freely throughout Europe as did the golden ecu first coined by Louis IX (St. Louis) in the thirteenth century.

The silver certificates

In the United States, from the old gold standard days until silver was withdrawn from circulation, one-dollar bills were almost exclusively "silver certificates," each one certifying that "There is on deposit in the Treasury of the United States One Dollar in Silver Payable to the Bearer on Demand." These, too, were not inflationary, being merely a more convenient form of subsidiary currency.

Probably few Americans noticed that, when the silver coins and silver certificates were withdrawn from circulation by President Johnson, the new Treasury bills bore the inscription: "The United States of America Will Pay to the Bearer on Demand One Dollar"—about as inane a promise as any government has ever made to its deluded citizens. Payable in what? More paper dollars?

But perhaps few Americans have ever noted that, until comparatively recently, when the Treasury bills were replaced by Federal Reserve Notes, the one-dollar bills bore the inscription "In God We Trust," but we didn't trust God for five dollars or any higher amount. The Federal Reserve System now trusts Him up to $100—no more.

This brings us to the subject of bank notes and the question of how far we—and God—ought to trust the Federal Reserve System.

Paper money

In the old days, prior to World War I and for some time thereafter, the national banks were permitted to issue bank notes, and those notes formed the greater part of the paper money in circulation. It was profitable business for the banks, as even the smallest banks in the country could invest in certain United States bonds that paid 2 to 3 percent interest, and then issue their own bank notes, engraved by the Bureau of Printing and Engraving, for the same amount, thus putting their money to double use.

Later, in 1913, Congress passed and President Thomas W. Wilson, sometimes known as "Woodrow Wilson," signed the Federal Reserve Act, which gave rise to two new forms of paper money—the Federal Reserve Bank Notes and the Federal Reserve Notes. Only the latter are now outstanding.

Some economists consider these bank notes, as well as the old national bank notes, to be inflationary, while political scientists have pointed out that under the Constitution only Congress has the right "To coin Money [and] regulate the Value thereof." Paper money should be backed 100 percent by gold, they say—and that would certainly have avoided the inflationary excesses that the world has known ever since paper money was first invented.

But most students of the subject today agree that the economic development of this country would have been severely hampered had it not been for bank credit to farmers, manufacturers, retailers and others, and that "bank money," including that issued under the Federal Reserve Act, has been a major factor in the progress of this country over the past hundred years.

So long as the Federal Reserve Notes and bank notes were issued chiefly as a means of providing credit to the privately owned national and state banks, so that they in turn could extend credit to their customers, the paper money was not normally inflationary. It was "elastic" or "flexible," with the volume of notes rising or falling according to the volume of trade. In other words, the T of the monetary equation—the quantity of transactions—absorbed the increase in M (money), without provoking a rise in P (the price level). Velocity remained practically constant all through those good old days.

Although the Federal Reserve Board has been rightly criticized for its failure to take timely action to forestall, or at least limit, the extent of the 1929–32 depression, and although it has been claimed that a flexible currency is apt to exaggerate the booms and slumps in the economy, there are few economists or bankers today who would like to see the system abolished. Most people would agree that the Fed has been on the whole consistently well managed, and has done an excellent job within the limits of its authority.

The invisible hand

Now, back to the "old economics" and the "new economics," and the differences between them. What has been said thus far about money and the money equation would be accepted, with minor refinements of wording, by economists of every political coloration. In fact, the differences between Keynesians and anti-Keynesians, between economists of the old and new schools, are peripheral. In perhaps 80 percent of the body of economic thought, there is no substantial conflict of views, although academic economists will continue to argue about how many angels can stand on the point of a pin, as is natural among students of moral philosophy.

But in the matter of inflation, money and prices, the subject of this study, the cleavage between new and old is abysmal.

Bear in mind that "old" is not necessarily obsolete, and that "new" is not necessarily superior to "old." Some people still believe that Bach, Beethoven and Brahms are better than the Beatles—or even better than Barber, Britten or Bartók.

Briefly, the old economics held that prices and wages are self-regulating. And, in the Equation of Exchange, wages are a part of P, i.e., the price paid for personal services. If prices go up too high, people will buy less and prices will fall. If prices drop too low, people will stop producing and prices will rise. If wages rise too far or too fast, employment will drop and wages will fall. If wages fall far enough, people will start employing more laborers for tasks they could not have afforded when wage rates were higher—getting the crab grass out of the lawn, for example.

In this best of all possible worlds, there was an "invisible hand" that governed all these things more effectively, more wisely, than any individual or any government could plan. All that was necessary was that the government must keep its cotton-picking fingers out of the machinery.

There could be no such thing as unemployment if wages were allowed to drop far enough—say to ten cents a day. And there could be no such thing as overproduction, for whatever was produced meant that someone was paid wages or received income for that production, and this income would mean enough effective demand to absorb whatever was produced—Say's Law (Jean-Baptiste Say, 1767–1832). There could, of course, be excess production of some particular product, but general overproduction was an impossibility. True, there is probably no postulate in economics that has been so furiously debated as Say's Law, with scarcely two economists in agreement as to just what Say said, nor whether what he said was valid or not. But we need not go into that here.

For those who are surfeited by the overabundance of material things, production, as Say defined it, does not have to be in goods—it could be a sonnet or a sonata.

What about the effect of the invisible hand on wages? That's another thing. True, if wages are low enough, there will never be any unemployment, at least in theory. But can anyone believe that wages in this country should be allowed to drop until every last person who is without a job, and wants to work, finds employment? And can farmers and manufacturers be expected to continue producing and selling at a loss until the invisible hand manages to adjust matters and bring everything into equilibrium again? Sometimes that invisible hand works in a most dilatory way its wonders to perform.

These are what the economists refer to as the "rigidities" of the price system—rigidities on the downward side. And although labor unions have certainly contributed to forcing wages and prices up, they can hardly be blamed for not acquiescing in wage cuts sufficiently drastic to do away with unemployment. How far down would they have to go?

Nor can businessmen be blamed for refusing to sell at prices that are not sufficient to cover their costs. To the contrary, there is no reason whatsoever why a manufacturer or anyone else should be prohibited from charging whatever he wishes for his products or services. If a candy manufacturer wants to charge $10 a pound for his chocolates, or a baker $2 for a loaf of bread, or if a hairdresser charges $75 for a permanent, or a plasterer $40 an hour, there is no reason why anyone should interfere. For there, indeed, is where the invisible hand takes over. The limiting factor is the price that customers are willing to pay for such products or services.

Monopolies in restraint of trade

Adam Smith and John Stuart Mill have told us that if ever you see two or more merchants or manufacturers conferring together, you may be sure they are concocting some scheme to restrict production, raise prices, or divide markets.

But today in the United States combinations among producers or others to maintain prices, regardless of supply and demand, are illegal and properly so. Our antitrust legislation, despite its manifold defects, is generally recognized as having been one of the factors responsible for the tremendous economic growth of this country in this century. More recently, similar legislation has been a key element in the astounding development of West Germany over the past thirty years.

But antitrust legislation does not apply to labor unions and, even without the unions, it would be unrealistic to expect workers to accept for their services whatever they can get, according to the laws of untrammeled supply and demand.

The consequence is that a business recession does not bring a drop in wages—as it would if there were an absolutely free market—but a rise in unemployment. So that when the economists speak of rigidities on the downward side, they are thinking chiefly in terms of the rigidity of wage rates. And those of us who realize that high wages, *and low wage costs per unit of output*, have been the secret of this country's past prosperity may well be thankful for that rigidity.

On the upward side, unless wages rise faster than is warranted by increased productivity and are kept at artificially high levels—which probably would not happen were it not for labor union interference with the invisible hand of the free market—they would not normally result in either higher prices or unemployment.

This oversimplification of classical economic principles may make it sound as though the old-school economists were a particularly unrealistic lot of theorists. Could they really have believed in the invisible hand of a free-market economy adjusting everything for the best in this best of all possible worlds—in labor willingly accepting lower wages when demand slackened, in manufacturers and others automatically increasing wages when demand increased, and in the impossibility of general overproduction?

Of course not. The classical economists were at least as intelligent, at least as realistic as their modern counterparts. But they were attempting to work out the general principles of *economic theory*, a task they performed so well that this body of theory constitutes the basis of perhaps 80 percent of all economic theory today, and should serve as the guideline to practical political action in the world of reality.

But in Adam Smith's time labor did not pack the political clout that it does today. So that in times of stress labor did accept, was forced to accept, starvation wages that were worse than slavery. That is why Adam Smith launched his most devastating thunderbolts against the manufacturers and merchants and their conspiracy to interfere with the invisible hand accomplishing its task of increasing the wealth of nations.

Later economists, still in the classical mold, continued to direct their attacks against the price-fixing monopolies of merchants and manufacturers. And in the United States these attacks were responsible for the antitrust legislation that helped to make this country the most dynamic, most prosperous nation in the world.

Or at least it was the most prosperous until, drunk with our own affluence, we squandered our wealth in a messianic desire to save the world through such ill-fated enterprises as the Alliance for Progress, the Bay of Pigs, and the Vietnam War.

Arthritis in the invisible hand

When the 1929–32 crash and the New Deal destroyed, at least temporarily, the monopoly power of industry and of Wall Street, and put a permanent crimp in the public-be-damned attitude of big business, the labor unions moved into the vacuum of power. And it was not long before some of the classical economists began to launch their attacks on the excessive wage demands and slowdown tactics of labor, and on labor's political power which prevented the invisible hand from doing its stuff. For if there is one axiom on which all classical economists are united, it is Lord Acton's warning that "if there is any presumption, it is ... against holders of power, increasing as the power increases. ... Power tends to corrupt and absolute power corrupts absolutely."

But by that time, there were so many government interferences with the economy, not only in the United States but elsewhere, that the free market no longer worked as freely as it should, and the world's economies were managed by government controls ranging from the absolute dictatorships of Nazi Germany, Fascist Italy, and Communist Russia, to the negotiated regulations of the NRA and other alphabetized agencies of the New Deal.

4. The New Economics

It is astonishing what foolish things one can believe
if one thinks too long alone, particularly in economics.

John Maynard Keynes (1936)

By this time, too, the new economics of John Maynard Keynes and his disciples began to take over the economic thinking of most of the free world. Keynes's *General Theory of Employment, Interest and Money* appeared in 1936, and was as revolutionary in its consequences as Adam Smith's *An Inquiry into the Nature and Causes of the Wealth of Nations* (1776), or Charles Darwin's *Origin of Species* (1859), or Sigmund Freud's *Studien über Hysterie* (1895).

The Gospel according to Keynes

In its essentials, so far as this study of inflation is concerned—for the New Economics is too vast a subject to be boiled down into a few pages—the Keynesian Gospel, as developed and refined by the Master and his Disciples, comes down to five points: (1) the alleged interconnection between employment and money, leading to the belief that inflation inevitably brings more employment and that stable prices or deflation mean more unemployment; (2) that an increase in interest rates will attract investment, internationally as well as at home; (3) that savings and investment are not necessarily equal quantities, two sides of the same coin as it were, because, from an economic point of view, when someone invests his savings by banking them or buying stocks or bonds or other property from someone else, there is no increase in the national investment, just a switch from one owner to another; (4) that, consequently, there is a gap between individual or corporate saving and increased real investment, and this, it is alleged, is the cause of unemployment and recession, so the way to prevent recession and unemployment is for the government to take up the slack by spending more and more, without increasing taxes — and even lowering taxes in order to increase government "investment" without reducing private spending or investment; and (5) that this government deficit spending is not inflationary because of the "multiplier effect" which means, according to the New Economics, that every dollar "invested" by the government creates two or more dollars of increased aggregate investment, because these dollars will be paid to someone else who will pay them to someone else, and so on in ever-widening circles like the ripples on a pond.

Of course, some economists, such as the late Willford Ishbell King, the father of the national income accounts in the United States, have said that, to the extent that Keynesian economics is valid, it is not new, and to the extent that it is new, it is not valid. And this book will show that, of the five Keynesian postulates, only the third is in fact valid.

But, to be fair, Keynes was an extraordinary and highly original man, and his contributions to economics have revolutionized, for better or worse, not only economic thinking but political action in the United States, England, much of Western Europe, and all of Latin America. To be even more fair, there is scarcely a single new idea in Keynes' *magnum opus* which was not anticipated by Lauchlin Currie, whose name is all but forgotten outside of Latin America, and in this country is unfortunately and unfairly linked with that of the late Harry Dexter White, allegedly a "Communist."

But it was Keynes's genius that put the theories all together in a new Gospel, and through the genius of Paul Samuelson and his fabulous million-copy, ten-edition textbook, *Economics*, this Gospel has been indoctrinated into the minds of practically every economist in the United States since 1951. And, through the international student body of the London School of Economics and Political Science, it has spread like wildfire throughout Latin America, where practically every economist in the universities, the finance ministries, the central banks, and the development agencies is a dyed-in-the-wool Keynesian.

In the course of spreading the Gospel according to John Maynard, his Apostles have been forced to attack the fallacies and heresies of the nonbelievers, the classical economists, and in so doing have come up with what the classical economists would consider the even more egregious fallacies and heresies of the new faith.

The "fallacy of composition"

The Keynesians sometimes begin their books, therefore, with a little discussion of the "fallacy of composition"—the belief that, because something is helpful or harmful to an individual, it is therefore necessarily helpful or harmful to society or the nation as a whole.

As an example, Professor Samuelson begins his book by pointing out that if one person stands on tiptoes to watch a parade, he may see it better, but that, if everyone stands on tiptoes, no one will see it any better. From this he deduces that "what is prudent behavior for an individual or a single business firm may at times be *folly* for a nation or a state." And he gives six examples which may or may not be true, or which may be true under certain circumstances but not in others, but which his students and the students of his students accept as Gospel truth under all circumstances.

So indoctrinated are they in the new faith that they cry "fallacy of composition" if anyone argues that some action that would obviously be harmful to us as individuals might likewise be harmful to society in the aggregate.

Never stop spending

From this, of course, they deduce that, although it is folly for an individual to keep on spending more than he earns, it would be folly for a government *not* to spend more than it takes in through taxation, whenever unemployment reaches more than some arbitrary level—say 4 percent—because of the Keynesian connection between money, employment, interest rates and prosperity. And, because of the alleged multiplier effect, government spending is not inflationary.

What a bonanza that idea has been to profligate governments all over the world! They no longer have to tax and tax, spend and spend. They can spend and spend, borrow and borrow at the central bank, and still reap a harvest of votes at the next election from the grateful recipients of welfare and other forms of government largess.

It is in Latin America that this new Gospel has been most enthusiastically received, and in one South American country, which shall remain nameless, a new Minister of Finance, a brilliant graduate of the London School of Economics, announced to the legislature that "we shall no longer have *unplanned* deficits which in the past have led to inflation and depreciation of the peso; we shall have a *planned* deficit, and this will not be inflationary"—or words to that effect. (The peso was once worth $1 U.S., and at the time of the speech it was worth 10 cents; now less than 2½ cents in depreciated American money will buy you a peso).

The speech was welcomed with resounding cheers. And the speaker went on from his country's Finance Ministry to even higher honors as chairman of the Inter-American Committee on the Alliance for Progress. As a result, his Keynesian ideas have taken root, not in one Latin American country alone, but throughout the hemisphere, largely at the expense of the American taxpayer.

This incident is reminiscent of the time, in August 1923, when the

German Reichstag was complaining of the "shortage of money" and the President of the Reichsbank assured the legislators that the bank was going to print bank notes in higher denominations, and would soon be able to issue *in a single day* an amount in bank notes equivalent to two thirds of the then total circulation. Note circulation then stood at 63 quatrillion (fifteen zeros)! The announcement was greeted with wild applause.

Yet the German and Latin American legislators were men of intelligence, and so was the Latin American dignitary who insisted that a *planned* deficit would not be inflationary.

What difference it makes whether a deficit is planned or unplanned eludes me. But it does not escape my recognition that the only way a central bank can lend money to the government is to print it, and keep on printing and printing while the government spends and spends. Or create a bank deposit out of thin air in exchange for the government's IOUs. And in every South American country, save oil-rich Venezuela, this policy has brought monetary debasement, the flight of capital and economic disaster.

Budget magic

The United States, since the early 1960s, has taken a leaf from the Latin American book—or from the Book of Keynes—and has not only been printing money or creating bank deposit money hand over fist but has copied the Latin American nations by concealing or at least minimizing the budget deficit by the simple expedient of removing some $30 to $50 billion of deficit items from the budget entirely, including "off-budget" agencies and losses on government-guaranteed loans—a sort of bikini accounting that seems to reveal everything while concealing the essential.

Fannie Mae, Ginnie Mae and Freddie Mac—as the Federal National Mortgage Association, the Government National Mortgage Association and the Federal Home Mortgage Corporation are familiarly known—are not included in the federal budget. Nor are the Federal Land Banks, Federal Intermediate Credit Banks, Banks for Cooperatives, Federal Home Loan Banks, or the Student Loan Marketing Association (with over a billion dollars in defaulted loans), the Export-Import Bank (up to 1978), the TVA, REA, Amtrak (with nearly a billion dollars in guarantied loans) and the Federal Financing Bank. The last-named agency borrows on behalf of the Postal System, the Farmers Home Administration, the Export-Import Bank, the Environmental Financing Authority, the U.S. Railway Association and other federal agencies.

Imagine concealing the deficits and the borrowing of the Postal System by excluding the post office operations from the federal budget and reporting its debt anonymously as part of the indebtedness of a practically unknown and certainly unpublicized "bank." Have you, a well-read and intelligent person, ever heard of the Federal Financing Bank? It is down in the budget for $13.9 billion for 1979–80, more than twice the amount budgeted for all the battleships, aircraft carriers, submarines and other vessels of the United States Navy, plus over $50 billion in borrowed money. And the Postal Service had an *admitted* deficit of $688 million in fiscal 1977, *excluding* government appropriations of $1.7 billion—a real deficit of $2.4 billion, while the 1980 budget calls for expenditures of $1.7 billion, the actual future deficits being a matter for surmise. Talk about bikini accounting!

During the same fiscal year, 1977, Amtrak (the National Railroad Passenger Corporation) had a *published* net loss of $536 million in fiscal 1977, not included in the government deficit and not counting federal operating subsidies and grants of some $1.7 billion and Treasury-guarantied loans of $900 million that Amtrak cannot pay. And the General Accounting Office reports that, because of mismanagement, the cost of repairing the New York–Boston lines will not be $1.7 billion, as originally estimated, nor $2.4 billion, as the administration admits, but $3.65 billion! It would take a staff of a hundred qualified investigators to go through the entire gamut of federal government and agency spending and unearth equally glaring examples of bikini accounting in practically every area.

The outstanding debt of the various federal agencies added up to over $180 billion at the end of 1978, approximately a quarter of the gross public debt of the United States, not counting the unrevealed total of government-guarantied indebtedness of agencies, municipalities and individuals that the Treasury must make good in event of default—an event that is eventuating with increasing frequency. Moreover, the unfunded, unconfessed liabilities of the federal government under its inflation-escalated military and civilian pension plans, and under the present welfare aspects of Social Security (more on this in Chapter 14), are not included in the budget figures for the national debt—omissions that, if perpetrated by any private corporation, would send the perpetrators to jail for life.

President Ford's Assistant for Economic Affairs informed the author that his advisers believed it proper to exclude the federal lending agencies from the budget and national debt because their loans could be regarded as "investments" that would in time be repaid. But he admitted that the pressure of agency financing on the capital market tended to force up interest rates and create a credit "crunch" just as much as Treasury financing.

And, certainly, when the Postal Service deficits are paid for by the Federal Financing Bank, they can hardly be regarded as "investments," and when the defaults on the lending agency loans are reaching alarming proportions—it costs the government some $500,000 *a day* for maintenance charges alone on the houses whose mortgages have been foreclosed, and there are some 800,000 foreclosures a month—it is clear that Congress and the public are entitled to a franker disclosure of the government's debts and deficits.

When this double set of government accounts was first set up— one for routine expenditures and one for "investments"—there was at least some plausible justification for the distinction. There was no expectation that the emergency loans made by the original federal financing institutions under FDR would be defaulted, and it was only natural not to include their lending operations as expenditures in the general budget. But political interference and mismanagement under seven subsequent administrations were inevitable, and defaults have mounted—even in the Export-Import Bank, whose 1977 Annual Report to Congress boasts that no loans were written off during the year. But their balance sheet shows $328 million of delinquent loans, and it is only by reading the notes to the accounts that one learns that the total of defaulted loans adds up to $571 million, a default ratio of over 5 percent. And nowhere in the report do they reveal the amount of loans written off as uncollectible. Bikini accounting—yet Eximbank is certainly one of the best managed of all the federal lending agencies.

At the least, therefore, the defaulted loans and deficits of *all* federal agencies, rigorously defined by proper accounting practices such as those the SEC and the Fed insist upon in the case of private enterprises, should be charged to the general budget. And now that not only the lending institutions but the Postal System, TVA, Amtrak and other operating agencies are omitted from both the budget and the debt ceiling, the duplicitous accounting practices of the federal government are reduced to absurdity. Another leaf taken from the Latin American book where every country maintains two sets of accounts and includes the most extravagant and unprofitable government enterprises and buildings among its "investments."

The credit crunch

Of course, from the viewpoint of monetary stability—the soundness of the dollar—any outlay of funds not covered by revenues but financed by bank borrowing is monetized (added to the money supply) and hence inflationary.

In 1978 new Treasury and agency securities floated in the money and capital markets added up to $89.5 billion, the issues of state and local governments combined to $48.6 billion—a total of $138 billion in new governmental issues. By comparison, *all the domestic corporation stocks and bonds combined floated in the market in that year amounted to only $46.5 billion (est.), and one quarter of that amount was for refunding—only $35 billion (est.) of new corporate financing.*

This flood of federal, state and municipal financing has practically monopolized the available supply of money on the security markets, forcing up interest rates for everyone—corporations, homeowners, private borrowers. The Council of Economic Advisers, with the usual governmental bikini accounting, attempts to minimize the impact of government borrowing by comparing the amount of federal financing, not with the total amount of new issues floated on the *securities* market, but with the total of all funds borrowed in all *credit* markets, including mortgages, installment sales, retail charge accounts, etc., so that they can show that federal financing (in which they fail to include government-guaranteed borrowing) only takes 16.5 percent (est.) of the available funds. It should be obvious, however, that when a corporation tries to raise money through the sale of stocks and bonds, it is competing with other *securities* and not with *retail credit,* etc.

Lenders are now becoming aware of the fact that lending money at 10 percent when annual inflation is higher than that figure means that in reality they are charging a negative rate of interest. So don't blame the Federal Reserve Board alone for higher interest rates. The Fed is helpless in the face of the avalanche of government spending and borrowing and the consequent inflation. The true explanation of high interest rates and the stagnation in residential building and business investment in general is to be found in the overwhelming amount of new governmental borrowing competing for the lenders' dollars. And it is to corporate financing that we must look for any real increase in domestic fuel production, and in other productive investment, industrial production, jobs and national prosperity.

Corporations have done their best to meet the capital funds shortage by distributing an ever-shrinking percentage of their net profits to the shareholders, and plowing back into the business an ever-increasing percentage and dollar amount of those profits. In 1970 cash dividends amounted to $24.7 billion and undistributed profits to $14.6 billion— 37 percent of after-tax income. By 1978 dividends had risen to $49.3 billion, in depreciated dollars, while undistributed profits plowed back into productive use were $68.9 billion—58 percent of net income.

But vast additional amounts of capital investment are needed if we are to finance new sources of fuel and recover from the prevailing depression, with more jobs and more prosperity for all. And sufficient new money cannot be obtained so long as the United States Government and its multiple agencies, as well as the states and the cities, are driving interest rates up and drying up the securities market for new issues, with their ever-mounting deficit spending and borrowing.

The "full-employment" budget

Along with the now-you-see-it-now-you-don't magic of concealed federal expenditures, our Keynesian economic advisers have introduced another modern miracle—the full-employment budget. Instead of trying to reach a balanced budget by balancing expected revenues against expected expenditures, they calculate what the revenues would be *if* there were full employment, with every industrial and other plant working at full capacity.

"Full employment" used to be arbitrarily defined in terms of a 4 percent unemployment rate. At present, "high employment," as the new budgeteers now call it, is computed at 5.1 percent. On that basis, instead of a $29 billion officially admitted budget deficit in fiscal 1979–80 (actual total deficit, $127 billion), the deficit will only be $8 billion! Thus we can keep on spending and spending with nary a worry as to the future. The 1979 Budget Report used a 4.9 percent unemployment figure to represent "high employment," declining to 4.7 percent by 1983 and, on that basis, it confidently predicted a "high-employment" surplus of $65 billion for that year. The 1980 Budget Report predicts an unemployment rate of 4.8 percent by the end of 1984, but prudently omits a prognostication of the alleged "high-employment" surplus at that time.

Our government wizards believe that if the government *spends* at a full capacity level, it will automatically get the country to *work* at full capacity and government revenues will then catch up with expenditures— as though the fact that you can *pull* a toy wagon with a piece of string means you can *push* it with a piece of string.

Much as if the family wage earner were to say: "Let's spend $15,000 this year. Of course, I shan't earn that much because I'll only be working 150 days this year, but if I *were* working 365 days, eight hours a day, I would be earning $15,000. So let's spend it, and buy that new automobile."

Outraged cries of "fallacy of composition" from the Keynesians. Governments can wave their hands, say *hoc est corpus* or *abracadabra* and work a miracle; individuals can't. It's all because of the multiplier effect; when the government spends a dollar, it creates two dollars or more of increased investment and purchasing power.

This sounds like hocus-pocus to the old-fashioned economist who, from long observation of governments at home and abroad, would be inclined to say that the dollar left in the hands of private individuals or corporations is more likely to be wisely spent and fruitfully invested—the multiplier effect—than the dollar wrung from him by taxation or created by the printing press, and then squandered by the government.

For remember—governments do not create wealth. They can only rob Peter to pay Paul through taxation, or rob Peter and Paul alike through printing-press money and inflation.

Lesh have a li'l more inflashun

Anyway, the Keynesians argue, inflation, at least a mild inflation of 5 percent or 4 percent, like another little drink, won't do you any harm. Samuelson has come down from the 5 percent a year advocated in his first edition to the 2 percent he suggests in his ninth, but he has been equally positive in proclaiming the benefits of mild inflation in each successive edition.

Inflation won't hurt, the Keynesians tell us, because what one person loses by inflation, another gains. It makes things easier for the debtor—his wages go up and he can pay in 50-cent dollars what he borrowed in 100-cent dollars. And harder for the creditor—he gets paid in 50-cent dollars what he lent in 100-cent dollars.

The profit and loss balance out. Society as a whole loses nothing from inflation. If prices go up, so do wages. If creditors—the rich—lose, then debtors—the poor—gain, unless it is galloping inflation, which not even the Keynesians approve of. They fail to tell us, however, how once an inflationary government gets the bit in its teeth, you are going to keep it down to a walk and not have it take over, hell bent for leather.

One might as well argue that society loses nothing when the crook, the bank robber, the embezzler ply their trades. Robbery merely transfers money to the needy poor from the comparatively rich.

The evils of inflation

Inflation robs more millions of people of more billions of dollars than the combined activities of all the embezzlers, gangsters and crooks put together. The value of every savings bank account, insurance policy, retirement pension—the reward of hard work and thrift—is diminished and, over the long run, practically wiped out.

Even a 3.4 percent drop in the purchasing power of money, such as occurred in 1972, if continued year after year—and 3 to 4 percent is well within acceptable Keynesian limits—is confiscatory.

An inflationary rate of 3 percent a year means that the dollar one saves at the age of twenty will be worth 25 cents when he retires at the age of sixty-five. And, over the long run, 3 percent is a normal return on savings accounts; it is higher than the return on insurance policies and nearly as high as that on real estate investments after taxes. Thus, at 3 percent inflation, the interest on one's investment is close to a negative rate of return. How Samuelson could have once argued for 5 percent inflation is beyond me.

It is only debtors who profit from inflation. And the biggest debtor of all, the biggest profiteer, is the government! Perhaps the only good thing you can say about inflation is that it enables every American to live in a more expensive neighborhood without having to move.

Even corporations, with their huge bonded indebtedness, lose by inflation because, although they can pay off their bonds with cheaper dollars, they also pay income tax, year after year, on "profits" which to some extent, perhaps entirely, are not really profits, but losses disguised by the fact that the dollars they use in their accounting are worth less year after year.

The stock of goods they sell at a net bookkeeping profit of 10 percent may cost them more to replenish than their gross selling price, and they may actually have a 10 percent loss instead of a profit, although their accounts will never show it. The investment in plant and machinery for which they may charge depreciation at the rate of 5 percent a year may cost them three times the amount of their investment to replace at the end of twenty years. Hence, public utilities and other companies with heavy capital investment may actually be subject to piecemeal confiscation, although their books may show a profit every year, and they must pay income tax on that psuedo-profit. That certainly was the case during the inflationary decade from 1941 through 1950, and has proved true again in every year since 1972.

Inflation and the "bottom line"

In 1978, for the first time, the Securities and Exchange Commission required corporations to report—either in their annual reports or in the 10-K forms filed with the SEC—what their balance sheets and operating results would look like if their annual accruals to depreciation were shown at present replacement costs instead of at a percentage of original cost.

Most corporate managements refrained from including this information in the annual reports to stockholders, believing it to be misleading. But Exxon, the largest of the oil companies, in the 1977 "Notes to Financial Statements" (not in the 1978 report), gave "historical costs" (book values on a conventional accounting basis) and "replacement costs" (present-day values, estimated for the most part by applying appropriate price indexes to the book values). On the whole, based on a study of those data and of the annual reports and 10-K forms of six major oil companies that I have examined, I would say that, from an investment viewpoint, replacement cost analysis is of no practical value whatsoever in the case of the oil companies, because of the nature of the depreciation and depletion allowances that are standard accounting procedure in that industry, and the impossibility of placing a fair value on properties where a $50 million exploration investment may in one case prove to be a bonanza and in another a total loss.

On the other hand, I would say that, in the case of the public utilities and of most industrial companies, it gives a more realistic perspective on true earnings if the annual charge for depreciation is computed on the basis of present-day replacement costs, no matter how theoretical and subjective such estimates may be, rather than using the conventional accounting basis of historic cost, which assumes that plant and equipment can eventually be replaced at the costs of ten or thirty years ago. And this view is supported by a 1979 proposal of the Financial Accounting Standards Board—the official rule-making body of the accounting profession— which will require publicly held corporations to provide supplemental earnings data on an inflation-corrected basis, beginning in 1980.

Remember that "generally accepted accounting principles" assume a reasonably stable value for the currency in which the accounts are stated and that, with technological improvement, good management can take a moderate degree of inflation in its stride. But if inflation is a continuing process, even at as low a rate as 4 percent per annum, prices will double in eighteen years—less than the average depreciation accounting "service life" of the plant and equipment in most companies. And if a company then computes its depreciation expense on the basis of historic cost, and prices its goods or services on that basis, it is really digging into capital—a piecemeal erosion of its investment.

But for anyone who has not had long experience in a country where continuous and steep inflation is the rule, it is hard to escape the fallacies of the "Money Illusion" and to grasp that a dollar is no longer a dollar.

I have examined the annual reports and 10-K forms of twenty-three representative companies, and I would say that the manufacturing companies whose 10-K reports I studied were in decidedly better shape than the utilities, with an average "bottom line" of $5.28 earnings per share according to the books, and $2.85 on a replacement cost basis. Whereas the utilities showed an average bottom line of $3.30 according to the books, and only 84 cents with expenses computed on a replacement cost basis, meaning that the companies had to dip into capital to pay dividends and, in some cases, to pay interest on their obligations.

Industrials are also in a better situation than the utilities because their prices are in general not subject to regulation, and even a long-continued inflation is not necessarily a threat to their solvency. In fact, it would practically wipe out their long-term debts, although it would indeed entail a shortage of working capital—an inevitable concomitant of inflation.

Industry, mining, trade, all suffer from this succession of feast and famine. In every country where inflation has become deep-rooted, businessmen have complained of a shortage of working capital and investment capital. But under the influence of the Money Illusion, they have failed to realize that the profits they have shown on their books are not truly profits, and that when they have paid out dividends from these pseudo-profits they have really been eating piecemeal into their capital, all because of the debasement of the currency. For the individual, inflation robs him of all incentive to save and to provide for the future. Yet thrift is the basis of investment, and investment is the foundation of economic growth and prosperity.

The growth of the gross national product is dependent upon private investment in business, and business investment in new plant and equipment. The nation's total need for additional capital investment in business, agriculture, mining, oil, gas, power, etc., is estimated at some $5 trillion over the next ten years (not allowing for further inflation). This is three times the capital needs of the previous decade. And it compares with a total present worth of all the assets in the country today—land, buildings, machinery, household goods, clothing, everything—estimated at some $5.7 trillion.

The Commerce Department estimates that new fixed investment in business each year should average 12 percent of GNP. Yet our actual scale of business investment in 1978 was only 6.9 percent per annum, and one tenth of that investment is devoted to meeting health, safety and environmental goals—desirable ends, but contributing nothing to the expansion of plant or increased productivity, i.e., to the long-term growth of GNP.

The growth rate in investment in constant dollars—not its percentage of GNP—has dropped from 8 percent per annum in the five-year period 1964–68 to 3.9 percent in 1969–73 to 2.7 percent in 1974–78. As a consequence, the growth rate in GNP has dropped from 4.8 percent per annum to 3.3 percent to 1.7 percent over the same periods.

Using a different measure of investment, the OECD (formerly

OOEC) reports that the United States now ranks seventh among the major industrial countries in average private investment as a percentage of GNP—after Japan, Germany, France, Canada, and even after Italy and the United Kingdom with their notoriously depressed economies. And seventh, too, in the average annual growth in productivity (output per man-hour), with an average improvement in the United States of 3.3 percent per annum contrasted with 10.7 percent in Japan!

An American "think tank," the Hudson Institute, after completing a study of nineteen leading industrial countries, concludes that the larger the government sector, the slower the rate of real growth of the national economy, basically because government "investment" is not productive and crowds out productive private investment. And inflation has been the inevitable consequence of government "investment" throughout the so-called free world.

Fallacies in the Keynesian thesis

But, the Keynesians argue, they are not advocating a perpetual merry-go-round of government spending and borrowing, but continuous, never-ending prosperity ensured by government deficit spending whenever unemployment reaches a certain level. But this ignores the fact that practically nowhere in history has any government that has become accustomed to spending beyond its means during a depression voluntarily cut down on its spending when good times return and tax revenues increase. That, in all countries of the world, this overspending has invariably produced an increase in the money supply and inflation. And that no country has ever been able to keep inflation within prescribed limits, so long as a deficit spending policy is followed; that, on the contrary, the controlled inflation of today becomes the galloping inflation of tomorrow.

But, say some economists, it is always possible to escape the ill effects of inflation by making all contracts in terms of a cost of living index—"indexation," they call it. Wages, pensions, insurance policies, savings deposits, could all be made payable, not in a fixed number of dollars, but in an amount that would vary from month to month or day to day according to the fluctuations of some generally accepted index of the value of the dollar. Prices in the stores and supermarkets, the prices agreed upon for the delivery of steel, building materials, textiles, automobiles, shoe repairs, wages, rents—everything—would have to vary in accordance with that index, so that no one would lose. It's all so simple!

But what about the hundreds of billions of dollars of existing contracts—life insurance, mortgages, corporate bonds? And people who don't travel around with an IBM computer in their pockets might not find index number contracts and supermarket shopping quite so simple, and might conclude that an economist must be a fellow whose business it is to make a mess of things and then make a wreck out of the mess. That is what some Keynesian economists did in Chile some forty years ago—tied all wages to a cost of living index—and it proved to be the worst inflationary device ever invented, with wages and prices chasing one another in a mad spiral that is continuing to this very day. And we are now copying the Chilean example in wages, pensions and Social Security!

Not many years ago, one of America's outstanding economists, Professor Milton Friedman of the University of Chicago, after a brief trip to Brazil, came back with this inflationary idea from Latin America and is the man largely responsible for giving currency to the idea of "indexation," of tying all prices to index numbers—an idea that might appeal to a theoretical economist but, if he realized what havoc inflation and indexing have wreaked in Brazil and elsewhere in South America, he might have some misgivings about applying the same system to our own economy.

Why not simply aim for a reasonably stable dollar and a reasonably stable level of prices? That might not be wholly attainable—unless we adopt the method suggested in Chapter 18—but at least we could hope to come closer to achieving it if that is our goal, rather than if we aim at a constant "mild" inflation, with computerized daily adjustments in wages and prices.

Employment and prices

But, say the new economists—and this is the clincher, based on the alleged tie-up between money, prices and employment—we must make a choice between a little, mild inflation with full employment, or price stability with unemployment. And they "prove" the connection between employment and a rise in prices and wages with a device called the "Phillips curve," invented some twenty years ago by a former professor at the London School of Economics.

The Phillips curve is a line drawn on a chart with the percentage of unemployed shown horizontally at the bottom of the chart, and the percentage rise in wages and prices shown vertically at the side of the chart. Obviously, the chart being drawn the way it is, if your eye follows the curved line, you will see that the higher the percentage rise in wages and prices, the lower the percentage of unemployment, and vice versa.

But nothing is *proved* by drawing a picture on a piece of paper, and I could cite dozens of instances, including the present situation, where the actual facts of inflation and unemployment thumbed their noses at Professor Phillips and behaved exactly the opposite of the way his celebrated curve says they should behave.

I found, however, that the bright young economics students at The University of Michigan were so indoctrinated by their Keynesian professors that they were practically hypnotized by the curved line and were utterly bewildered when a visiting Harvard professor of economics, Gottfried Haberler, too old to be a Keynesian, told them things that left them aghast—"contrary to everything we have ever been taught." And contrary to at least 229 learned discussions—perhaps hundreds more—of the Phillips curve published over the past twenty years.

At a panel discussion at the U of M, headed by two university economists—not run-of-the-mill teachers, but two of the outstanding economics professors in the country—one of the speakers pointed to the great success of President Johnson's Keynesian economic advisers.

Government spending and the federal deficit had been increased by billions of dollars and, as a consequence, he said, unemployment in the country was lower than it had ever been before. Someone in the audience objected that Italy had a balanced budget, yet unemployment in Italy was even lower than in the United States. Another person in the audience—the economist of the United Auto Workers—interjected that the Italian unemployment problem had been solved by the fact that so many thousands of Italian workers had been shipped to Germany, where there was such a terrific rise in production that they were importing laborers from all over the world. The chief panelist on the stage accepted and elaborated on this explanation.

So I rose to inquire whether the low unemployment figure in the United States might not be similarly explained, not by the budget deficit and Keynesian economics, but by the fact that 300,000 Americans (this was in March 1967) had been taken from the work force and shipped to Vietnam—with the added advantage, from a strictly economic viewpoint, that many of these people would never return to the work force.

No, said the panelist, 300,000 workers represent too small a percentage of the total labor force to be significant. It is the budget deficit that in accordance with Keynesian doctrine had been responsible for the drop in unemployment.

I did not pursue the question. The audience had not come to hear me, but the two distinguished economists and a beloved Michigan congresswoman on the podium. But I might very well have added that 300,000 workers represent a very significant figure when compared to the number of *unemployed*; that it was a far higher figure than the number of Italians working in Germany; that 300,000 soldiers in Vietnam meant several times that number of workers in the United States producing war equipment; that unemployment had always been practically nonexistent in wartime; and that Germany, with a balanced budget, was enjoying the greatest period of prosperity it had ever known, with unemployment nil despite the thousands of workers imported from elsewhere in Europe and even from Asia Minor.

This points up how unfair it was to put all the blame for the sticky high rate of unemployment on President Nixon, considering that he brought home from Vietnam over 500,000 young men looking for jobs. And, in all, reduced the size of the Army and of the number of workers in the defense industries by 2.5 million.

The fallacy of the Phillips curve

When the Michigan discussion took place in the spring of 1967, the further escalation of the Vietnam War and its gradual de-escalation under President Nixon were unknown eventualities. But I might have added—if I had been making a speech and not merely posing a question as a well-behaved member of the audience—that there was no proof, Phillips curve or no Phillips curve, of any inevitable connection between employment and inflation, although there was indeed a distinct connection between government deficit spending and a rise in prices. The more the government spent, to the extent that the extra spending came from government borrowing and was not taken from the citizens through taxation, the greater the money supply and hence the demand for goods, and the higher prices would rise—demand-pull inflation. And the more prices rose, the more the government had to spend just to keep even—a vicious spiral if ever there was one.

I might also have pointed out that, during one of the greatest periods of expansion, prosperity and high employment this country has ever known—the years from 1923 to 1929—the Bureau of Labor Statistics wholesale price index remained practically stable, actually dropped a bit, in fact. While, at the end of Franklin Roosevelt's second term, after seven years of deficit financing ("pump-priming," as Roosevelt called it) and a rise in prices never before or since equaled in this country in time of peace (22.3 percent in a single year), unemployment remained at 14 percent and did not drop to more manageable levels until after the outbreak of World War II.

Moreover, in other countries of the world, particularly in Latin America, long periods of inflation had been accompanied by disastrous economic crisis and unemployment (or underemployment), and, conversely, periods of virtually stable prices were at the same time marked by rising prosperity and diminishing unemployment.

The 1977 annual report of the Inter-American Development Bank contains a statistical summary of its member countries showing the rise in

GDP (gross domestic product) and in consumer prices for various periods. For 1971–76, the latest period shown, I find that the three countries that had the highest rate of growth of GDP (Venezuela, Honduras, Panama), averaging 4.3 percent per annum, had the lowest rate of increase in the price level, 6.2 percent p.a. The three countries having the highest rate of inflation (Chile, Argentina, Uruguay), averaging 154 percent p.a., had the lowest rate of production growth, 1.4 percent p.a. And unemployment, of course, in all countries of the world, is a corollary of a low rate of production growth.

Ten years ago, following Germany's remarkable economic recovery in 1948–58 after that country had put a stop to its skyrocketing inflation (see Chapter 7), the then president of Germany's central bank told a group of bankers at the Federal Reserve Bank of New York:

> *There are perhaps two principal lessons to be learned from the German experience. The first is that currency stability can be achieved and preserved, even under the most adverse circumstances. The second, and even more significant, is that a monetary policy firmly committed to currency stability not only does not conflict with a high rate of economic growth but indeed is essential to its achievement.*

So the Phillips curve, the alleged trade-off between inflation and economic growth and high employment, is utter nonsense, notwithstanding which the professors in their ivory towers keep feeding it to their students and, worse still, to the press, the politicians and the public.

Six centuries ago, William of Ockham (1285–1349) laid down as a rule of logical reasoning the "law of parsimony," the principle that no more causes or forces should be assumed than are necessary to account for the facts (*pluralites non est ponenda sine necessitate*—complexity must not be assumed without necessity). This rule came to be known as "Ockham's razor" because with it he cut down the fallacies of other philosophers of his time. And it has never lost its validity to this day. If there are several possible explanations of any fact or phenomenon, the simplest and most obvious explanation is most likely to be the valid one.

Why, then, search for some abstruse relationship between prices and employment, and seek to prove that relationship with Phillips curves and other theoretical props, when the facts show that, except in time of war or war's aftermath, there is no necessary correlation between a rising price level and low unemployment? That, from the beginning of recorded history, war has always brought scarcities, high prices and full employment—a correlation that is obvious, simple, logical and "parsimonious."

The choice is not between inflation with little unemployment or price stability with high unemployment, as the Keynesians tell us. The choice for us is between having 500,000 American soldiers in Vietnam with little unemployment at home, or the soldiers back home with fairly high unemployment until they can get settled. Which do you prefer?

And, throughout the world, inflation has in fact—except in wartime—brought with it a drop in investment and production and a rise in unemployment, aggravated—not alleviated—by government spending programs.

5. Some Facts and Fallacies

Intellectuals are no more dishonest than other people, but their resources for self-deception are greater.
George Orwell (1945)

The facts, of course, are the things I believe; the fallacies are what those who call themselves "intellectuals" believe, with their vastly greater capacity for self-deception. And you will notice that in this book, as author, I invariably win my arguments against the intellectuals on points or by knockout. With that explanation out of the way, let's get down to some of the current fallacies in economic thinking.

So far as inflation is concerned, the major fallacy is that there is any necessary link between inflation and growth, that if we want to stop inflation we must put up with a certain amount of economic stagnation and unemployment—the fallacy of the Phillips curve adumbrated in Chapter 4. There is no such tie-up, no such trade-off. In fact, the contrary is true. A stop to inflation, if brought about by the methods urged in this book in Chapters 15 and 16, would mean an almost instantaneous end to economic stagnation and a slower but certain drop in unemployment—the "miracle" of monetary stabilization demonstrated in Chapters 7 and 8.

There are also the fallacies of foreign aid and other major fallacies discussed in Chapter 11 and elsewhere, all of which have a major bearing on the current inflation in the United States.

The present chapter has to do with rather minor fallacies, with the "tools" of economic analysis, if you will, and these should be borne in mind when reading about the facts and figures of inflation and growth. One example is index numbers.

Index numbers
The more complex index numbers are, the less accurate and—while they may serve a useful purpose to those familiar with their method of compilation—the more dangerous they are for the layman to use. The price

indexes for primary products, the staple commodities of world trade, are reasonably reliable because the commodities used are identical or practically the same from one decade to another, such as electrolytic copper, raw sugar of 96° polarization, cotton of specified staple lengths, standard grades for wheat and coffee and so forth.

There can be some argument as to the weights used for each commodity—its changing importance as people shift from cotton, wool or silk to the synthetic fibers, or from copper and steel to aluminum and plastics—and as to whether to use the weights prevalent in the base period (the Laspeyres formula) or the weights proper for the current period (the Paasche formula) or Fisher's "Ideal Index." And the computation of the index must be mathematically valid (such as a weighted aggregative), not like some of the popular stock market indexes which are not.

The "Dow," for example, is a mathematical absurdity based on a simple arithmetical average of the market quotations for thirty stocks. Under this simplistic computation, a high-priced stock is given double the weight of a stock selling at half that price. So that if, for example, Eastman Kodak—which reached a high of 151 in 1960–76—drops 65 percent in value, as it did, and if 1960–76 highs are used as a base, that drop would show up as twice as important as a 65 percent rise in AT&T, which sold at a high of 75 in 1960–76. And the Dow would drop, not rise, even though AT&T's assets are double those of Eastman, its earnings seven times as large, and its importance as an investment medium perhaps twenty times as great.

Serious students of the market use the Standard & Poor's or the NYSE index, not the Dow as a guide—"Holier than Dow," as it were. And so, from December 1977 to December 1978, the first two indexes (industrial) went up 3.65 percent and 5.7 percent respectively, while the Dow Industrials dropped 13.3 percent, which is misleading. But brokers must follow the Dow because their customers do, and because the popular predominance of the Dow index and of the mathematically untenable Dow theory is such that they actually influence market behavior over the short term at least.

Even with respect to the mathematically correct commodity price indexes, one must be wary. The Bureau of Labor Statistics wholesale price index is beyond doubt the best and most reliable of all the general price indexes and the only one that can be used for long-term comparisons. So it is significant that the annual report of the Council of Economic Advisers, transmitted to Congress in January 1978 as the Economic Report of the President, shows the wholesale price index for "all commodities" up 92.2 percent in December 1977 compared with the 1967 base year.

But it is even more significant—and shocking—that the CEA annual report for 1979 drops the wholesale price index for "all commodities" and substitutes a "producers' price index" for "totally finished goods," which enables the administration to claim that prices only went up 85.5 percent in December 1977, and 102.4 percent by December 1978, from the 1967 base year. Whereas if they had used the traditional "all commodities" index—which is the only one that can be used for comparison with the FDR, Truman and Nixon-Ford inflationary periods—they would have to confess that prices had gone up 98.2 percent and 117.4 percent, respectively. Avoiding that admission, they simply dropped from the index the raw materials which had gone up 151 percent. And, as raw materials are the only items that are subject to monetary controls, the raw material sector of the index is the truest measure of the debasement of the dollar.

The Federal Reserve Bulletin, following the administration lead, has likewise displaced the old wholesale price index and similarly shows only the producers' price index for finished goods, compounding the deception by heading the columns: "Producers' Prices, formerly Wholesale Prices."

To find the historical wholesale price index for all commodities, one must turn to the Survey of Current Business, whose compilers faithfully give the old figures as well as the new. Here, as elsewhere, the government's bikini accounting is seldom to be attributed to the hardworking and competent bureaucrats who compile the statistics, but to the use made of those statistics by our political leaders.

Furthermore, even when using the traditional wholesale price index, one must ask whether there is any identity between the commodities used in the index today and those used ten years ago or even five years ago. I can recall when Pennsylvania Vacuum Cup Tire Company put out its then amazing 3,000-mile guaranty; today, 40,000-mile guaranties are not uncommon. If tire prices have risen tenfold—and they haven't—is there really any increase in the price of tires? Or a decrease? What resemblance is there between the long johns of yesteryear and the shorts and panties of today? Between silk stockings and nylon; between the $300 Ford of 1923 and the $5,000 Ford of 1978; or between the TV sets and cameras of today and those on the market even five years ago? Perhaps some of the price rise shown in the index should really be shown as a price drop. Although, conversely, I can think of dozens of products on the market that are inferior to those of ten or twenty years ago. So better take even the best of the index figures with a grain of salt.

When it comes to the more general indexes, such as the consumer or cost of living series, one must be even more skeptical. It is silly to worry about fractional gains or losses in such indexes when their accuracy is such that they should be written "plus or minus 5 percent." And forecasts as to what these indexes are going to show six or twelve months from now are meaningless—as when the President's Council of Economic Advisers gives its annual prediction as to what the inflation rate will be by the end of the year. Any such forecast is based on the sum of a series of ifs, each if the product of a statistical assumption multiplied by another series of ifs. And although the Economic Advisers are intelligent and well-meaning persons, there are factors that simply cannot be quantified and placed in a computer, yet which may have a far greater impact on future prices than any of the factors that these economists have taken into consideration in making their predictions—for example, the situation in the Middle East, political events at home, the weather here and in a dozen other places of the world.

If the wisdom of these economic advisers were commensurate with their learning, they would confine their activities to their proper function, which is to advise the President, and they would make sure that their forecasts were not published or taken down on tape.

When the Office of Management and Budget makes a six-year "projection" of unemployment, prices, GNP, personal income and corporate profits, and actually publishes those projections, it is being wholly irresponsible. To project past trends six years into the future is absurd.

Aside from the folly of economic prediction by government agencies, the danger of the cost of living and other general indexes is that our "money managers" are attempting to use them as a guide to governmental and Federal Reserve economic policy, when the fact is that these general price series include not only prices for actual physical goods but prices for services—the barber, the hairdresser and so forth—as well as interest rates, rents, insurance premiums and scores of other items that simply are not amenable to monetary management.

Many of the services included in the general index are not comparable in quality with the services rendered ten or twenty years ago. For example, a penny postcard now costs ten cents, and the general index reflects that rise. But the postal service is not a fifth as good as it was when postcards cost a penny. So shouldn't we say that postal rates have multiplied fifty-fold over the past fifty years? Or perhaps the government would argue that postage is the one thing that hasn't gone up—a five-cent stamp still sells for a nickel.

Interest rates, included in the living cost indexes, often move in exactly the opposite direction from prices, although that has not been true in recent times. But when the Fed—the Federal Reserve Board—wants to "cool" an inflationary trend, it is accustomed to raise interest rates—its "target" rate for federal funds and its own discount rate for interbank loans. It thus contributes to *raising* the cost of living index—not that its action was necessarily wrong but that this index or any other general index is not an appropriate one for the money managers to use as a guide in controlling inflation.

Life insurance, and theft and fire insurance rates, likewise included in the cost of living index, depend in part upon the return the companies get upon their investments. So when the Fed raises interest rates, the companies get higher revenues and can reduce their premiums. But their premiums also depend upon mortality rates, and the increase in fires and crimes, and the monetary managers have no way of affecting those contingencies. Unless indeed the high interest rates drive farmers and businessmen to suicide or to arson, which is probably not the intention of the Fed's directors.

The prices the barber, the hairdresser, the tailor, the cobbler charge for their services are simply not subject to the influence of higher interest rates, bank reserve requirements, credit restrictions, "open-market operations" (buying or selling government obligations), balanced or unbalanced federal budgets or other instruments that the money managers in the Fed or in the government have at their disposal. Services constitute a greater and greater proportion of the total number of items that are included in the cost of living and other general price indexes. So there is simply no point in the money managers trying to stabilize in terms of those indexes. They can't do it.

Many tangible goods, too, are impervious to monetary or fiscal (budget-balancing) controls. When a cosmetics manufacturer charges $10 for ten cents worth of ingredients, attractively packaged and expensively advertised, or when a Fifth Avenue candy shop charges $10 a pound for its chocolates, the retail price is completely divorced from any pressures of actual cost or economic law, save only the ultimate law of demand—of bankruptcy if the public won't buy $10 chocolates or $10 cosmetics. And with increasing affluence, more and more products in the index come into the category of luxury goods sold largely on the basis of snob appeal, where the higher the price, the greater the demand.

In short, a very large proportion of the items included in the cost of living and other general indexes are simply not amenable to monetary management. There is nothing the money managers—Keynesian or otherwise—can do to affect these general indexes except by disastrously overreacting on those items in the index that are susceptible to monetary and fiscal pressures.

The dangers of index numbers

Let us assume that, because of inordinate wage increases in the service fields—government or private—or exorbitant oil prices, the cost of living index shows a tendency to go through the roof. And let us assume that the money managers use all the "cooling" measures they have at their disposal—higher interest rates, restrictions on credit and so forth—to counteract that trend. And that they actually do succeed in keeping the cost of living index absolutely level in spite of the rise in service wages and oil prices. What then? Well, obviously, this means that all other prices in the index have to be pushed downward, and the farmers and all the rest of the population affected are simply not going to allow that to happen.

To make matters worse, there is practically nothing that can be done to increase productivity in the service industries and thus bring down the cost of services reported in the index. All the invention and innovation that management can bring to the task will not enable the barber to give any more haircuts today than his grandfather did two generations ago; the waiter cannot wait on any more customers or the bricklayer lay any more bricks—fewer, in fact, for, although one man should be able to lay 1,000 to 1,200 bricks a day, and a highly skilled Dutch mason can double that speed, the labor unions have cut the permitted output to a fraction of that figure.

So that, not only is it impossible for the money managers to stabilize the purchasing power of the dollar in terms of a cost of living or consumer index, but the closer they come to that objective, the more disastrous it will be to farmers, miners, fishermen and others, as well as to the economy at large.

In the words of the old song, the economists and money managers can push the damper in, they can pull the damper out, but the smoke goes up the chimney just the same.

Interest rates

The weapons most generally used by today's money managers to hold down inflation are an increase in interest rates and raising bank reserve requirements to curtail credit. As is plain to anyone who has ever built a house and taken a mortgage on it, a rise in interest rates and increased credit restrictions are the most damaging things that can happen to the economy. Public utilities know this, manufacturers and businessmen know it, everyone seems to know it except perhaps the money managers—and surely even they must know it is true, but perhaps hope it isn't.

My own conclusion, based on long experience in many countries of the world that have faced or failed to face the problems of inflation, is that raising interest rates and restricting credits are very effective means of controlling speculative overexpansion in business, but not for combating inflation, because if used for that purpose they can only result in adding the problem of recession to the existing problems of inflation, particularly if the government fails to balance its own budget and thus throws a monkey wrench into the whole economy by adding to inflation through the issuance of its paper IOUs that increase the money supply, crowding private enterprise out of the lending market.

Furthermore, high interest rates do not, as the money managers allege, attract investment, whether domestic or foreign. Where a country's currency is indubitably sound, then indeed an increase in interest rates, say from 3 to 4 percent, will generally attract a flow of investment capital. But when rates go beyond say a norm of 6 percent as a consequence of inflation, because investors demand an additional return to compensate for the diminishing value of their money, then soaring interest rates not only fail to attract new investment but also scare investors to the point of capital flight.

We then have the vicious cycle of rising prices, higher interest rates to compensate for inflation, unbalanced government budgets because of higher prices and higher interest on government debt, the issuance of new deficit-financing obligations, still higher interest rates to attract investment in those obligations, more inflation which is merely another way of saying the debasement of the currency, capital flight because of fears of further monetary debasement, the shortage of investment capital because of government borrowing and the timidity of investors, business recession, unemployment, further government deficits to spur business and increase employment, a consequent increase in the money supply and more inflation, and so on in endless sequence.

Anyone who has followed Latin American affairs over the past thirty years knows that this sequence is inevitable and disastrous, as we can see in the United States today, and even more notably in Italy and South America, where capital flight is a major factor in the economy. (See Chapter 6 re capital flight from Latin America.)

The fallacies in GNP

Another fallacy in the spectrum of economic theories is the belief that the progress of a nation can be measured accurately by gross national product (GNP) or gross domestic product (GDP) in an era where so much of the GNP and GDP is made up of government spending.

When a corporation invests $100 million in a new petrochemical plant, it adds no more to GNP than when the government spends $100 million to build some monstrosity such as the Rayburn Congressional Office Building, which cost $88 million in 1966, or the Hart Senate Office Building, whose cost was originally estimated at $48 million but is expected to cost $160 million by the time it is finished—$1,600,000 per senator! And there are two other Senate office buildings, which will remain in operation.

Yet the manufacturing plant will add many times $100 million to the nation's productive capacity, which will flow back into the economy year after year in the form of wages, profits, taxes, demand for raw materials and consumer satisfactions, whereas the government "investment" means a direct subtraction from the nation's resources and productive powers, whether it is financed through deficit borrowing or through taxation. This points up the fallacy in Keynesian thinking when economists assume that government spending involves the "multiplier effect" and hence is not inflationary, in contradistinction to private spending.

If prosperity were just a matter of increasing the GNP, then there would be nothing like a war to achieve that aim, for the cost of war adds just as much to GNP, dollar for dollar, as the cost of a new factory or power plant. Professors James Tobin and William Nordhaus of Yale, disturbed at seeing President Johnson's economic advisers take credit for the fantastic growth of GNP, when it was chiefly because of the war in Vietnam, decided to compile a new index in which they would make deductions for what they called the "disamenities" of life, including war, congestion, pollution, noise, crime, racial discord and so forth. And Professor Samuelson gave this idea his blessing by incorporating it in his ninth edition of *Economics* under the acronym NEW (net economic welfare).

Not that the idea is really new; Jeremy Bentham (1748–1832) proposed a method of calculating the quantum of happiness—"felicific calculus." But when economists try to give mathematical, and therefore seemingly objective, form to what can only be their own subjective likes and dislikes, we are indeed headed for trouble. So let's be wary of substituting NEW or felicific calculus for GNP despite the fact that GNP today embodies more fallacies than practically any other economic concept.

Throughout Latin America, one reads of the year-by-year increase in GNP while anyone who has known that part of the world for any length of time can see the steady increase in all the evidences of poverty—the proliferating shantytowns that surround and penetrate every major city in that area, the widening gap between the ultrarich and the desperately poor. The growth in GNP is almost entirely accounted for by the magnificent government buildings that rise on every side, the great highways practically devoid of profitable traffic and other vast public works and enterprises that represent a direct subtraction from the real wealth and well-being of these underdeveloped countries. Or, in many cases, a direct and futile subtraction from the pockets of the American taxpayer.

It is not surprising that Keynes, as the Messiah of the New Economics, should have written that pyramid-building, earthquakes and wars may serve to increase wealth—that if the government were to fill old bottles with bank notes, bury them in abandoned coal mines and cover them over with rubbish, leaving it to private enterprise to dig them out again, unemployment could be solved, and the real income and capital wealth of the community increased!

That sentence epitomizes the essence of the New Economics—the economics that has been indoctrinated into the minds of all the students and teachers of economics in this country over the past three decades.

Small wonder that the same administrations that brought us deficit spending as a way of life also brought us the Korean police action, the Vietnam War and in fact every war that this country has engaged in, in this century, together with the high GNP, low unemployment and high taxes that are the inevitable concomitants of war. It all fits in with the Keynesian theories and works marvelously—until our money runs out, or until the people decide that war or Rayburn-Hart pyramid-building is not a satisfactory road to wealth. And by that time, any incoming administration is faced with the painful task of putting the pieces together again, and taking the blame for increased unemployment when the troops come marching home.

Models—the unsexy kind

As a means of refining their economic theories and "proving" the validity of their reasoning processes, the new economists—the "econometricians," as they like to call themselves—have taken to the game of constructing "models." The economic processes of a nation in real life are too complex, they argue, to make it possible to analyze cause and effect with certainty. So they construct theoretical "models" to facilitate their analyses.

The idea dates back to François Quesnay (1694–1774) and his disciples, the Physiocrates, who gave us the doctrine of "laissez-faire." But the modern-day technocrats have carried the process to a much more "scientific" (read "incomprehensible") stage by inventing models of a theoretical economy or slice of the economy, vastly simplified and based on a series of assumptions as to the occurrence of this or that event and this or that consequence. In hundreds of economic journals in this country and throughout the world, econometricians vie with one another in parading their little models with their fascinating figures across the stage of public opinion to demonstrate this or that consequence of this or that cause. And they apply the most complex mathematical processes to the trends shown by their little models, using the most advanced computerized techniques to reach their conclusions.

All of this might have impressed—or at least confused—me had I not taken a course in computer programming at The University of Michigan in 1966–67 in order to keep abreast of the brilliant young students of the Graduate School of Business Administration. And I learned what is, or should be, axiomatic: that with a computer, "garbage in, garbage out."

Although the input and output of these models, hundreds of them devised every year—all highly mathematicized and computerized—is garbage, the new economists, particularly the younger ones who are forced to "publish or perish," seem to think they actually "prove" something, forgetting that their models are nothing but abstractions, based on assumptions, founded on theories completely divorced from real life, and proving nothing save the ingenuity of their makers.

This is not to deny the utility of econometric models in industrial forecasting—for a particular industry or a particular section of the economy—as a guide in planning purchases of supplies or investment in new plant, for there the compiler and user of the model are acquainted with the input and have a reasonable grasp of the contingencies that lie ahead. But not for an entire economy, where the input is outdated and the contingencies unknown.

Input-output analysis and statistical error
The same might be said of the technique of "input-output analysis" devised by Professor Wassily Leontief, which is useful—indeed essential—in any large industry, and in government in the planning of its own operations. But as a guide to the general economy, where one must rely on dubious and outdated statistics, its only utility in a free-market economy is to keep a number of bright and inexperienced people busy in a field where they can be expected to wreak the least possible damage to the economy, and as a stimulus to improving the timeliness and quality of national statistics.

So when you read of any investigation of inflation and its problems based on input-output analysis, forget it.

And, as to statistics in general, Professor Oskar Morgenstern (b. 1902) in an amusing and scathing book, *On the Accuracy of Economic*

Observations, writes that, when the Marshall Plan was introduced, one of the major European figures in its administration told him: "We shall produce any statistic that we think will help us get as much money out of the United States as we possibly can." Which is no more unscrupulous than our own government misleading Congress and its own citizens with its bikini accounting.

Notwithstanding which, we are compelled to use the government debt and budget figures *faute de mieux,* precisely as we are forced to use the GNP figures, even though Morgenstern tells us that each such figure should be written plus or minus 10 percent. And from my own experience, I would say that in many cases, plus or minus 50 percent would be closer to the mark.

6. Let's Take a Look Around

Lenin is said to have declared that the best way to destroy the Capitalist System was to debauch the currency. By a continuing process of inflation, governments can confiscate, secretly and unobserved, an important part of the wealth of their citizens. . . . Lenin was certainly right. There is no subtler, no surer means of overturning the existing basis of society than to debauch the currency.

John Maynard Keynes (1920)

With Keynes and Lenin in agreement on the evils of inflation, one wonders why economists—instead of trying to simplify the complexities of the American economy through the use of theoretical models—don't simply turn to some real economy, where the actual inflation has been so vast, so overwhelming in its impact, as to blast out all crosscurrents and countertrends, thus making it possible to study the causes and effects of that one particular phenomenon almost in isolation.

A striking example was Germany after World War I, when a trillion to one inflation was so catastrophic that no other event of the time could have had any appreciable effect on the ultimate calamity.

Or Bolivia, where, over a four-and-a-half-year period, a 2,200 percent rise in living costs was caused by a 1,700 percent increase in bank note circulation, which in turn was triggered by a 2,000 percent increase in bank loans, 90 percent of which were to the government—which certainly made it easy to pinpoint the source of the inflation.

As to what was cause and what was effect in the Bolivian inflation, the central bank could not compel the government to borrow, but the government could and did compel the bank to lend. And the only way it could lend was to make a deposit in the government's bank account, which, when the government paid its bills and payrolls, was converted into cash. So the increase in the money supply—bank deposits and currency combined—consisted chiefly in printing-press money engendered by government borrowing.

The same causes and the same consequences have been seen in every country of South America where inflation has been rampant. Just as we see in the United States today.

Inflation no harbinger of prosperity

Contrary to the suppositions of the Keynesians, inflation has *not* brought prosperity to Latin America. Even in the highly fallacious and often misleading figures for GNP, which are the only mathematical guides available, those countries that have had the least inflation, the least growth in money supply, have had the greatest rise in gross national product.

Statistics compiled by Dr. Robert Vogel of the Council of Economic Advisers reveal that for the twenty-year period 1950–69, the five Latin American countries that had the highest rate of growth in the money supply (an average of 35.9 percent per annum) and the highest rate of inflation (34.8 percent per annum)—Uruguay, Bolivia, Brazil, Chile, Argentina—had the lowest rate of growth in real income (2.9 percent per annum).

Conversely, the five countries—El Salvador, Venezuela, Guatemala, Costa Rica, Honduras—that had the lowest rate of increase in the money supply (6.9 percent per annum) and the lowest rate of inflation (1.3 percent per annum), had the highest rate of growth in real income (5.0 percent per annum). In those five countries the growth of the money supply was barely sufficient to take care of the rise in real income (i.e., GNP in terms of real purchasing power), and the rate of inflation was therefore minimal.

The correlation between the growth of the money supply and the rate of inflation in the five countries where inflation was rampant is too close to be coincidence. And the reverse correlation between inflation and the growth of GNP should suffice to discredit the fine theories of the Keynesian economists here and in Latin America if only they would heed the injunction of this chapter head—"Let's Take a Look Around"—instead of playing games with their "empirical analyses," their "Phillips curves" and their neat little mathematical "models."

But they won't. Because they would have to unlearn all the things that have been indoctrinated into them ever since they first began boning up for their doctoral dissertations. And in moral philosophy it is a rare man indeed who can bring himself to admit in his mature years that all the opinions he so vigorously maintained in his youth, and taught his pupils, are a snare and a delusion. I can think of a few such apostates—Paul of Tarsus, Thomas Aquinas and John Henry Cardinal Newman. There may be others. But they were not economists.

High interest rates and capital flight

Another phenomenon to be observed in Latin America is that, contrary to everything one learns from the economics textbooks and that the Federal Reserve Board still believes, high interest rates do *not* necessarily attract capital. Interest rates in the inflation-ridden countries of South America vary from 12 percent to 48 percent per annum and in one country over 1,000 percent! Notwithstanding which, the flight of capital from those countries to safe havens in Switzerland and elsewhere has been so great that total Latin American flight capital abroad is estimated to exceed the total amount of foreign investment in those countries. And the annual flight of capital is reported to be greater than the annual amount of United States aid, plus all the foreign aid given by other countries and by the multinational lending agencies.

In other words, were it not for the flight of capital, engaged in by the Latin Americans themselves, foreign aid would be superfluous. And it is not just the ultrarich, the "oligarchs," who have engaged in that trade but the politicos in government who have received and profited from foreign aid, and their friends who can conceal their operations because of their political influence.

And, if it were not for constant, endemic inflation, there would be no flight of capital, because the opportunities for investment would be at least as great in Latin America as anywhere else in the world, were it not for the well-intentioned but meddling governments that, over the past forty-five years, have wrested control of economic activities from the comparatively capable hands of private enterprise and turned it over, on an increasing scale, to the hands of the corrupt and incompetent people who are the friends of the politicos or of the military.

Of course, neither the high interest rates nor the flight of capital is surprising when the people of Latin America realize, as many of them do, that the pesos they own today will be worth only a few centavos tomorrow. The high interest rates are really negative interest rates, just as an 8 percent rate is a negative rate in the United States today.

Unemployment and underemployment

Another lesson to be learned from studying the experience of other countries—and particularly those countries of Latin America where government deficit-financing and inflation are rife—is that high employment is not a necessary corollary of inflation. To the contrary, the countries where inflation has been most pronounced have the highest ratios of unemployment, and, even more insidiously, of *underemployment*, by which is meant a situation where able-bodied people are engaged in productive work for only a few hours a week, or are performing tasks that can by no stretch of the imagination be considered productive—shoeshine boys begging in the streets, three clerks in the store checking on one another and doing work that one clerk could perform, supernumerary household, office or factory help, valets, butlers, chimney sweeps and so forth. When was the last time you saw a chimney sweep in the United States—aside from Dick Van Dyke, of course?

On the whole, there has always been less *underemployment*— valets, beggars and so forth—in the United States than elsewhere in the world. By the same token, there has always been a higher percentage of *unemployment* in this country than elsewhere (aside from wartime).

And this endemic unemployment—not the extremes of unemployment witnessed in 1930–37—is actually evidence of prosperity, not of hard times. In the prosperous years from 1923 to 1929, and in every period of good times, when a workingman can always be sure of finding a job, there are always many men and women who are temporarily unemployed because they move from one job to another, without even making certain that the new job will be available before giving up the old. It is part of the spirit of enterprise that made our pioneer forebears leave the Atlantic seaboard on their trek westward and populate the state of Michigan and other lesser states en route and to the West. And this mobility in jobs and places is characteristic of this country today—a sign of affluence and not of poverty. Although it can be the latter, too, as was evident in the westward trek of the "Okies" in the 1930s.

In recent years we can see another area of voluntary unemployment, likewise attributable to prosperity—perhaps we should say excessive affluence. For example, the young people who—generally supported by their parents—renounce material aims and live as dropouts, drifters, hippies, members of communes, drug addicts and sometimes criminals, as well as the people of every age who would rather live on welfare than work for a living, or those who take part in strikes, walkouts, protest marches and demonstrations, and are thus voluntarily absent from the labor force. Manifestly, these voluntary unemployed form only a small part of the potential working force, but they may constitute a fairly large percentage of the total number of unemployed.

Even if the Keynesian postulate of the tie-up between inflation and high employment were true, which it is not, it would be invalidated so far as this country is concerned by the large number of people who are voluntarily unemployed. And bear in mind that the employment and unemployment statistics, and the questionable definitions of both, make these figures probably the least reliable of all our untrustworthy statistics.

The minimum wage

There is one cause of unemployment—not voluntary—that finds its origin in the minimum wage laws. There are many people who could be employed at $1.30 an hour who will not be given jobs if they must be paid $2.90 an hour (the present national minimum).

Because of that legislation, we can expect to see a great many raspberries not picked this summer (and last summer they were $3.00 a pint in the Washington stores!), a great deal of maple syrup not packed next spring, and boll weevils allowed to remain undisturbed in the cotton fields.

Minimum wage laws do not raise wages. What they do accomplish, and they do this most effectively, is to deprive the least educated, the least efficient, least motivated workers of any possibility of finding jobs. As Billy Carter says, "Every time the minimum wage goes up, we have to lay off a few more people; a lot of people simply are not worth the minimum wage."

A leading black columnist puts it more elegantly and admits that any increase in the minimum wage means fewer opportunities for blacks and particularly for black teenagers. But he adds that one of the chief problems is the exaggerated idea that so many young blacks have of their own abilities, based on the fact that they have college *diplomas* although they are far from having a college *education* (italics are his), and because they refuse to be content with any job that doesn't pay $25,000–30,000— "a white-collar job, you know, where I can tell a few people what to do."

In a 1965 speech at Howard University, Lyndon Johnson pointed out that prior to the New Deal the unemployment rate for blacks and whites in the United States was approximately the same and that, as late as the Truman Administration, the unemployment rate for black teenage boys was actually less than that for whites. But that, thanks to ever-increasing minimum wage rates, and to lack of education as well as racial anger and a feeling of hopelessness, the unemployment rate among blacks—particularly among the young and least qualified—far exceeds that among whites. And he added that a *majority* of all black children have been raised on federal welfare. Which, as might be expected, has engendered the feeling that they have the *right* to be supported at public expense rather than the *obligation* to work for a living.

One of the best-known black economists also contends that the workers who bear the heaviest burden under minimum wage laws are the young, because of their lack of work experience, and the racial minorities such as blacks, who are disproportionately represented among the low-skilled workers. In any event, the adverse impact of minimum wage laws falls chiefly on the poor or, as the sociologists say, the "underprivileged." Or, according to Professor Galbraith, "those who are unencumbered by the burdens of wealth."

Certainly, it is illogical for Congress to inveigh against high unemployment and the high cost of living, and then directly contribute to both situations by raising minimum wage rates.

Prices and money supply in the United States

Let us see what has actually occurred here over the past ten years—from 1969 through 1978, a short enough period so that no drastic change in the velocity of money is likely to have taken place.

Let's take a look at Chart 1. The money supply (the broad, solid line—the Fed's "M_3") went up from a base of 100 for June 1969 to 241.3 by June 1978. And, over the same period, wholesale prices (the broad, broken line) rose from a base of 100 to 196.8. (To carry the figures beyond those shown on the chart, by mid-1979 it is estimated that the money supply rose to an index of 299, while wholesale prices rose to an index of 219.)

But during that same span, GNP in constant dollars—i.e., the actual *volume* of gross national product—rose to 128 from the 1969 base. So that an 18.8 percent rise in the money supply would have been justified by the increase in GNP, and would have produced no increase in prices *if the rise in the volume of money had been limited to that percentage.* Remember the money equation: $MV = PT$.

CHART 1—Money Supply and Wholesale Prices in the United States

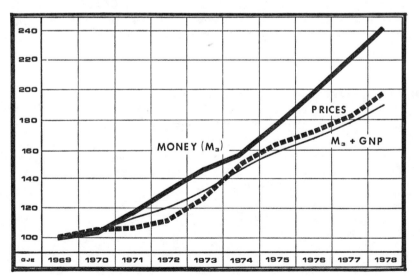

So I have divided the money supply ratio for each year by the GNP ratio for that year—in effect removing from the picture the *necessary* increase in the money supply called for by the increase in gross national product. The result is shown by the narrow solid line. Note how closely that line—the *inflationary* rise in money supply—tallies with the broken line showing the rise in wholesale prices (the June 1979 figures are shown in italics):

	Inflationary rise in money supply ($M_3 \div$ GNP)	Rise in wholesale prices
1969	100.0	100.0
1970	103.5	103.8
1971	114.0	107.0
1972	120.4	112.0
1973	127.3	126.4
1974	139.7	150.1
1975	159.4	164.2
1976	167.5	172.0
1977	179.0	182.1
1978	189.0	196.8
1979	*227.5 (est.)*	*219.0 (est.)*

In other words, setting aside that part of the increase in the money supply needed to carry on the nation's business, the rise in the money stock coincides almost exactly with the rise in prices. Which is not surprising, as Professor Fisher's money equation is a truism, an arithmetical truth as simple as $3 \times 4 = 2 \times 6$, and not requiring proof were it not for those economists and others who claim that there is no necessary relationship between the money stock and the general level of prices.

The creation of money

It may be a little difficult for the layman to grasp why currency and bank deposits are both regarded as exactly the same thing in computing the money supply. It is easy to see that it is inflationary if the Federal Reserve or the Treasury prints a billion or a trillion dollars in paper money—clearly there is then too much paper money "chasing" a given amount of goods. But why is it bad—inflationary—for bank deposits to increase? When we, as individuals, put money in the bank, we are *saving* our money. And this is good, not bad—how can it be inflationary?

Let's go back to fundamentals and examine how money is created under the Federal Reserve System. Let's assume the government has to meet a $100 billion deficit—not an improbable assumption. To meet its payrolls, buy supplies, pay interest, it needs either cash or money in the bank. And to get money in the bank the government must print Treasury obligations, either long-term bonds or short-term bills or notes. The Federal Reserve Banks and the commercial banks buy these obligations either directly from the Treasury or through security dealers.

Now, "money in the bank," as you know, is not really money in the bank—it is the amount of your or the government's or someone else's bank deposit. The bank does not keep $100 in cash for every $100 in deposits—it keeps a reserve against demand deposits of 10 percent to 22 percent in the case of the metropolitan banks (the "reserve city banks"), and 7 percent to 14 percent for all other banks; 3 percent to 10 percent in the case of time deposits. These reserves are either in the form of cash in the bank's vaults or deposits in the regional Federal Reserve Bank. So when the government sells $100 billion of obligations, it puts the $100 billion it receives into one of its various bank accounts, and bank deposits throughout the nation are thus increased by $100 billion. And because the banks generally put these funds into the Federal Reserve Banks, the banks' reserves throughout the nation are automatically increased by the same amount.

But with $100 billion more of bank reserves—created by the Treasury IOUs—the banks can increase their loans and investments up to a theoretical limit of $567 billion (i.e., a total of $667 billion, assuming an average 15 percent reserve requirement—66⅔ is the reciprocal of 15 percent). And the loans and investments will in turn mean more deposits because the borrowers put the money into *their* bank accounts. Theoretically, up to the $667 billion limit, provided the banks can find borrowers and depositors for this amount.

In order not to count the same money twice, the banks' reserve balances at the Fed and the cash in the banks' vaults are not counted as part of the money supply. Money supply therefore consists of currency in circulation with the public and demand deposits with the banks, plus time deposits and other accounts that can be used as money.

And "printing-press money" includes not only the *printed* dollar bills but the increase in the government's bank accounts resulting from the sale of its *printed* IOUs. Both are the product of the printing press, created out of thin air.

Of course, a similar expansion of the money supply—the same inflationary pressure—can take place when states and cities and private individuals and corporations borrow from the banks as when the government borrows. Except that only the federal government is in a position practically to compel the Federal Reserve Bank System to buy its obligations and print money—or increase deposits— without limit. Cities and states, corporations and individuals, can only borrow up to the limit of their borrowing capacity, as determined by the lenders. And, in general, the corporate borrowing is not inflationary because it goes at once into productive use, with a "multiplier effect" that increases the volume of goods and services bought and sold many times more than the increase in the money supply.

How much of the money supply consists of cash, and how much of bank deposits, depends upon what the general public decides and demands. At Christmas shopping time each year, much more cash comes into circulation, but by January that extra cash money is back in the banks. More cash money is needed on Fridays—paydays—than on Mondays. And there are many other factors—some temporary, some permanent changes in public habits—that can affect the volume of actual currency in circulation.

If the foregoing explanation of why bank deposits are considered part of the money supply seems complicated, look at it this way: We are interested in the money supply because the money supply determines the pressure behind the rise in prices. And you can see that bank deposits, credit cards, etc., can all be used instead of actual cash money—in fact, are far more important than cash in handling all the nation's transactions. So our definition of the money supply must include everything that can be used for money in the formula "too much money chasing too few goods."

Cash and bank deposits are interchangeable, indistinguishable and equally inflationary. This is true despite the fact that, from your point of view as an individual, an increase in bank deposits means savings, and savings are definitely beneficial for the individual as well as for the nation. For, of course, savings are invested by the banks and savings and loan associations in loans to agriculture, industry, commerce, commercial and residential building, etc. And these savings involve the "multiplier effect" that is lacking when the money is squandered by the government.

But would the increase in your personal bank account constitute savings if you had borrowed the money you put in the bank account and then squandered that money? Of course not! And this is what happens when the government borrows against its IOUs, which is why any increase in the money supply beyond the needs of the economy is inflationary, regardless of whether the increase is in currency or bank deposits.

Prices and money supply abroad
The foregoing chart and discussion are a pretty crude demonstration that would be given a "flunk" in any mathematics or economics course. But I did not wish to burden this book with ten pages of charts and figures in order to prove what should be accepted as axiomatic. The fact is that in any economy as complex as that of the United States—except under unusual circumstances such as the planned "reflation" during the first year of the Franklin Roosevelt Administration—it is almost impossible to

isolate cause and effect and *prove*, with the mathematical certainty of a QED, that this or that factor is the original cause of any spiraling sequence of cause and consequence.

Proof is lacking—but let's take a look around, as the title of this chapter suggests, to see whether there is *evidence* of the relationship between money supply and prices in the experience of other countries of the world. For, unless this relationship is universal, or at least a general phenomenon, we must look elsewhere for an explanation of the rise in prices.

Let us take as examples the three countries that have most expertly managed their economies and finances since World War II, the countries whose currencies are regarded today as the soundest of all in a troubled world—Germany, Japan and Switzerland. And, for comparison, let us take the two major industrial and trading countries of the world most thoroughly imbued with Keynesian monetary doctrine, in other words, those countries whose currencies, finances and economies have been most woefully mismanaged over the past three decades or more—namely, England and the United States.

You question that? Well, from the outset of World War I until well after the end of World War II, the United States was beyond question the greatest, the strongest, the wealthiest nation in the world. Its per capita wages, income, ownership of automobiles, gross national product—every index of national prosperity—were so far in advance of every other country of the world that there was simply no comparison. Today, however, the United States is surpassed in per capita GNP by Sweden, Switzerland, West Germany, Canada and Denmark, and, of course, by Kuwait, Qatar and the United Arab Emirates; in economic growth—the annual percentage change from 1960 to 1970—the United States ranks seventeenth or eighteenth, and by now probably twentieth; and its wages, including fringe benefits, are now below those of Sweden, Belgium, Netherlands and West Germany.

A sixth-rate country or worse, instead of the leader of the world! Fortunately, the productive capacity of the United States, the tremendous drive not of Washington or New York but of Middletown, U.S.A., our powers of recuperation, are so enormous that it is still not too late for us to recover our former position of preeminence if we can succeed in ridding ourselves of the excessive burden of government under a welfare state.

As to England, certainly one of the greatest countries of the world up to the outbreak of World War I, and still one of the world's leaders in science, civilization and merited prestige, its economy has been on a generally declining course ever since the general strike of 1926 and the beginnings of a welfare state under which the incentive for hard work was removed because one could live tolerably well on the dole. The United

Kingdom now ranks twenty-fourth among the nations of the world in per capita GNP. The productivity of the English labor force is now lower than that of any other major industrial country; it ranks tenth in wages (Japan is ninth); and it is even more burdened than the United States by excessive government expenditures, taxation and inflation.

Chart 2 demonstrates the close relationship between the money supply and the rate of inflation over the past twenty years in each of these five countries. The figures are taken from *International Financial Statistics* published by the International Monetary Fund in order to give at least some measure of uniformity and continuity, and the consumer price indexes have been used to show the general level of inflation. Money in circulation includes demand deposits, while, in the United States and United Kingdom, time deposits have also been included because they are more volatile (more often withdrawn and used as money) in those countries than elsewhere.

Chart 2
Money Supply and Consumer Prices in Five Major Countries

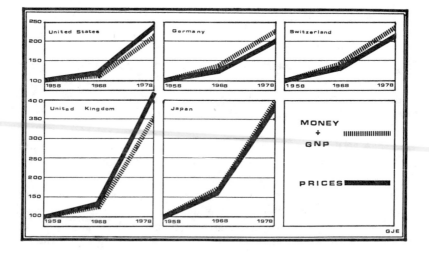

The relationship between the increase in the money supply index divided by the GNP index (as we did in Chart 1 for the United States), and the rise in prices *in every one of these countries*, from 1958 through 1978 as well as at the midway point, is too close to be mere coincidence, viz.:

		Money in circulation ÷ GNP index	Consumer price index
1958	United States	100.0	100.0
1968		110.0	120.0
1978		226.0	234.0
1958	United Kingdom	100.0	100.0
1968		120.4	134.0
1978		359.0	419.0
1958	Germany	100.0	100.0
1968		137.4	125.0
1978		248.0	200.0
1958	Japan	100.0	100.0
1968		170.5	162.0
1978		397.0	396.0
1958	Switzerland	100.0	100.0
1968		140.5	131.0
1978		239.0	212.0

The money supply and government deficits
Well and good. It is clear that, not only in the United States but elsewhere in the world, the increase in the money supply, in excess of that necessary to keep up with the rise in GNP, is closely related to the rate of inflation, both in countries that have had the least inflation (Germany and Switzerland) and in countries that have had the most inflation (United States, Japan and the United Kingdom).

But which is cause and which is consequence? Did inflation simply mean that more money and bank deposits were needed to take care of the higher prices? Or was it the increase in the money supply that caused the inflation? And, if so, was the increase in the money supply caused by private borrowing or government borrowing?

In the first place, while it is true that inflation *can* be caused by the undue expansion of credit to the private sector, it is also true that the banks and savings institutions, for their own protection, are generally unlikely to extend credit beyond the reasonable needs of the borrower. Nor are business borrowers in general likely to borrow beyond those needs. The judgment of banks and borrowers is not infallible, as was shown in the expansionary trends of 1928–29—in this country, the low-margined loans by brokers to stock market speculators, and in Europe, the speculative ventures of some of the leading banks such as the Kredit-anstalt whose eventual failure triggered the 1931 crash. But, since then, Europe has learned a lesson, while the brokers in the United States have been chastened and are closely monitored by the SEC and the FRB, and the number of banks in the United States has been drastically reduced—from over 25,000 before the 1929–32 catastrophe to some 15,000 since that time. And the quality of their management has for the most part been improved as a consequence, aside from the fact that the Fed is now keeping a closer control over interest rates, reserve requirements, and loans to brokers, thus directly limiting the capacity of the banks to lend.

Bank credit in the United States to the private sector is therefore *elastic*, expanding as business needs require, and contracting when those needs have been satisfied. So long as that principle is followed—i.e., so long as the money supply (M) is not expanded at a greater rate than the volume of transactions (T)—the increases in money will have no effect on prices (P). From all the evidence we must conclude that, except in isolated instances, credit to the private sector has not been, by and large, the vehicle of American inflation in recent years.

The government, on the other hand, is the one vehicle in the economy that is all motor and no brakes. So long as its expenditures were restricted to the amount it could raise through taxation, as was true when we were on the gold standard, there was a limit on government expansion, because there is a limit to the burden of taxation that the citizens are willing to put up with. California proved that point beyond question in its 1978 referendum. And the biennial elections keep the House of Representatives fairly well attuned to the wishes of their constituents. But when the government can spend and spend, and borrow and borrow, there is no such limitation. To the contrary, there is every political incentive for greater and greater government expenditure in the almost certain expectation of getting more and more votes from a grateful constituency.

And when the government's ability to persuade the private sector to buy more and more government bonds reaches its limit, the Treasury must turn to the Federal Reserve Banks to find a market for its obligations. And the Fed is then placed in a delicate position.

If it refuses to purchase any further issues of Treasury bills, notes, certificates and bonds, it is courting economic disaster—a crash in the government bond and money market which would have immediate and serious repercussions on the economy. Not to mention the risk of arousing the anger of the administration and Congress and the probable curtailment of its quasi-independence from political pressure. So the Fed has been practically forced to absorb all the Treasury and government agency issues that cannot be placed elsewhere, thus avoiding the immediate disaster but paving the way for the ultimate catastrophe.

Any securities purchased by the Fed are immediately "monetized," i.e., their purchase means an immediate and commensurate increase in the money supply, plus an ultimate increase of up to six or seven times that. And, out of $120.4 billion of the Fed's portfolio of loans and securities on December 31, 1978, $118.6 billion was in obligations of the federal government and federal agencies—98.5 percent!

It is true that the commercial banks hold $186.3 billion of federal government and agency obligations (18.9 percent of their total loans and investments), plus $117.3 billion of state and municipal obligations (11.9 percent of the total), plus $679.8 billion in loans to the private sector (69 percent of the total), and that all of this credit is "monetized," just as the Fed's loans and investments are—i.e., converted into cash or bank deposits.

But, over the past ten years, bank loans to the private sector have only increased 127 percent, thus barely keeping pace with the 124 percent rise in GNP, meaning that only some 3 percent of the bank loans to the private sector can be considered inflationary. Remember that if the increase in the "money supply"—currency plus bank deposits—is the same as the rise in GNP, there is no inflationary pressure ($MV = PT$). While, over the same ten-year period, bank holdings of state and municipal obligations have increased less than the rise in GNP—98 percent—so the states and cities are not to blame for inflation.

But the commercial bank holdings of government and agency obligations jumped 189 percent in those ten years, far exceeding the rise in GNP. And those holdings—the bank financing of government deficit spending—are clearly inflationary.

So, taking into account the fact that 98.5 percent of the Federal Reserve System's loans and investments consists of federal obligations and that the bank loans to the private sector can only be responsible for 3 percent of the inflationary pressure, it is manifest that government borrowing—deficit spending—has been the cause of some 95 percent of the inflation that has plagued the United States over the past decade. We must blame not the labor unions, not big business, not the Arabs, not the oil companies—but the United States Government!

To forestall criticism, it may be admitted that the mathematics in the foregoing exposition is not as rigorous as I would like to make it, but is is clear that even the most thorough mathematical proof—which would take pages of text—would arrive at the same conclusion: It is the deficit financing of the federal government that is responsible for some 95 percent of the inflation from which the country is suffering today.

Experience in other countries

Again, let's take a look around. Have government deficits in other countries—government borrowing from the central bank—been the major factor behind the increase in the money supply shown in Chart 2? Here we would not expect to see the same uniformity of results that we noted in demonstrating the relationship of the money supply to inflation that we found in Chart 2. In one country, government borrowing may have been chiefly to blame; in another country the culprit may have been private speculation or borrowing beyond the needs of the rise in GNP.

Chart 3 shows this dramatically. Switzerland has been omitted, as Switzerland is one of those fortunate countries where the government is not addicted to unlimited deficits. There, the increase in the amount of money in circulation, and consequently the increase in prices, over the past twenty years has been almost exclusively the consequence of the vast inflow of foreign funds into that country—the flight of capital from Latin America, Italy, the United States and elsewhere, from the fast-depreciating currencies of those spendthrift countries to the soundest currency in the world today, the Swiss franc. And, from February 1978 to January 1979, Switzerland took steps to put a stop to this influx, which, because of the consequent rise in the value of the Swiss franc, had adversely affected Switzerland's ability to export and its attraction as a tourist center. During that period, Americans and Latin Americans could no longer increase their deposits in Swiss banks or their purchases of Swiss franc securities held in Switzerland—at least, not legally. Switzerland did not *want* any more dollars!

As the individual charts show, the ten-year cumulative government deficits, from 1958 to 1967 and from 1968 to 1977, have been a large factor in the increase in money in circulation in all four countries. Again the figures have been taken from the IMF statistical bulletin, and the analysis is not as precise, the evidence not as conclusive, as was shown in the case of the United States, where we could prove, almost apodictically, that government deficits and government borrowing were practically the sole cause of the increase in the money supply and hence of the inflation. But a conclusive investigation of the facts in four foreign countries would go far beyond the scope of this book.

Chart 3—Cumulative Government Deficits and the Increase in Money Supply

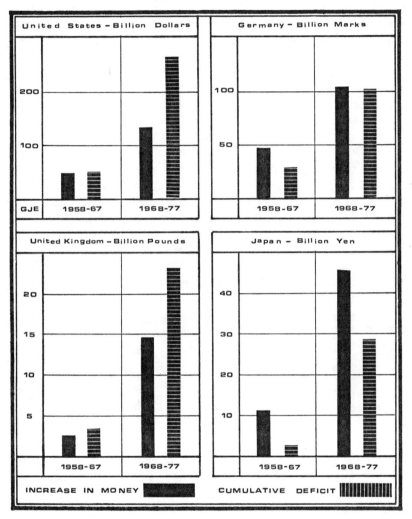

The charts do, however, indicate—not prove—that in Germany the government deficits under the country's present socialist regime have been practically the sole cause of the increase in the money supply. That the same was true in Japan in 1978, but that, in prior years, private borrowing must have been the main cause of monetary expansion, and we know from personal observation on four visits to that country that this expansion has been in part speculative, but chiefly to support Japan's phenomenal increase in GNP: to an index of 504 in 1978 (1958 = 100), compared with 219 in Germany, 197 in the United States, 190 in Switzerland and only 162 in the United Kingdom.

In England and the United States—the Keynesian countries—the charts reveal that the cumulative government deficits have far outstripped the increase in the money supply, although this would not be true were we to take a more meaningful definition of money (such as M_3) than that chosen by the IMF. But, in any event, the chart and figures do show that, in those countries, not only is the government solely to blame for the increase in the money supply (and thus for the inflation) but the private sector has been cramped as a consequence.

The figures behind the charts are given in the following table and, to complete the data through 1978, an eleven-year summary is included in italics, pointing to the same conclusions:

		Increase in money in circulation	*Ten-year cumulative government deficits*
1958–1967	United States	47	50 Billion dollars
1968–1977		133	265
1968–1978		*150*	*309*
1958–1967	United Kingdom	2,349	3,579 Million pounds
1968–1977		14,886	22,414
1968–1978		*16,757*	*32,100 (est.)*
1958–1967	Germany	42	29 Billion marks
1968–1977		109	107
1968–1978		*138*	*133*
1958–1967	Japan	10,184	2,556 Billion yen
1968–1977		45,631	28,657
1968–1978		*49,749*	*42,047*

The Fed as the holder of the fort

Returning to the analysis of the situation in the United States, the Federal Reserve System has not always been the vehicle of inflationary financing for the government. When I was manager of the Foreign Department of a New York bank in the mid-1920s, the Fed's chief function was the rediscounting of commercial paper or purchasing such paper in the open market. "Rediscounting" meant that when a client of a commercial bank shipped merchandise abroad, that client—the exporter—would draw a bill of exchange for its value against the foreign importer, generally payable in sixty or ninety days after presentation of the bill of exchange with its accompanying shipping documents. The bank would *discount* that paper, i.e., give the exporter 80 to 100 percent of its face value, less interest and commission; and would then *rediscount* the paper at the Fed, or give the Fed its own note for the total of the day's operations in such bills of exchange. The bank made its profit out of the low rediscount rate charged by the Fed and the higher rate the bank charged the exporter. To some extent, domestic trade was handled in the same way, but chiefly through the Fed's purchase of commercial paper on the open market.

The Fed was thus fulfilling its intended function of providing credit on an elastic basis against actual business transactions, and these operations meant that credit expanded and contracted commensurately with the volume of business, so that they did not tend to raise prices.

In those days, United States Government expenditures plus agency deficits amounted to only 3.76 percent of national income, not 36.4 percent, as is the case with the 1980 budget. The government balanced its budget, and government borrowing was therefore not a vehicle of inflation.

The situation has been sadly reversed today. The Fed, despite its excellent and knowledgeable management, has been unable to hold the fort. It has fought a gallant delaying action but has been unwilling—and properly so—to precipitate a crisis. Thus, at the present time its chief function, as seen from the composition of its assets, has not been to finance the country's industry, trade and agriculture, but to finance the deficits of successive spendthrift administrations, beginning with Roosevelt's New Deal and continuing, on an ever-ascending scale, to the present time.

In that respect, the record of the Fed is better than that of the Latin American central banks only in degree. And, in South America, it can be *proved*, because of the dominant position of government in the economy, that government deficit financing is practically the sole cause of the inflation that has been rampant in those countries.

So, to sum up, the evidence is well nigh conclusive that in this country, at the present time, the deficit financing of the federal government is the root cause of the expansion of the money supply *beyond the growth requirements of the economy*, and that it is therefore directly responsible for the rise in prices. If the government were to balance its budget, and to carry out all the measures suggested in Chapter 15, inflation would end almost overnight—the "miracle of stabilization" that has been witnessed in every country, large and small, that has dared to live within its means.

The future of the Fed

If ever the time should come when our government can lay down the law to the Federal Reserve System, and *compel* it to buy the Treasury bonds, bills and notes, and yet reduce interest rates, we shall have come to a sorry pass. Yet many people have from time to time inveighed against the independence of the Fed, demanding that it be completely responsive to government needs. There are only two other countries in the world whose central banks enjoy as great a measure of independence as the Fed—West Germany and Switzerland. And Arthur Burns, ex-chairman of the Fed, attributes their relative freedom from inflation to that fact.

The Fed, as you may remember, is not a government central bank, but a group of twelve regional banks owned by the private member banks, each Federal Reserve Bank being controlled by a board of nine directors, three of whom are chosen by and represent the member banks, three chosen by the member banks but nonbankers and representative of agriculture, industry or commerce, and three appointed by the Board of Governors of the Federal Reserve System. The Board of Governors consists of seven members appointed by the President of the United States, with the advice and consent of the Senate, for fourteen-year terms, which ensures some degree of freedom from political pressure.

It is well to recall right now that the only thing that stands between us and galloping inflation is the limited independence of the Fed. Remember that, in South America, where inflation has run wild, it is because the central banks are wholly at the mercy of the governments which can and do force them to lend without limit. And if ever our Federal Reserve System is made subordinate to Congress or to the administration, we can look forward to the permanent Latin-Americanization of our banking and monetary system and inflation without end. Look at the appalling record of defaults to our government-controlled lending agencies and their constant need for additional capital to keep them in business—the consequence of the political pressures that are inevitable in any government-managed enterprise.

Despite all the flaws in the record of the Fed—and there have been many, as is unavoidable in any human institution—the system is and always has been better administered than the federal government or any government-controlled agency.

"Automatic" control of the Fed

One proposal that has been put forward as a means of controlling the operations of the Fed and maintaining the stability of the purchasing power of the dollar is that advanced by Professor Milton Friedman, formerly of the University of Chicago and now with the Hoover Institution at Stanford. Dr. Friedman is generally known as a conservative and a "monetarist"—the former because he believes in a free-market economy with the minimum possible intervention by the government, and the latter because he is convinced of the importance of the money supply as a determinant of prices and hence its vital significance in the economy. But Professor Friedman is a man of such diversified abilities that to label him is to libel him. It would be better to describe him as the outstanding student of monetary theory in academic circles.

He proposes, as his solution to the money question, that the Fed should be required by law to maintain a constant rate of growth of the money supply, at the rate of 3 percent or 5 percent a year, depending upon which definition of the money stock is used. In that way, he claims, the money supply would keep pace with economic growth and business needs, and would therefore be "neutral," tending neither to push prices up nor to pull them down. The fact that the adjustment would be made automatically by the Fed, in accordance with a fixed rule, would remove the question from politics or from errors of human judgment.

The idea undoubtedly has theoretical merit but remember that, if we were once again on a gold standard with no government deficits to be financed by the Fed or the banking system, monetary management and control of the money supply to curb inflation would be totally unnecessary; the Fed could and should establish discount rates and reserve requirements to deter speculative business and banking expansion or contraction, but the money supply would automatically expand and contract with the needs of the economy. Furthermore, no fixed percentage of monetary expansion that is valid now will necessarily be valid even two years from now with changing trends in monetary velocity, electronic debits and credits in lieu of check payments and other developments beyond the range of human predictability. Remember, too, that those people who display such zeal and zest for economic experimentation and for managing the monetary supply and the economy inevitably end up by mismanaging both.

Yet I realize that some of our leaders—in the administration and in Congress—will always be unhappy over the independence of the Federal Reserve System whenever the Fed's views of financial and monetary policy run counter to the political pressures of the moment.

7. How Other Countries Have Conquered Inflation

The suddenness of Germany's recovery was even more striking than its scope. It was not spread out over months or even weeks, but has a specific date . . . the day the currency reform went into effect. Only those who were on the spot can bear witness to the literally instantaneous effect it had upon the reappearance of merchandise and customers in the stores.

Jacques Rueff (1963)

This *instantaneous* end to inflation and the beginning of economic recovery in West Germany, pointed out by France's leading economist, has been true in *every* country that has dared to face squarely the problem of uncontrolled inflation. A *gradual approach*, the slow tapering off of inflationary pressures, has never worked, and indeed has only tended to make matters worse.

So before straying from the injunction to "take a look around," we might examine how the great monetary stabilizers of the twentieth century accomplished their miracles, because this will show *why* none of the measures thus far taken in this country have been effective in staying the price rise—and perhaps even point to what should be done here if we wish to follow their example. What *should* be done; whether or not it *could* be done and how it *can* be done is another more ticklish question which we shall come to in due course.

The great monetary stabilizers of history

I refer to the miracles of monetary stabilization wrought by Hjalmar Horace Greeley Schacht in Germany after World War I and by Ludwig Erhard under the inspiration of his economic mentor, Dr. Wilhelm Röpke, after World War II—and the word "miracle" is correct, for that is how stabilization has been acclaimed in every country where it came *practically overnight* after years of inflation.

We might also learn from the accomplishments of Charles de Gaulle with the assistance of his economic adviser, Jacques Rueff; and those of Finance Minister Hayato Ikeda in Japan; of Gesualdo A. Costanzo, the United States Treasury adviser in Greece (1947); and of Princeton Professor Edwin Walter Kemmerer in eleven countries of the world, five of them in South America: Peru (1922), Colombia (1923), Chile (1925), Ecuador (1927) and Bolivia (1928). I can speak from personal observation of those five countries, and from personal contact with Dr. Kemmerer in the last four. True, all these South American countries sooner or later reverted to their inflationary ways, but only because they abandoned the sound principles laid down by Dr. Kemmerer.

I do not include myself in the list of the great stabilizers of the century—although it is true that when I stabilized the Bolivian currency in 1956–57, stabilization came almost overnight and was widely acclaimed as a miracle—because all I did was to follow in the footsteps of Drs. Kemmerer, Schacht and Erhard.

I shall discuss the Bolivian stabilization at some length in Chapter 7 because it holds invaluable lessons for us in the United States, and because I can speak more authoritatively on that subject than on any other. But if I deserve any credit whatsoever for that accomplishment, it is not because of any originality as an economic adviser—there was nothing original in my work—but because, as a lawyer, my forte is that of stubborn, tactful persuasion. And I had to convince a Revolutionary Marxist President that he had to reverse practically everything that his Marxist predecessor and "comrade" had done in the four previous disastrous years.

The great stabilizers were all exponents of the "old economics"

All of the great monetary stabilizers were either pre-Keynesians or followed principles diametrically opposed to those advocated by Keynes and his disciples. As classical economists, they insisted upon balanced budgets, upon the government living within its means at home and abroad, without borrowing from the central bank or printing more paper money of its own.

And they did *not* resort to price controls, because they knew from all previous history that price controls and freezes and "rollbacks" simply will not work. They never have, they never will, and they never can. All that price controls can accomplish—and they do that very well—is to disrupt the economy and produce scarcities, as we can see right now in our own country, most notably in the case of oil and housing.

Identical problems but tailor-made solutions

Lest some might think that the monetary experiences in Germany, France and Japan, and particularly in the smaller countries of Latin America, have little relevance to our own problems, it may be said that *in any country*, our own included, there are only three real problems—the economists and the politicians and the people who say "it can't be done."

The problem of monetary and price stabilization itself is identical *in every country*, whether the preceding inflation was mild (say 138 percent as in the United States from 1967 to mid-1979, est.) or galloping (say a trillion or billion to one, as in Germany and Brazil), and regardless of whether the country is an economic giant or an economic midget.

In fact, stabilization is a far more difficult task in a small country such as Bolivia, with its scanty resources and limited recuperative powers, its history of almost perpetual revolution, and an endemic corruption so extreme that an English historian has written that the remuneration of government officials is too small "to offer any temptation to honesty."

But although the *problem* of stabilization is identical in every country, the *solution* must be tailor-made to fit each particular situation. And the approach would vary according to the extent and origin of the preceding inflation, the basic economic strength of the particular country—its capacity to generate foreign exchange through the balance of payments—and, above all, the political structure, bearing in mind that "politics is the art of the possible" and that politicians are people who sometimes make the possible impossible!

German stabilization in 1948

As to the problem of the economists, Dr. Erhard writes that the Allied authorities in Germany had prohibited him from *altering* the price controls imposed by the occupation economists, but that it had never occurred to them that someone might decide not just to *alter* price controls but to *abolish* them.

When this was precisely what Erhard did, in line with his insistence on a free-market economy, General Lucius Clay, head of the American mission, summoned Erhard to his office and asked him whether it was true that he intended to balance the budget, abandon all price and other controls and restrictions and return Germany to a free-market economy, subject only to the untrammeled forces of supply and demand.

When Erhard answered in the affirmative, Clay replied (the conversation was related to me orally but is believed to be substantially accurate), "My advisers tell me that, if you do this, prices will rise sky-high and there will be chaos in Germany."

"That's all right, General," Erhard is reported to have replied. "Don't worry. My advisers tell me the same thing, but I'm going right ahead."

Which he did. The result was that Germany, on a free-market basis and with a balanced budget, achieved one of the most remarkable eras of economic recovery that the world has ever seen and, as the late Dr. Rueff pointed out, the recovery was practically instantaneous. Clay backed up Erhard against the advice of his own economic adviser, who later became head of President Johnson's Economic Council, but Erhard writes that, from then on, "in the coming months and years, the Allies tried to influence German reconstruction according to their ideas"—which did not fit in at all with Erhard's insistence on a free economy.

Some economists, stubbornly Keynesian in their outlook, have analyzed the German miracle as though it had not been the consequence of a balanced budget and a free economy, but insist that stabilization had occurred because the government had "syphoned off" excess paper money from circulation—the inflation had been of the demand-pull variety, caused by too much money chasing a limited supply of goods. And when the excess money was withdrawn, they contend, stabilization occurred automatically.

But the retirement of paper money, in Germany as elsewhere, was merely the final step in the stabilization process. It had nothing to do with the essence of the stabilization plan, but was merely a matter of convenience, of substituting an entirely new currency for the old, which had become so worthless that it took a shoe box full of bank notes to pay for a pair of shoes.

The government exchanged 1 new Deutschmark for 100 old Reichsmarks, and retired the old bank notes completely from circulation, precisely as Schacht had done a generation earlier when he exchanged 1 new Rentenmark for 1 trillion old marks. Or as De Gaulle had exchanged 1 franc nouveau for 100 old francs, or as they did in Bolivia, where 1 new peso was exchanged for 1,000 old bolivianos. And in all cases this was merely a matter of convenience, because adding machines and pocketbooks were not big enough to accommodate the hundreds or thousands or trillions of old money. It had nothing to do with the process of stabilization.

"Syphoning off" excess bank notes

Many economists, wedded to the idea of the unbalanced budget, are adamant in insisting that the thingamajig that did the trick was the bibbidy-bobbidy-boo of syphoning off bank notes from circulation. In Greece the American economic advisers actually persuaded the Greek

Government to try that very thing, and obligingly handed over millions of dollars of United States aid so that the Greeks could buy up their own currency.

The Greek Government blithely printed more and more bank notes in exchange for American dollars until, finally, an able Treasury economist, Dr. Gesualdo A. Costanzo, now vice-chairman of Citibank in charge of all foreign operations, put a stop to the thing and stabilized the Greek currency by balancing the budget, stopping the printing presses, removing all controls, and insisting on a realistic foreign exchange budget so that the government was forced to live within its means abroad as well as at home.

When I was in Bolivia, a high State Department officer, who had been in Greece but apparently failed to grasp the implications of the Greek experience, recommended that I use $5 million out of the $25 million stabilization fund that it had taken me so much effort to raise, to buy up $5 million worth of bolivianos—which at the time would have meant some 70 trillion paper bolivianos. Wow! I didn't have shoe boxes enough for that.

To emphasize the absurdity of the proposal, when I later reported to the State and Treasury Departments some of the ridiculous schemes that had been proposed to stop the inflation, I likened this particular scheme to exchanging good American dollars for cigar-store coupons. And I told the story of my experience as a sergeant and interpreter in World War I.

My troop was quartered in St.-Nazaire in a billet previously occupied by some Marines, apparently from the Halls of Montezuma. My captain called upon me to interpret the angry complaints of a laundress and her daughter who had taken in washing for the Marines and had performed other services on the side—although perhaps this is not an accurate description of their position at the time. The two women had a large packet of United Cigar Store coupons (which looked like money) to show for their exertions, and to their dismay they had been unable to cash them at the bank.

This true story was later embellished, and published in the *Stars and Stripes,* by having the ladies run out of the office, waving the cigar coupons and screaming that they had been raped!

My story fell flat as yesterday's omelet, and it was not until later that I learned that several of the State Department and foreign-aid officers present at the meeting had participated in the Greek tragedy—or comedy, if you are a Greek and not an American taxpayer.

The true solution to inflation

But to prove that buying up paper money is not the cure for inflation, we should look, not to the American economists who have analyzed the

German miracle, but to the writings of Ludwig Erhard himself and to those of his close friend and adviser, the late Wilhelm Röpke. In fact, one paragraph of Dr. Röpke's is so pertinent to inflation in the United States today that it is worth quoting at length, at the risk of boring some and offending others:

> . . . the German accomplishment was nonetheless—in economic terms—no miracle at all, if the essence of the reform of 1948 is clearly understood. Its success was on the contrary precisely what its architects had expected. The real miracle lay in the fact that, in this particular country and in a world still under the spell of inflationism and collectivism, it proved possible politically and socially to return to the economic reason of the market economy and to monetary discipline. . . . Outside Germany there still appear to be some die-hards who—either out of ignorance of the facts and interrelationships or against their better judgment—resist admitting that here is to be found the most convincing case in all history against collectivism and inflationism and for market economy and monetary discipline. . . . The essence of the German economic reform corresponds to the sickness which it was intended to cure. If the sickness was repressed inflation (meaning the attempt to curb inflation by price controls, rationing and other interferences with a free market), the therapy for it had to consist, on the one hand, in the elimination of inflationary pressure and, on the other hand, in the elimination of the apparatus of repression and the restoration of market freedom, free prices, competition and entrepreneurial incentives. Freedom in the realm of goods, discipline in the realm of money—these were the two princi-ples on which rested the German economic revival from 1948 onwards. . . . It was not always easy to maintain, uninterrupted, the course of such a noninflationary economy. The temptation was strong to give in to an anachronistic Keynesianism [emphasis mine] and to fight the persistently high level of unemployment, due to the continuing streams of refugees from the East, with a program of inflationary (government) investments. The American occupation authorities exerted, over a considerable period, strong pressure on the German government and the German central bank in this direction.

Considering that the American economists who were behind the pressure on the German Government to fight inflation with government spending are the very ones whose advice under Kennedy-Johnson started the inflationary tide in this country and who are now loudest in demanding more government deficit spending and price controls or "jawboning" here, it would be well to ponder the astounding success of Germany, with its balanced budget and free-market economy (at least at the beginning of the German boom), and our difficulties in the United States with our deficit financing.

To emphasize the little understanding that academic economists in this country have of the problems of inflation and their solution, one of the ablest of American economists characterized the lectures of Jacques Rueff in this country as "damned nonsense," which may possibly have been true so far as Rueff's apperception of the facts of economic and political life in this country was concerned, and his consequently specious recommendations for action. But the fact remains that Rueff—the first economist elected to the elite, forty-member French Academy—was General de Gaulle's adviser in the stabilization of the French franc, putting into effect precisely the same principles as those used by Röpke and Erhard in Germany, and that his views on those principles and on gold as a necessary international medium of exchange, as expressed in his lectures, are eminently sound. And the application of those principles *did* stabilize the currency in his country, something that the economists here have thus far failed to do. To stabilize a currency means to stabilize its purchasing power—in other words, to put a stop to inflation.

The meaning of "galloping" inflation

Let's pause for a moment to explain just what "galloping" or "rampant" inflation means.

One of the chief political leaders in Bolivia—later my violent Trotskyite adversary—quite logically raised the question of the stability of the dollar when I spoke of stabilizing the boliviano in terms of dollars, which were stable at the time.

Under his questioning, I admitted that, from 1940 to 1953, but chiefly during the Truman Administration from 1945 on, wholesale commodity prices had gone up more than 100 percent under the strictest of price controls. In other words, the purchasing power of the dollar had fallen more than 50 percent. But I added that Eisenhower had removed all price controls and, despite Truman's insistence that prices would shoot through the roof, they had in fact risen only a fraction of 1 percent and the purchasing power of the dollar had been practically stable ever since. (This was in 1956.)

To show the extent of the Bolivian inflation in comparison with the 100 percent inflation in the United States, and to give the Bolivians some encouragement by explaining the far worse inflation in Germany, I prepared a little chart on a 5″ by 8″ card that I used in several speeches to the Bolivian senators and representatives, labor leaders and others. Later I used a similar chart in my lectures at Harvard and Michigan. (See Chart 4.)

Visualize that chart as being five inches high, and showing the more than two to one (an index of 216) inflation in the United States from 1940 to 1953. On that same scale, the Bolivian inflation, from 2.4 bolivianos to the dollar to 14,000 to the dollar, would need a chart 1,250 feet high—taller than the Empire State Building!

The 1923 German inflation of a trillion to one—one million million—would call for a chart nearly 40 million miles high, equal to 85 round trips to the moon and back—170 trips!!

That should suffice to put our relatively modest inflation—a rise of 27 percent in wholesale commodity prices under Kennedy-Johnson (8 years), some 55 percent under Richard Nixon (5½ years), a further 17.6 percent under Gerald Ford (2½ years), and 27 percent to mid-1979 under President Carter (2½ years)—in somewhat better perspective. It is serious, but not yet "galloping." At the same time, the German inflation

CHART 4—Inflation in the United States, 1940–53

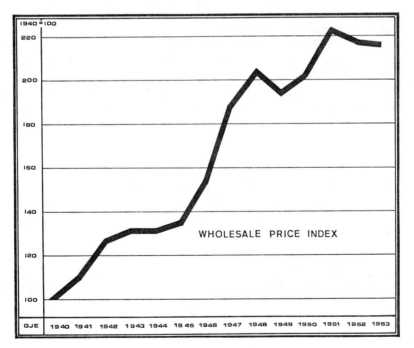

should warn us of the direction in which we are headed if we continue to follow the deficit spending policies, the attempts at *gradual* recovery from inflation and the palliatives that led to Germany's catastrophe.

But even then, remember that Germany survived her trillion to one debauchment of the currency in 1923, and her hundred to one debasement in 1948 and, after having been defeated in two world wars, is now far better off than we are. In fact, Germany's economic record over the past twenty years has been better than that of any other major country in the world, except perhaps Japan, with France and Switzerland not far behind. Those countries have been living within their means in pre-Keynesian economic bliss, and their currencies are the soundest in the world. In recent years, it is true that the worldwide "energy crisis"—*for which the United States is to blame because of our uninhibited demand for oil*—has hit those countries hard as they are practically 100 percent dependent on imported oil. But the setback there was temporary; the inflation problem here may not be.

Think about it. Those four countries must have been doing something right—and perhaps we may be doing something wrong.

Is the American "stagflation" unprecedented?

Dr. Arthur Burns of the Federal Reserve Board and several other professors or ex-professors of economics have been assuring us in recent years that the present situation in America, of inflation plus economic stagnation, is "without precedent in history" and they even coined a new word for it—"stagflation."

But it is by no means unique. In most of the Latin American inflations over the past fifty years, and in every one of the eleven instances in Europe, Japan and Latin America cited in this chapter, the same sequence of causes and consequences has been evident that is now present in the United States:

> Government overspending and deficit financing
> Printing-press inflation through borrowing from the central bank
> Rising prices and wages
> A credit shortage caused by the government borrowing in excess
>   of the lending capacity of the market
> Higher interest rates for the same reason, as well as because of the
>   ongoing depreciation of the currency
> A housing shortage as a consequence of the credit shortage and
>   high interest rates, as well as rent controls
> Economic stagnation
> Rising unemployment and underemployment

Increased welfare expenditures to counteract the effects of
  stagnation

And, once again, the vicious cycle of government overspending
  and deficit financing

The only reason this combination of inflation plus stagnation is unprecedented in the United States is that this is the first time in this country that government overspending has reached such extremes and continued for so long a time—for over forty years to be exact. Until, as a consequence of thirty years of foreign aid and welfare and the longest, costliest war in our history, our currency has become nothing but a paper fraud, with a frightening *minus figure* in our gold and foreign exchange reserves, as we shall see in Chapter 10, and *nothing* behind the dollar but the government fiat: "Let this piece of paper be money."

It is indeed strange that all the professorial economists who have guided our destiny over the past forty years—men of undoubted intelligence and theoretical knowledge—tell us that the present combination of inflation, stagnation, high interest rates and unemployment is without precedent, when in fact the only thing without precedent is that for the first time they are brought face to face with the fact that all they have ever learned and taught of Keynesian theories and Phillips curves is *obsolete and fallacious.*

If only they would take a look around, they would see that the situation here is practically identical to that of each of the eleven instances cited in this chapter where a nation has licked inflation and stagnation combined. And they might then come to the realization that the same processes—a balanced budget and a balanced foreign exchange account— that enabled those countries to overcome inflation and depression would inevitably work here in the United States. And far more easily and more certainly here because of this country's vast recuperative resources. Thus, if we have the wisdom and courage to follow in the footsteps of those nations, we could, like them, succeed in overcoming our present problems, not gradually and over a period of years, but practically overnight— the "miracle of stabilization" that has occurred in every country that has dared to face the problem.

8. Lessons From the Bolivian Stabilization

The struggle against inflation calls for enormous moral courage, a profound and unbreakable conviction, and the spirit of self-sacrifice which will discard dangerous and easy remedies in favor of the authentic and enduring interests of the people. To those brave and farsighted men who have undertaken to conquer inflation in Bolivia, I therefore pay the spontaneous homage of my admiration.

Raúl Prebisch (1957)

When I stabilized the Bolivian currency, my chief problems—aside from the incompetence of United States State Department and aid officials in Washington, and the not unexpected corruption, incompetence and communism prevalent in Bolivia—came from two highly intelligent Keynesian economists who were responsible for having brought the Bolivian currency down from 190 bolivianos to the dollar (it was once worth 40 cents U.S.) to 14,000 to the dollar at its nadir.

One was the President of Bolivia, formerly a professor of economics at the University of San Andrés in La Paz, the other his economic adviser, sent down by the World Bank, who also lectured at the University, and had once been president of the Hungarian central bank during a period when the Hungarian pengo dropped to 1.4 nonillion (10 to the thirtieth power) to one!

Both of these gentlemen would undoubtedly insist that *they* were not responsible for the disastrous debasement of the currency, and they could certainly muster up an impressive list of other reasons for the inflation. But, come to think of it, American and English Keynesians would also deny that unbalanced budgets and the rise in the money supply had anything to do with the rise in prices and the critical economic situations in those two countries. The rise in the money supply, they would say, is always a *consequence* of inflation, not the *cause* of it, and government deficit spending was necessary to prevent unemployment. If the temperature rises, you wouldn't blame the thermometer, would you?

So it is perhaps not surprising that I display some animadversion toward the Keynesian philosophy. I have seen it in operation in its purest form—an ordeal from which the Keynesian economists in England and the United States have been happily spared.

Bolivian conditions prior to stabilizaton

Now let's see what the situation was in Bolivia when the United States Treasury and State Departments, alarmed by the fact that our foreign aid was going down the drain because of galloping inflation, asked me to go to that country to help the President of Bolivia stabilize the currency. And let's see what measures were taken to remedy that situation.

Not that the Bolivian economy bears the slightest resemblance to that of the United States, but because the forces that make for monetary inflation—inflation caused by printing paper money and paper IOUs to finance government deficits—are the same everywhere in the world and because the measures we took in Bolivia are substantially the same as those that have been taken by *every nation* that has successfully overcome the scourge of monetary inflation. And monetary inflation—*debasement of the currency*, to put it in its true terms—is what we are suffering from in the United States today, plus the wage-push or cost-push pressures that are inevitable and natural consequences whenever prices rise as the result of monetary debasement.

When I arrived in Bolivia in midsummer of 1956, the political, social, economic and financial chaos was unbelievalbe, although I was by no means a stranger to that troubled country. The nation was run by a Marxist Revolutionary government, composed of Trotskyites, Communists, ex-Nazis, left wing-socialists, anarcho-syndicalists and just plain crooks.

The President, members of his Cabinet, and his top political allies were each importing a truck a month at the official exchange rate of 190 bolivianos to the dollar when the actual rate for the past twelve months had varied from 6,000 to 14,000 to the dollar. In other words, they could bring in a $6,000 truck at a cost to them of between $80 and $190—and "live comfortably on the proceeds," as I was told by the President himself!

This was the Keynesian professor of economics who had hornswoggled Milton Eisenhower into increasing American aid to Bolivia, and under whose guidance the galloping inflation had begun and was continuing, despite the phony "stabilization measures" taken three years before my arrival on the advice of "experts" from the International Monetary Fund and World Bank.

From one third to two thirds of United States aid was going into the pockets of these political gangsters and their friends, much of it being smuggled out of the country. And much of the rest of American aid proved to be one of the major causes of the then rampant inflation thanks to the fact that the United States Government required the Bolivian Government to provide "counterpart funds" in bolivianos for every dollar of aid provided by the United States. This kept the Bolivian printing presses working full-time, grinding out billions of dollars of cigar-store coupon currency.

Rent controls, price controls, controls of every kind, as well as rationing, had been enacted. The President-elect said he was prepared to enforce those controls with bayonets if necessary—just as in Germany, from 1933 to 1948, the death penalty was prescribed for evasion of the controls. And—in Bolivia as in Germany—none of the controls worked!

Instead, farmers stopped producing; laborers worked only a few hours a day; bread, meat, all the essentials of life were in such short supply, and black markets charged such exorbitant prices, that the most profitable business for the poor people was waiting in line at the official rationing places for twenty-four hours a day, and then *selling their places in line* to others only a little more prosperous than themselves.

The three great tin-mining companies had, for over sixty years, provided the major force behind the nation's decidedly limited economic development; accounted for 80 percent of the exports; paid 80 percent of the taxes—and ran the country. These enterprises were confiscated outright, and were being run by the most corrupt and incompetent gang of politicos I have ever run into, backed by a "people's militia" of miners, armed with guns and dynamite.

Ostensibly under a Marxist "land reform" program, every farm of appreciable size—not just the large estates—had been confiscated. But actually the farms had been seized by armed bandits, the "peasants' militia," which was the second largest armed force in the nation. The Army and police forces had been disarmed and reduced to impotence.

Imagine the United States taken over lock, stock and barrel by Black October, the Black Panthers, the Mafia and their ilk—not the Benevolent and Protective Order of Ilks—and you may have some faint idea of the chaos and corruption that prevailed in Bolivia when I arrived there to stabilize the currency.

My mission in Bolivia

I was neither given—nor wanted—any advice or instructions as to how I was to accomplish my mission of stabilizing the Bolivian currency, certainly not from the high officials in the State Department who kept on dishing out United States aid to Bolivia in the face of those conditions. But I had several things working in my favor.

In the first place, I had known Latin America firsthand for nearly forty years, and Bolivia for over sixteen. And I knew exactly what the causes of inflation had been in every country of Latin America since the turn of the century. I had known Professor Kemmerer and knew what he had done on his five South American missions, during a time when I was chief of the Latin American Section at the United States Bureau of Foreign & Domestic Commerce.

In the second place, the Undersecretary of the Treasury of the United States—a distinguished banker and economist, who was largely responsible for my appointment—had made it clear that there would be no more United States aid until Bolivia "had put its house in order." So the Bolivian President was practically forced to appoint me as economic adviser and accept the conditions that I laid down as a precondition for taking the post.

In the third place, and most important, two months after my arrival, and two days after my official appointment by the Keynesian President as Executive Director of the National Monetary Stabilization Council, a new President was inaugurated, Hernán Siles Zuazo. He was a Marxist, but luckily not an economist and, above all, he was a man of integrity and courage. It was a privilege to serve as well as economic adviser to the President under that statesman during the remainder of my stay in Bolivia.

Drafting the Bolivian stabilization program

Meanwhile, during the two months after my arrival and before my official appointment, I had drafted legislation creating the National Monetary Stabilization Council, completed a forty-step stabilization program, and a detailed six-month agenda to carry it out. All those plans and legislation were cleared with the incoming and outgoing Presidents and with their respective advisers, as well as with the heads of the People's Militia and the Peasants' Militia who were scheduled to be the president of the Senate and the vice-president in the new administration. This was accomplished in the most frenzied two months of intensive labor that I have ever undertaken. But speed was more essential than meticulous planning, for the monetary, financial and economic situation was disintegrating at such a vertiginous rate that, if it were done, then 'twere well it were done quickly.

The forty-step chronological plan was later replaced by a substantially identical fifty-step program that I arranged by subject matter and implemented by detailed legislation drafted over the course of the next five months. All this was cleared in Bolivia and Washington, where I managed to raise a $25 million stabilization fund, with contributions from the Treasury, the United States foreign-aid agency and the International Monetary Fund. I had arranged for an additional $5 million to be contributed by a consortium of New York banks, but there was no time to complete that operation, which, in the event, proved to be unnecessary.

Shortly after I returned from Washington with the money, and with the program all approved, the American Monetary Stabilization Mission was completed with the arrival of two colleagues—a central banker and a tax consultant—who were able to help in the implementation of the program and with advice on the necessary supplemental legislation.

The final fifty-step program was drafted in collaboration with Dr. G. A. Costanzo (who had previously stabilized the Greek currency) and his assistants from the International Monetary Fund. And I may say that, without his help and that of a member of his team who remained in Bolivia during the remainder of my stay there, I could never have completed nor carried out the stabilization program in time to be of any use.

The essence of the stabilization program

The essence of the program was: (1) to consolidate the budgets of the government and of all government agencies and operations—the tin mines, petroleum company and so forth—and arrive at an overall balance, so that there would be no more borrowing from the central bank and no more printing-press money; (2) to set up a realistic foreign exchange budget—an estimated embryo balance of payments—so that the government would be living within its means internationally as well as domestically; (3) to eliminate all restrictions and controls on foreign exchange, prices, imports, exports, and establish—to the extent that this was possible under a Marxist regime—a free-market economy; and (4) to eliminate the existing multiple rates of exchange—official, import, export, free market—and establish a realistic exchange value for the boliviano, which would thereafter be allowed to fluctuate freely in accordance with supply and demand until such time as a rational fixed rate could be determined, and a new currency issued at a ratio of 1,000 new pesos for one of the old bolivianos.

The other features of the program were all ancillary and of no interest to anyone not actually engaged in a monetary stabilization program in some other country of the world. Such persons are referred to an 800-page book I wrote at The University of Michigan (*Inflation and Development in Latin America*, Graduate School of Business Administration, Ann Arbor), which describes the stabilization process in all its gory details and, believe me, they were gory.

Universal applicability of the Bolivian plan

But the essential elements in the plan—the balanced budget, the limitation of the government's expenditures abroad to amounts that would not strain the country's balance of payments, and the removal of all price and foreign exchange controls and special privileges—are *identical* to those found in *every* successful stabilization plan enacted over the past sixty years in any country of the world—*mutatis mutandis*, as we lawyers say, meaning changing such details as must be changed to meet changes in circumstances.

And these essential elements are those that *must be adopted in the United States* if we are to have an end to the present era of controls and inflation—and stagnation, unemployment and taxation without end.

Those economists and government officials in this country who, with all modesty, have been saying that mankind does not know how to control inflation should exercise an even greater degree of modesty and admit merely that *they* do not know how to cope with it. For the great monetary stabilizers referred to in the previous chapter have all clearly demonstrated that mankind does indeed know how to stop inflation, and that the only real problems are the economists and the politicians and the faint of heart.

Consequences of the stabilization program

What happened in Bolivia after the stabilization program was enacted? One day of chaos worse compounded, a few days of bewilderment and uncertainty, and then—the "miracle of stabilization." The black markets, the long queus of peasants waiting on interminable lines, the smuggling and misuse of United States aid, all vanished as if by magic. Bread, meat, fruit and other essentials began to come back from secret places under the shelves or in the smugglers' warehouses. And, within eight days, as one newspaper put it, Bolivia had its first Christmas with free prices—and, for the first time in years, under the influence of free competition and supply and demand, the stores and peddlers had ample stocks of holiday merchandise for all.

Within seven months, prices and living costs had fallen 22 percent below the December stabilization level. The program had succeeded. And, for a brief moment, graft had been wiped out—a "return to morality," as the newspapers put it. With complete freedom of imports, exports and free competition, smuggling became unprofitable to the point that at one meeting of the Stabilization Council at the Presidential Palace, we ran into a delegation from the smugglers' "guild"—the third-rate politicos and their friends—demanding an end to that "damned Eder program," as the President told me with a smile.

And over the course of the following six months the Vice-President was thrown out of office because of some skullduggery revealed in my report to the Cabinet, and the president of the Senate was forced to flee for his life from an angry mob of Indian women. I was twice threatened with assassination and violently denounced by the politicos whose livelihood had been taken away by the "return to morality."

But that break with Bolivian tradition—the "era of morality"— was not of long duration. Before I had left Bolivia the smugglers were back in operation at their own special marketplaces and the politicos were back in business. And United States aid has since been going down the drain at a greater rate than ever before.

And now—seven revolutions later—the stabilization of the Bolivian peso has finally come apart at the seams. And if ever the troubles in Indonesia are over and tin prices drop from their present dizzy height to more usual levels, Bolivia will be worse off than it was before, because the country has been so long dependent on the crutch of foreign aid that it will be unable to stand on its own feet again for a generation.

But the currency stabilization was successful. The peso has been reasonably stable in terms of dollars for over twenty years; it is now quoted at 20 to the dollar. And with an end to inflation, economic recovery came gradually, with less unemployment and far less underemployment.

Would the Bolivian plan work here?

The question is: Could the same program—*mutatis mutandis*—be used in the United States and would it work?

Unquestionably! It *would* work, and it would work far better here than in Bolivia, for the United States has far greater resources, far greater recuperative powers, than Bolivia or any other country in the world.

But the legislation requisite for the success of the plan would have to be radically different in the United States than in Bolivia, and geared to our system of laws and government structure. The only indispensable element, and this has proved true in every country, large or small, that has succeeded in breaking the vicious spiral of rampant inflation, is that the Congress must be willing to submit to a self-imposed legislative moratorium on spending until the inflation is under control. How this may be achieved in the United States is deferred until Chapters 15 and 16, for the problem of inflation must be expounded more fully before we get to a proposed solution.

The structural political hurdles

But, in view of the tense relationship that developed between the Nixon Administration and Congress as an aftermath of the Watergate affair, perhaps I should interject right here that representatives and senators are neither evil men nor profligates, and that a President is not invariably in the right in his conflicts with Congress. It is just that a collective body such as Congress is collectively irresponsible—not like a President who has to shoulder full responsibility for the consequences of his acts. Each of the spate of money-spending bills presented by the more than five hundred legislators has some merit, some at least plausible justification, taken by itself. It is in the aggregate that these bills add up to more than the nation can afford.

And, to go from generalities to specifics—one instance out of thousands—at midnight on October 17, 1972, when the Senate was overriding the President on the Water Pollution Act, the distinguished senator who was leading the debate declared: "Well, it only costs $350 million in fiscal 1973, so there is no problem!" Ignoring completely the fact that it would cost some $18 *billion* over the following three years, and that is indeed a problem—inflation incarnate!

In all my years of experience in Latin America I have never run across a more outrageous example of fiscal irresponsibility than that illustrated in this instance. Do you wonder that past administrations were unable to curb the inflation in the face of the collective irresponsibility of Congress?

And can any administration stop inflation when Congress passes a bill that, by raising the personal exemption and that for dependents from $750 to $1,000, is expected to relieve some 3.7 million people from paying any income tax whatsoever? When we know as a matter of fact—getting away from the clamor of the rabble-rousers and the uninformed—that no further privileges should be granted to those in the lowest tax brackets nor to the tax-exempt. That the wealthiest half of the people in the United States pay 94 percent of the income taxes; that the 52 percent of the households in the lower brackets—those with aggregate earnings of less than $10,000 a year—pay only 6 percent of the tax. Households earning over $30,000 a year, ranging from the comfortably well-off to the very wealthy, receive 22 percent of all income reported, but pay nearly 40 percent of the taxes.

Congress has already enacted one tax break after another favoring the lowest bracket taxpayers and, as a reaction to the California tax "revolt," they are likely to distort the distribution of taxes still further.

Some would call it demagoguery, but I prefer to stick to my term, "collective irresponsibility," for I am certain that the overwhelming majority of our senators and representatives would repudiate such tactics if they realized, as I am trying to point out in this book, that government deficits are practically the sole cause of inflation in this country and of the consequent stagnation and unemployment.

So, henceforth, when some politician or television pundit—one of those who, like Samuel Butler's Dr. Downie, "could say nothing in more words than any man of his generation"—declaims in stentorian tones: "Do you mean to say that this nation, the richest in all the world, cannot afford to spend $50 million to save the youth of this country from untold suffering and wipe out poison ivy?" Or to wipe out or accomplish whatever else it may be that ought to be accomplished or wiped out—then the answer must be: "No, this nation cannot afford to do that—not if it is to carry out the other tasks that Congress has mandated."

This matter of collective irresponsibility is indeed one instance where the charge of "fallacy of composition" is a valid criticism—the sum of the parts can be disastrous even though the individual spending bills may have some merit.

And as I have pointed to "collective irresponsibility" as the besetting sin of the legislative branch, let me point out the inherent vice of the executive branch—the arrogance and corruption that is so often engendered by unrestricted power, the assumption by the Executive of powers not delegated to it by the legislative branch nor mandated by the Constitution. And this undue expansion of presidential power may be as productive of inflationary pressures as the spending proclivities of the Congress.

Despite reiterated admonitions by one administration after another that Congress must cut down on its spending legislation, my own impression is that the growth of the federal budget, from some $3 billion under Hoover to more than $300 billion under Nixon, $349 billion under Ford, and $630 billion under Carter, is more the work of the Executive and its lobbying bureaucracy than it is of Congress.

But, wherever the blame lies, our only hope of retrenchment, and of putting an end to the present inflation, is for both branches of government to work together to curb both the "collective irresponsibility" of Congress and the unlimited expansion of executive and bureaucratic power. Ways and means of accomplishing this formidable task are discussed in Chapter 16.

9. The Gold Standard and Its Paper Substitutes

It is not robbery if princes exact from their subjects that which is due to them for the safeguarding of the common good, but if they extort something unduly, it is robbery, even as burglary is. Hence, St. Augustine says: "If justice be disregarded, what is a king but a mighty robber, since what is a robber but a little king?"

St. Thomas Aquinas (1267)

Ever since money was first invented, kings and governments have been robbing the people by "clipping" gold coins, lowering their weight, or debasing the gold content by using less gold and more copper—so much so that George III was known as "Red-Nose" because of the coppery glint of his profile on the golden guineas. Or they have debased the currency in other more subtle ways so that subjects or citizens would not blame the government for higher prices, but could always blame the speculators or the bankers or the foreign imperialists. But debauchment of the currency is what inflation is all about—simply a more honest, less polite name for what people usually call "inflation."

The Roosevelt and Nixon devaluations

When Franklin Roosevelt "raised the price of gold," he did it openly. Many people criticized him, a few praised him, but his action did serve to increase the disastrously low price of cotton and other basic commodities in the United States, and brought this country out of one of the worst depressions it has ever known. Proof of this statement is given in Chapter 10.

And when President Nixon twice "raised the price of gold," it inevitably raised the price of all international staple commodities in the United States, and hence the general price index and the cost of living.

But what Roosevelt and Nixon did was not really *raise the price of gold.* The price of gold, like that of any other commodity, is determined by world supply and demand, and not by what the President of the United States may declare or decree.

So when President Roosevelt "raised the price of gold" from $20.67 an ounce to $35 an ounce, all that he was really doing was to say that the dollar was no longer worth one twentieth of an ounce of gold, but one thirty-fifth of an ounce. And that he *could* do. It was *debasement of the dollar*, pure and simple—which is not to say that it was a bad thing to do at that time and under those circumstances. Personally, I don't think it was.

And when President Nixon "raised the price of gold" to $42.2222 ounce, although it is true that the price of gold *in dollars* was raised, all that the President, with the consent of Congress, really did was to proclaim that the dollar was worth one forty-second part of an ounce of gold—again *debasement of the currency.*

The dollar today is simply not the same dollar that it was forty-five years ago. Intrinsically, at the official price, it is now worth one half of what it was worth then. At the market price, it is worth less than one tenth of its former value. And if you expect prices in today's dollars to be the same as prices used to be in yesterday's dollars, then you really do believe in miracles. Again, as Irving Fisher used to say, you can't buy as much with a little piece of gold as you can with a big piece of gold.

The merits of the gold standard

One of the most satisfactory things about the gold standard was that your measuring stick did not vary from year to year. Prices, of course, did vary, as we saw in the disastrous slump from 1929 to 1932.

Because, with the gold standard, prices for each and every commodity depend upon the ratio between the supply and demand for gold, and the supply and demand for each particular commodity. And the general price index—the purchasing power of the currency—varies according to the aggregate of all those prices.

The gold standard did not work perfectly, as we all know. Booms were followed by slumps, some of them disastrous—a "sloom followed by a bump," as one Spoonerism-prone economist once stated. But the bumps were never as catastrophic as the crises caused by fiat money, as we have seen throughout the course of history in many countries of the world. And it is fiat currency that we have today.

One of the reasons why the gold standard worked as well as it did for so many centuries—at least relatively well, in comparison with any other system thus far in general use—is that the annual production of gold throughout the world is only about one thirtieth of the total monetary gold stocks of the world at any given time. So that the price of gold—the ratio between world demand and world supply—was less affected by a single year's production than was the price of wheat or cotton or copper or practically any other commodity.

Gold has always been in demand. Moths and rust do not corrupt it, and it has proved to be a better *repository of wealth* than silver, tin, jewels, laces, tobacco, beads, shells or any of the various media that people have used as money in times past.

And, as a *medium of exchange*, which is the second function of money, gold is and always has been eminently "sound"—immediately exchangeable for goods and services of every kind, a common denominator in the marketplace that served well in the transition from barter to a money economy and for centuries thereafter.

The failures of the gold standard

But in the third function of money, to serve as a *yardstick of value* in which money contracts extending over months and years can be measured as reliably as distances can be measured by the standard foot or meter, gold has been a woeful failure.

And modern life requires a monetary measure that will be stable— or at least relatively stable—as long as the term of one's life insurance policy, or mortgage, or a corporate bond.

The failure of gold as a permanent measure of value has been due in part to sudden changes in the supply of gold, such as the successive discoveries of the yellow metal in Colorado, California, Alaska, Canada and South Africa, and the invention of the cyanide process to extract the metal from the ore. Each of those events meant that gold became more abundant and cheaper—hence, prices for all other commodities in terms of gold increased.

But, chiefly, the failure of the gold standard has been attributable to three other factors of tremendous importance: (1) the invention of paper money, not backed 100 percent by gold; (2) the increasing use of bank and other forms of credit in many countries of the world, but particularly in the United States, where checks are used more widely than anywhere else, largely because of certain safeguards in our Negotiable Instruments Law, not found in the British Bills of Exchange Act or in Civil Law countries; and (3) adoption of the "gold exchange standard," whereby countries other than the United States could use dollars as a substitute for their gold reserves, thus saving the expense of storing gold and, instead, receiving interest on their dollar deposits.

All three developments meant that each ounce of gold in the

world's monetary stocks could perform many times the number of services that a single ounce of gold could perform if there were no paper money, no credit, and no gold exchange standard. And all three developments increased the world money supply just as effectively as if vast new stocks of gold had been discovered, say on the moon.

Hence, prices went up and will probably never come down to previous levels again, for no one wants to propose the dreadful crisis that would ensue if all paper money and all credit were to be eliminated.

However, the late Jacques Rueff, the great French economist, did advocate abolishing the gold exchange standard. This system was created at the Geneva Monetary Conference in 1922 in order to relieve the world gold shortage caused by the fact that during and after World War I so much of the world's gold had come to the United States. The gold exchange standard "economized" the use of gold by allowing countries to maintain their reserves in foreign balances—dollars.

Rueff blamed the gold exchange standard for the world crisis of 1929, because it removed the brakes on excessive expansion which would have been imposed by a true gold standard, under which a country could not increase the import side of its balance of payments unless it had the actual resources to do so. And governments could not expand their domestic or foreign expenditures beyond the limits imposed by their tax capabilities.

He also rightly blamed the gold exchange standard for the eventual overconcentration of the world's gold stocks in the United States, and for the consequent "double mortgage" on our gold stocks which, he claimed, imposed a serious threat to American solvency. He wrote this in 1961 and his prescience is noteworthy, for the dangers, which American economists pooh-poohed, have since materialized.

Eurodollars and SDRs

The use of the dollar as practically the only currency acceptable on a worldwide basis came so rapidly and accelerated so quickly that it proved a terrible strain on America's resources. And when the United States so mismanaged its affairs that the dollar ceased to be a "hard" and acceptable currency, the gold exchange standard crashed and some $250 to $700 billion of "Eurodollars" and other demand liabilities that the United States is unable to redeem in gold, is hanging over the market today like a false-gilt sword of Damocles. The spread between those two estimates, taken from equally impressive sources, is evidence of how little we know of the precarious position of the dollar today.

Eurodollars are created when one of the oil-exporting nations (OPEC), or any other exporter who has no immediate use for the dollars to which he is entitled in payment for his exports, decides to transfer his dollar claim to some bank in Europe. And the exports need not be to the United States, for much of world trade between other countries is conducted in dollars. In other words, the exporter opens up a dollar account in a European bank which may then lend the "dollars" to a bank or corporation or individual, perhaps in another country. No actual dollar currency is involved, just claims to dollars which can at any time be presented for payment in the United States. These claims are massive in amount and constitute one of the favorite high-interest investment media in the world today, the high rate being in part a consequence of worldwide doubts as to the future of the dollar.

Or the Eurodollar deposits may be created by someone who has a dollar account in a bank in the United States and who transfers his account—his right to be paid in dollars—to a European bank or to a branch of an American bank.

Similar foreign accounts are kept in other currencies—pounds, marks, Swiss francs, etc.—and total "Eurocurrency" accounts, inclusive of the Eurodollars, are estimated at $300 to $900 billion. There are no reliable figures for the total of Eurodollars or Eurocurrency outstanding, but the Bank for International Settlements—an interbank clearinghouse in Switzerland, and certainly the best-managed and most trustworthy of all the international financial agencies—makes estimates of *reported* accounts, of which somewhat more than half are located in London.

What $250 to $700 billion of Eurodollar claims means as a potential threat to the stability of the American dollar may be gathered from the fact that actual currency in circulation in the United States is only some $99 billion and the basic money supply (currency plus demand deposits—M_1) is less than $360 billion—a potential inflationary push of perhaps 100 percent or more if ever the chickens come home to roost.

The future of the Eurodollar is becoming increasingly problematical. Will holders in Europe present their dollar claims for payment in the United States and, if so, will they be met? Or will the dollar shrink to perhaps half its present value?

Many countries are beginning to take steps to prohibit the continuing accumulation of dollar accounts. Switzerland officially barred any further dollar investments during the 1978 year. And with England and the United States, along with practically all the "underdeveloped" countries of the world, continuing to spend far beyond their means as shown by their international payment balances, the shortage of internationally acceptable currencies has become acute.

To meet the situation, the member nations of the International Monetary Fund decided to create out of thin air a new medium of exchange, and the Fund's Articles of Agreement were accordingly amended in July 1969 to give member countries "Special Drawing Rights" (SDRs) in proportion to the amounts of their respective quotas in the Fund. (Each SDR was originally worth $1; it is now quoted at $1.30 U.S. See below.)

These SDRs, backed by nothing but a bookkeeping entry in the books of the IMF, constitute a new inflationary factor among the forces responsible for undermining the financial solvency of the world. Already, in just ten years, they have served to expand the world money supply—marginally, it is true, but this marginal increase of fiat currency is at least in part responsible for the worldwide increase in prices over those four years and may prove to be the straw that breaks the camel's back.

Why, then, did the IMF consent to this suicidal measure? The utilization of the SDRs tells the story. By mid-1975 the United States had used (i.e., borrowed) over 535 million of SDRs, the United Kingdom some 475 million, and ninety-one "less developed" countries of Latin America, Asia and Africa 950 million. By January 1979 the United States had borrowed 1,098 million, the United Kingdom 530 million, and the third world 1,632 million.

Bear in mind that, at the meetings of the Board of Governors of the IMF, these spendthrift countries far outvote the countries that have normally kept their international expenditures within the limits of their national revenues—Germany, Japan and Belgium (Switzerland is not a member of the IMF). And the more thrifty countries, rather than wreck the economy of the world, have been willing to absorb well over 4 billion of SDRs which they hold hopefully, prayerfully, along with many more billions of perhaps unredeemable Eurodollar accounts.

Thus far, more than 13 billion of SDRs have been authorized and, while this amount is small compared with the $250–$700 billion of Eurodollars and some $50–$100 billion of other Eurocurrency outstanding, it constitutes one more element of expansion in the world's inflationary position.

Nairobi and hereafter

In recent years the pressure of the profligate powers has posed a further threat to the solvency of the world's monetary structure.

In September 1973 the Governing Board of the International Monetary Fund, at the insistence of the underdeveloped nations that constitute a majority of the Fund's 138 member countries, agreed to hold a meeting of finance ministers and deputies in Nairobi, the capital of Kenya, in Equatorial Africa. Kenya, bounded by its fellow IMF members, Ethiopia, Somali, Uganda and Tanzania, was chosen as the meeting place because of its remoteness from the "Big Five" and the "Group of Ten" nations that had theretofore dominated the decisions of the IMF, and because that choice supposedly emphasized the interest of the more advanced countries of the world in their more backward compeers. A delegation of twenty foreign ministers at that meeting, with their many delegates and alternates, gave equal representation to the underdeveloped and developed nations of the world.

In June 1974 the Committee of Twenty resumed its deliberations in Washington, and there gave birth to the most monstrous creature that ever a committee has spawned—and it will be remembered that a camel has been described as a horse that could only have been invented by a committee.

In an interim agreement, which has now taken permanent form, it was resolved among other matters that:

1. The international measure of value used by the IMF and its member nations is the SDR whose valuation is not defined in terms of gold, but is allowed to "float" in accordance with the fluctuations of an average of the foreign exchange values of 16 currencies, weighted according to their importance in the world economy—i.e., the dollar counting for 33 percent, the mark 12½ percent and so forth. The June 28, 1974, value of this "basket" of currencies is the permanent base on which the daily fluctuations in the value of the SDR are calculated, starting from a base figure of $1.2056 per SDR—i.e., practically the pre-Nairobi gold value of the dollar ($1.20635) which in turn reflected the two official U.S. devaluations as, originally, the SDR was made equivalent to one pre-Nixon gold dollar.

2. A "substitution account" has been created in the IMF to absorb the "overhang" of dollars and pounds sterling held in the reserves of other nations. The language of the resolution is a newly created technical jargon—a kind of Committee of Twenty Esperanto or Volapuk so unintelligible that the General Counsel of the IMF has written a witty twenty-five-page pamphlet to explain it, pointing out that the terminology was purposely made ambiguous so as to enable "the proponents of divergent views to insist that their opinions had prevailed." In other words, to let the French public believe that they had not abandoned the gold standard while most other nations were sure that they had. Making the floating SDRs a flimsy raft indeed on which a shaky world will have to brave the monetary seas. And utterly annihilating the sole power of the

United States Congress "To coin Money [and] regulate the Value thereof."

For the value of the dollar internationally, and hence the whole economy of the United States, will henceforth depend upon the vagaries of sixteen floating currencies under the semi-anal control of a hybrid Committee of Twenty—half of the members being representatives of the underdeveloped countries—which has now acquired permanent status in the IMF bureaucracy. And this abrogation of the power of Congress to regulate the value of our own money was riveted down on April 1, 1978, when the Second Amendment to Article IV of the Articles of Agreement of the IMF entered into effect. It took no further act of Congress, nor the advice and consent of the Senate, to make that April Fool's amendment effective—at least in the eyes of the IMF—because the White House had already lobbied through Congress an amendment to the 1934 Bretton Woods Agreements Act, which automatically became effective as soon as the IMF amendment was approved and, of course, the U.S. representative at the IMF was instructed to approve it.

The 1934 Bretton Woods statute was entitled: "An Act to protect the currency of the United States," and, ironically enough, the amended statute now authorizes the Secretary of the Treasury to deal in gold and foreign exchange only in a manner "consistent with the United States obligations in the IMF." And, under the April Fool's amendment to the IMF charter, the United States, in common with other IMF members, is expressly forbidden to maintain the value of its currency in terms of gold.

It may be asked how many members of the general public knew of the amendment to FDR's 1934 statute, and how many members of Congress are even now aware of the fact that they have bargained away their constitutional duty to regulate the value of the American dollar. It may also be asked whether the 94th Congress, which amended the 1934 act, can constitutionally bind the present Congress to continue to subordinate, in perpetuity, the value of the dollar to the decisions of that misbegotten committee of the IMF.

3. The international monetary structure—the quantity of SDRs issued and the loans hereafter made by the IMF—is now for the first time linked to foreign aid from the IMF, the World Bank and other agencies. In pursuance of this plan, a special new "oil facility" and an "extended fund facility" have been created. More Volapuk which, translated, means that the IMF has already started making loans to countries whose balances of payments have been upset by higher oil prices, and will increase its loans to the underdeveloped countries for terms beyond the previous five-year limit. And, of course, adding to worldwide inflation by issuing as many more SDRs as the unlimited appetites of the spendthrift nations may call for. The representatives of the underdeveloped countries insisted upon

this tie-up between foreign aid and the monetary system as an absolute precondition for any general agreement, and the United States, in order to get an agreement, backed down from its previous insistence that international monetary solvency was a matter that could not be made dependent upon the future of foreign aid.

When, oh when will American negotiators learn that, in international affairs, the objective should not be *unanimous* agreement, but a *sound* agreement? That it is better to reach no agreement at all rather than concur in one that embodies unsound compromises and promises that are either meaningless or downright dangerous, the harbinger of future problems. That, in monetary matters, it would be better for the United States and for the world if ten or five or even three solvent countries were to reach an agreement establishing a truly sound and stable monetary system—in Washington's words, to "raise a standard to which the wise and honest may repair"—rather than acquiesce in a floating and uncertain monetary standard, agreed to by 138 nations, but which can lead only to a pentecost of calamity.

But, of course, at the conclusion of the meeting of the Committee of Twenty, the United States Secretary of the Treasury, although doubtless aware of the frailities of the interim agreement, felt compelled by diplomatic usage to characterize it as "comprehensive," "resourceful" and "practical." And at the same time he announced that the United States would return to a free gold market by December 1974—a promise later embodied in legislation which now permits private ownership of gold. A sensible move if meanwhile we had taken the measures that are absolutely essential to curb the decline in our vanishing dollar. But, under present circumstances, with no effective curb on our government spending spree, the consequences of a free gold market may well prove to be reminiscent of the agonized wail of the building contractor as he saw ten of his jerry-built houses crash down in a cloud of dust and flying lumber: "Goddamm it! I told you not to take the scaffolding down until you put up the wallpaper!"

And our monetary structure is now supported by nothing more substantial than wallpaper—by faith alone, and faith without works is dead.

Meanwhile Congress, the press and the general public, befuddled by the Volapuk of international monetary jargon and the exaggerated mysteries of international finance, fail to see that what is going on in the IMF, and in our own fiscal and monetary system, poses the greatest peril to this country and to the world that we have faced since the disastrous days of 1929.

And now that the government has put up at auction 2 million

ounces of gold, and managed to sell over a million ounces from our pitifully inadequate gold reserves—inadequate only because of our $25 billion balance of payments deficit—there is a frightening parallel between our present situation and that of Germany in 1922–23 when a persuasively self-confident Finance Minister, with the approval of most of the German economists, abandoned every last vestige of adherence to the gold standard, and brought the mark down to one trillionth of its former value. Until at last a new Finance Minister—Schacht—consigned all the memoranda and letters he received from the economists and self-appointed "experts" to the wastebasket, as he writes in his memoirs, and restored the country to financial sanity, thus beginning a period of economic revival and full employment that made Germany once again the richest and most powerful nation in Europe (unfortunately, as it turned out some seven years later).

Perhaps the most dangerous feature in our government's sale of gold—at superficial glance a brilliant scheme to get $160 to $253 an ounce for reserves officially established at $42.22 an ounce—is that this step constitutes an acknowledgment that the dollar is now equivalent to less than 1/200 of an ounce of gold instead of 1/42 of an ounce. Prices for international basic commodities in the United States are already quoted on a $130 to $250 gold value basis, but, in view of the two-to-six-year lag before a change in the intrinsic value of the dollar is translated into a rise in the price of all goods and services, it means that over the next several years the cost of living in the United States can be expected to rise to perhaps as much as four times the level of 1972 when we abandoned the gold standard.

A price rise, whether or not it reaches 300 percent, is inevitable now that we have officially debased the dollar to less than 1/250 of an ounce of gold, and regardless of what we do in the way of price controls or other measures, as is shown by the analysis of the mechanics of gold price changes and commodity prices in Chapter 10. But, as no nation has ever held inflation of that magnitude down to within those limits, and as there is no present expectation of the government reducing its expenditures at home or abroad, it means that universal distrust in the future of the fiat dollar may well result in its shrinkage to a fraction of its present value which could lead to the wreck of the American economy.

Lest any reader feel inclined to agree with the German intellectual leaders in the pre-Schacht era, and with our own academic economists, that the gold standard is obsolete, let him ask himself if he would risk gambling in a casino where the management can without warning change the value of the chips at any time, say from one dollar to one cent or to a trillionth part of a cent. And then let him ponder whether this is not precisely what happened in pre-Schacht Germany, and what is happening in the United States today with our fiat dollar.

But so deep-rooted is the aversion of economic theorists in this country and England to the gold standard that they can be expected to denounce the foregoing as nonsense. So, in deference to their sensibilities, let us take any commodity other than gold as a measure of value—tobacco, for example. And the theorists would find it hard to deny that a dollar that will buy a pound of tobacco will buy up to sixteen times as much of all other commodities and services as a dollar that will buy only an ounce of tobacco. Once that is admitted, it would seem hard to deny that a dollar that will buy 1/40 of an ounce of gold will buy up to six times as much as a dollar that will only buy 1/250 of an ounce.

And the world—outside of the unreal world of the economics professors—takes gold rather than tobacco as its measure of value and medium of exchange because not everyone in the world wants tobacco, while everyone in every country of the world wants gold and has faith in its continuing value—at least greater faith than in any other commodity that the world has ever used as a medium of exchange. And certainly greater faith than in the feckless promises of kings and presidents who can debase a fiat currency such as ours down to the last molecule of worthlessness.

So we are back full cycle to Irving Fisher's truism that a big piece of gold will buy more than a small piece of gold. And with the continuing auction of even a minuscule fraction of our gold reserves, we are back again to the situation Fisher found in Germany in 1922 when the country's highest officials, as well as economists, businessmen, the press and the general public, each had their own pet theories as to what to do about high prices, recession and unemployment. But none of them had the faintest conception that it was the debasement of the mark that was at the root of the problem.

And unless we can find some Schacht (or Erhard or Röpke or De Gaulle or Rueff or Kemmerer) who will ditch the advice of all the Keynesian professors of economics and lead us back on to the road of monetary sanity, we may well be headed toward the million or billion or trillion to one debasement of the currency that has afflicted so many nations that have resorted to fiat money.

Let us see what Ludwig Erhard once said back in those halcyon days of 1959 when the dollar was the soundest and "hardest" of all the world's currencies:

> *The dollar must be defended by all means. It is a tremendously important task. I am extremely happy to hear that President Eisenhower has set himself up as the first and foremost fighter for*

the stability of the dollar. I am also happy to see that the Federal Reserve System has assumed this duty as their most urgent and immediate responsibility. But where on earth should the planetary system of the world's currencies go, what should happen to it if the sun, which is the dollar, stopped being fixed and stopped being a reliable term of reference. I really think this is most serious. This is the thing that has to be faced all over the world not in the sense of questioning or doubting, but in the sense of reaffirming the ultimate decision that the dollar will stay and will stand and remain the absolute and reliable measure for all other currencies. Because if it isn't the dollar, we have no other measure, no other reference point in the whole world.

Dr. Erhard, then Vice-Chancellor of Germany, was visiting the United States at the time he made this speech, and was already aware of the pressure by "liberal" Keynesian economists in the United States for abandonment of the gold standard and a Keynesian policy of government deficit spending—the very same "liberal" economists who were with the American occupation in Germany and tried to wreck Dr. Erhard's heroic and successful plans for a free-market economy.

Gold as a brake on inflation

Whether or not the SDRs will in time toll the death knell of the *gold standard*, even in those countries that have thus far refused to gamble with floating fiat currencies, it would be well to reiterate that, at least up to the time of the introduction of the *gold exchange standard* in 1922, when the American dollar was called upon to bear the burden of the world's uncertainties, gold served extremely well in two of the functions of money—as *a medium of exchange* and as *a repository of wealth*. It failed in the third function of money—that of *a permanent and stable yardstick of value*. But, even in that respect, gold has proved superior to any other monetary medium or system that the world has yet employed.

The major advantage of the gold standard is that it imposes a definitive restraint on the spending proclivities of spendthrift governments as well as of the general public, which explains why so many governments are anxious to throw off those shackles.

It is true that with the invention of paper money and of bank credit these restraints are less immediate, but they do exist. So far as government spending is concerned, when the government has exhausted its gold and foreign exchange resources, *if it is not on the gold standard*, it can borrow from the central bank which can print more money or create bank deposits to satisfy the government's needs. But, under the gold standard, the issuance of paper money has certain limitations—domestically, in the shape of reserve requirements, and internationally in the fact that the government must be prepared to redeem every one of the paper money notes that it or the central bank has issued. And redemption must be in gold of a specified weight and fineness.

That these limitations are effective has been proved again and again throughout history, which is why the mercantilists of the seventeenth century placed so much emphasis on a favorable balance of trade—there was no other way in which the monarch could get the gold to pay for the wars that perpetually occupied his attention. And at home there was a limit to the amount of copper he could add to his gold coins without detection, and a limit to the amount he could borrow or extort from his subjects. So the gold standard did in fact impose a restraint on government profligacy, and there has never been any other restraint that man's ingenuity has devised that has been as good as gold.

And, so far as the general public is concerned, when a country is on a gold standard, its citizens are unable to import goods from abroad or spend their money on foreign travel or foreign investment once their country's gold stocks are depleted and they have reached the limit of their credit lines. Hence, both governments and citizens are unable to spend beyond their resources, and a gold standard and a nation's gold reserves thus provide the best assurance ever invented against overspending and the inflation that comes when a country tries to replace its diminishing gold stocks with printing-press money.

Why gold is essential in world affairs
There is another reason for a gold standard, and it is a reason that the Germans, the Swiss, the French and the Japanese all understand because those countries are by necessity world-trade-oriented, while we Americans, being almost self-sufficient, seldom raise our sights beyond our own borders. It accounts for those countries insisting that the world should and must return to a gold standard. It underlies the constant admonitions by the finance ministers and the bankers of those countries that the fact that the United States is not living within its means is upsetting the balance of the whole world.

In world trade, when a Frenchman or a German or an Englishman buys wheat or cotton from the United States, he cannot pay in francs or marks or sterling. The American seller generally doesn't want that kind of money. He wants dollars. So the foreign importer has to find some way to buy dollars.

True, at the present time, there are millions of American paper dollars and billions of Eurodollars floating around Europe today—potential claims on our gold stocks and grim skeleton in the closet of our money managers.

But this is, it is hoped, a temporary aberration. In general and over the long run, the only way the English, French or German importer can get dollars to buy American goods is to pay for those dollars in gold. Not directly, of course. There are thousands of transactions, some bringing gold into Europe and some taking gold out of Europe. But gold—not dollars, sterling, marks or francs—is the one universally accepted medium of exchange in the world's markets, and it is in gold that the final settlements of debit or credit balances must be made.

So, when it comes to world trade, not only is the gold standard desirable—each currency must have an equivalence, fixed or variable, in terms of gold—but it is the best standard that has ever been in general use. Until July 1969, all International Monetary Fund accounts were carried in gold dollars, the pre-Nixon $35 an ounce dollar, each dollar equivalent to 0.888671 grams of fine gold. Since then, the IMF inter-country accounts have been carried in SDRs, but each SDR was originally made the equivalent of 0.888671 grams of fine gold, so that gold was still the international monetary standard, and this was true at least up to the time of the untested, experimental market-basket approach referred to in the preceding paragraphs.

And gold is still recognized as the sole international standard even by those governments that have debauched their local currencies. For *all* countries recognize and use the International Telecommunications Union and the Universal Postal Union Gold Franc (equivalent to 0.21759 grams of fine gold) as the measure of value in the settlement of their international telephone, cable, radio and postal traffic balances. And gold will continue to be the international standard of value and measure of international settlements even after the IMF Committee of Twenty succeeds in under-mining the stability of the SDRs.

Anyone who has ever had any actual experience in international trade and finance knows that a standard not subject to the arbitrary whims of some political body is not only far superior to a politically variable standard but is absolutely essential if the world is to be freed from its current uncertainties and recurrent crises, caused by ever-present doubts as to the gold value of the dollar and of other major currencies in terms of dollars.

This is why our friends in Germany, France, Switzerland and Japan have been berating us for living beyond our means—condemning our "fiscal and monetary policies," as they politely phrase it. And they are right. And we are wrong to be annoyed by their lectures, and even more wrong in lecturing them on how to manage their own economies, as Washington has been doing for the past two years or more. For those countries have managed their affairs extremely well and they are concerned that the United States, which has managed its affairs so badly, what with Vietnam and foreign aid and deficit spending at home, will someday crash and bring all the rest of the world down with it. No nation is an island anymore, and an economic collapse in the United States would have dire repercussions all over the world, precisely as it did in 1929.

Foreign aid to the United States

Nor can we say that it is ingratitude for those countries to criticize our policies and ask for a return to the gold standard after all we have done for them in Marshall Plan and other aid after World War II.

Germany has given this country more billions of dollars of aid than we have ever given Germany. This they have done by buying up American dollars and revaluing the mark upward five times in the past ten years to prevent a crash in the United States, and hence in the world (the latest revaluation in October 1978), even though the revaluation of the mark made German goods less competitive in world markets, and even though they knew that the dollars they have been accumulating may eventually be just a lot of worthless paper or uncollectible accounts.

The West German central bank, the Deutsche Bundesbank, spent $50 billion in 1978 alone to support the American dollar, and Dr. Otmar Emminger, president of the bank, has stated that they have been forced to write off losses of 10.6 billion marks (some $6 billion) because of those operations and the depreciation of the dollar since January 1, 1978.

And, over the past ten years or more, Germans have invested billions of dollars in real estate and industrial plants in this country, greatly relieving the pressure on our balance of payments and the credit crunch in American capital markets. Such well-known firms as Bayer, Henkel, Hoechst, Portland-Zementwerke and Volkswagen have each invested over $100 million in plants throughout the United States, while Volkswagen has bought out a controlling interest in Chrysler's Brazilian operations at a cost of some $50 million, and Mercedes is installing a $7 million truck manufacturing plant in Virginia. And Thyssen A. G. has bought out the Budd Company for $295 million, while a single Hamburg real estate firm has acquired real property in the United States valued at $650 million. In fact, one quarter of all sales of farm property in the United States today represent purchases by foreigners!

France, Belgium, the Netherlands, Switzerland and even England have also helped, although on a lesser scale, with investments of $100 million or more by Michelin, Cie. Française des Pétroles, Union Minière, Petrofina, Beecham, Hoffman–La Roche, Solvay ($600 million jointly with ICI, Ltd.), Unilever ($482 million), Nestlé ($277 million), Sandoz ($190 million) and Royal Dutch Petroleum ($500 million). Plus lesser acquisitions, such as F.A.O. Schwarz, the finest toy store in the United States; Bond's, the largest men's clothing chain; the Hygrade Food Products Corporation; General Cable Corporation; S. W. Industries; etc.

The vice-president of the New York Federal Reserve Bank has been successful in negotiating "swap credit lines"—reciprocal currency arrangements—with the central banks of Canada, France, West Germany, Japan, Belgium, Switzerland, the Bank for International Settlements and seven other institutions. These reciprocal credits now total more than $30 billion!

And the "reciprocal" is merely to soothe our sensibilities. We do not have the resources to lend $30 billion. The operation has been strictly a "save the U.S.A." arrangement.

Saudi Arabia, a country of less than 5 million population and not so long ago a less-developed country, has purchased over $30 billion in United States Treasury notes, bills and bonds and invested some $75 billion in the United States. Iran, Kuwait and the other Arab nations have made similar although smaller investments, largely in hotels, real estate and stock market securities. Three of the largest New York hotels—the Roosevelt, Biltmore and Barclay—are now owned by Arabs. Iran has purchased a substantial interest in Pan American World Airways and a majority interest in their subsidiary, Intercontinental Hotels.

The Japanese have not been far behind, with hotel and other real estate acquisitions—a resort complex in Orlando, an electronics factory in San Diego and three automobile and motorcycle factories on the West Coast. They have also bought out Helena Rubinstein (cosmetics) and an 80 percent interest in a Michigan plant of General Electric, as well as luxury hotels in New York and Los Angeles and six in Hawaii. And, having bought Utamaro prints in the United States for as much as $37,000 and Samurai swords for $75,000 from Americans who had probably purchased them in Japan for perhaps one-hundredth part of that price, and having paid up to $600,000 for a single thoroughbred in auctions in Kentucky and elsewhere, they are now engaged in making philanthropical gifts to the impoverished Americans—$1 million to each of ten American universities, while Harvard is soliciting $15 million more.

A number of America's largest banks have been acquired by foreign investors—the La Salle Bank of Chicago bought by Algemene

Bank Nederland; the Bank of Montreal now negotiating for acquisition of 89 of the 104 branches of Bankers Trust New York Corporation as well as its entire installment loan operations; a controlling interest in New York's Marine Midland bought by Hongkong and Shanghai Banking Corporation; the National Bank of North America and the Union Bank of Los Angeles taken over by London bankers; Detroit's Bank of the Commonwealth and the Main Bank of Houston purchased by Saudi Arabian multimillionaires; and so forth, including the much-publicized take-over of a Georgia bank by a Saudi Arabian, and a substantial Kuwaiti-Saudi-Abu Dhabi interest in Financial General Bankshares, which owns thirteen banks.

Those countries and other nations as well have been helping us to surmount our foreign exchange difficulties by their heavy investments in this country. Sometimes in new ventures, which mean more jobs for American workers, sometimes by buying up existing businesses, which helps to relieve our capital shortage, such as the purchase by English investors of the chain that owns Gimbels and Saks Fifth Avenue, and of a controlling interest in the Grand Union food chain; and the Canadian purchase of Texas Gulf Sulphur; the French acquisition of a majority interest in Korvette's; and the German purchase of controlling interests in White Motor Corporation and A & P, the latter a $75 million deal.

And then, in November 1978, the International Monetary Fund and the central banks of Germany, Japan and Switzerland came to the rescue of President Carter's failing wage and price plan with a $30 billion loan to prevent the dollar from disappearing down the drain—at least for another six or twelve months.

Isn't it humiliating—the richest country in the world in serious economic difficulties, with less than zero in gold and foreign exchange reserves, all because of the profligacy of our government over the past fifteen years. And being helped and bought out by England, Germany, France, Japan, Canada, Belgium, Switzerland, the Netherlands, Italy, Saudi Arabia, Abu Dhabi, Kuwait and Iran—just another "banana republic"!

And think of the leverage those foreign countries must have in their negotiations with the United States Government considering, for example, Saudi Arabia's ownership of $30 billion in United States Treasury obligations that it could dump on the market at any time, and Saudi and other foreign control of banks in New York, Chicago, Houston, Washington, Atlanta and elsewhere. A leverage that may perhaps be exemplified by nearly $3 billion in military supply contracts for which Saudi Arabia was able to obtain Defense Department approval in favor of a single designated supplier without competitive bidding. Or by the practically tax-free status that an Abu Dhabi-Kuwaiti-Saudi consortium has been able to arrange for the acquisition of the Financial General Bankshares, through a complex Curaçao, Grand Cayman Island, London, Amsterdam, Luxembourg tax-shelter structure set up with the aid of a former congressman and a recent director of the Office of Management and Budget (who is now out of the deal following a federal grand jury investigation of his personal financial affairs in connection with the sale of his own bank stock to Saudi interests). Every year since 1973, the U.S. Secretary of the Treasury makes an annual trip to Saudi Arabia to confer with the officials of the Saudi Government, Central Bank, and Monetary Agency, who control some $75 billion of U.S. funds and have it in their power to wreck the American economy.

On the other hand, the very fact that so many investment-wise foreigners have put their money into American real estate and other investments reveals their confidence in the basic strength of the American economy. They know that the American dollar is nothing but fiat currency and they want no more dollars or Eurodollars. They know, too, that the financial recklessness and incompetence of the American government is a threat to the economy of the whole world. But they have faith in the ultimate survival of the United States and know that an investment in America—not in dollars, but in tangible assets—will over the long run prove safer and more profitable than investment anywhere else in the world.

And so I say: Don't sell this country short!

10. The Actual Mechanics of Money and Prices

Gret prees at market maketh dere ware,
And to gret chepe is holden a litel prise.

(A great demand at the market makes goods dear, and
too great a bargain is held of little worth.)

Geoffrey Chaucer (c. 1475)

Our present-day moral philosophers do understand and agree with the economics of Geoffrey Chaucer. But there is one thing that very few economists seem to grasp, simply because they have had no actual experience in international money and commodity markets and because the subject has scarcely been discussed in any book on economics—namely, the actual mechanics of international trade, whereby changes in the gold value of a country's currency are immediately reflected in the prices for the major basic commodities in that country, and later in prices for all commodities and services.

I covered the subject in detail as an expert witness on money and prices in a United States Court of Claims case, as well as in an article printed by the *Journal of the Royal Statistical Society* in 1938, and in a paper presented at a round-table discussion before the annual meeting of the American Statistical Association in the same year.

The Roosevelt devaluation of 1933

In all three studies, I took as my spectrum the period between March 1933 and February 1934, when President Roosevelt "raised the price of gold" 69.3 percent; i.e., in a series of sixty-four graduated steps, he devaluated the dollar to 59 percent of its former value. There has never been, before or since, a period in world history where a gradual process of step-by-step devaluation of the currency has made it so easy to study the effects of devaluation, free from other conflicting influences, as during that twelve-month span.

But, as there were only sixty-four days during the entire period when an official United States Treasury price for gold was fixed, I had to take, as the daily price of gold or gold value of the dollar, the price for gold on the London free gold market, multiplied by the free foreign exchange rate in that market for dollars.

The average difference between this computed price, and the official price on those days when the two could be compared, was less than 0.5 percent. This is not surprising, as the spread between the "gold points" at that time was only 0.845 percent; if free-market gold prices and United States Treasury prices had been more than 1 percent apart, the buyer or seller would have shipped gold instead of buying or selling foreign exchange. It is this—the actual cost of shipping, insurance and interest—that determines the gold points, the spread between buying and selling rates, when countries are on the gold standard.

Distinction between staple and nonstaple prices

In the second place—and this is the most important contribution made by my study—I divided the 784 commodities then contained in the Bureau of Labor Statistics Index of Wholesale Commodity Prices into three classifications, distinguishing between "world staples," "domestic staples" and "nonstaples."

The world staples are commodities traded in the world's markets on the basis of standard grades or "staples," for example, 1″ staple cotton (the length of the fiber), 96° raw sugar, etc. The English call these commodities "primary products" rather than staples.

Even if only a fraction of a country's total production of the product is traded on the world market, it is a "world staple" because, if an American farmer or miner can get a higher price for his wheat or copper in Liverpool or Hamburg than he can in Chicago or New York, or if a European importer can buy cheaper in the United States than in Europe, the operation will be made in the more favorable market. It is the *whole world supply and demand* that determines both the domestic price and the world price.

Domestic staples are primary products traded in United States markets, but not shipped from the United States to the international markets.

The category "nonstaples" embraces all of the 784 products not classified as staples, including such things as automobiles, steel rails and hundreds of other manufactured items. We can think of the nonstaples in general as manufactured or semimanufactured products, but I do not use that term because some of the staples are also partly manufactured or processed; i.e., the market price for the staples is fixed in the form in which that commodity first finds its place in the domestic or international markets. Thus raw sugar is used, not sugarcane; ginned cotton in the bale, not in the boll, electrolytic copper, not copper ore—and these products are all "manufactured."

How staple prices are determined

Now, the point is that there is a fundamental difference between prices for staple commodities and those for manufactured goods, the nonstaples.

When a farmer sells his crops, he may have put in thousands of dollars of labor, fertilizer and other costs—but the price he gets in the marketplace bears no relationship to those costs. He may have to sell below cost or, perhaps because there is a shortage of that particular commodity, he may sell at bonanza prices. Furthermore, the amounts of seed, fertilizer, labor, etc., that he has put into his fields are not the only factors that determine the size of his crops. Good weather or bad weather may double or halve the amount of produce that he has for sale, while a hurricane or flood may wipe out his crop entirely.

The important thing is that the farmer does not fix the price. The price is fixed by supply and demand, and it is *in the marketplace*, not on the farm, that supply and demand are determined. And this is true of all staple commodities, not just farm products. The price is not fixed by the producer but by bargaining between the buyer and seller. True, there are occasional monopoly situations or combinations between producers—as in the case of petroleum and coffee at the present time, and tin, rubber and other products in the past—where, at least for limited periods of time, the seller controls the market price. And there are even cases of almost absolute monopoly—diamonds, for instance—where such controls have lasted for decades. But these are the exceptions. On the whole in the vast majority of cases, staple commodity prices are fixed by supply and demand and in the marketplace.

This is why we must distinguish between "world staples" and "domestic staples." For the former, the price is fixed in the great international markets of the world—tin prices chiefly in England, for that is where the great smelters are; wool prices chiefly in Liverpool and Boston; and so forth. Prices for domestic staples are fixed in domestic markets. When we come to examining the effects of dollar devaluation, we shall find that this distinction is crucial.

How nonstaple prices are determined

Nonstaple prices, on the other hand, are not fixed willy-nilly in the marketplace, but *by the producer*. An automobile or dress manufacturer, for example, computes his costs, adds on what he considers a reasonable, possible profit, and that is his selling price. And this is true regardless of whether it is a small factory or a huge monopolistic enterprise.

To be sure, the manufacturer has to bear in mind the prices that other manufacturers will charge for their products—the pressure of competition—and in bad times or at the end of the season he may have to sell below cost. But, on the whole, his price is not a *"market price"* but *"cost plus profit."*

He is not like the farmer who never knows how much wheat a hundred pounds of seed will produce, nor whether the market price will be $1 or $2 or 50 cents. The automobile manufacturer knows that a given amount of steel and other materials will turn out 1,000 cars on the assembly line, not 2,000 cars or 500 cars, depending upon the weather.

And he knows what price he is going to put on those cars—his estimated cost plus his hoped-for profit. He may have to shade his price a bit; he may not sell all his cars. But the price is, in the normal course of business, fixed by him, not by the free interplay of supply and demand in some distant marketplace.

And, to the extent that he can calculate correctly, he produces neither too many nor too few cars for his market, and he is ready to increase production at any time—not just at planting time.

Moreover—and this is a vital distinction—the very factors that, in the case of staple commodities, will tend to raise or lower prices generally have exactly the opposite effect in the case of manufactured goods.

A great, unexpected demand for wheat or corn or copper will send prices for those commodities skyrocketing. But for the manufacturer, if he finds unexpectedly that he can sell 500,000 units instead of the 100,000 units he had counted on, his supply is flexible, and he can and generally will cut his prices substantially. Because, almost without exception in the case of manufactured goods, *increased production means lower overhead and lower prices*—the exact opposite of what generally happens in the case of the primary products, where *planned increased production generally means higher marginal costs.*

In the case of products new to the market, where a manufacturer has made a conservative estimate of his expected sales and probable costs, price cuts resulting from increased demand and production can be fantastic, as in the case of Cellophane, where Du Pont slashed the price of the product eighteen times within eleven years for a total price cut of 86 percent. Dacron, plastics, computers, Polaroid cameras, radios and TVs have all experienced drastic cuts in costs and prices, which have brought about increased demand, which in turn made it possible for the manufacturers to make still further price cuts. It is an exceptional primary product where this situation can arise. Generally it is the exact opposite, and I can recall many cases in my experience where a moderate increase in demand or short supply of a primary product has brought about an extraordinary price increase. For example, I remember selling a tagua shipment in New York at double the price of a previous shipment, because fashion changes in men's clothes meant a greater demand for ivory-nut buttons instead of bone buttons.

The classical viewpoint

The conventional, classical economist would hold that the difference I have pointed out is merely one of degree. In both cases—staples and manufactured goods—they will aver, the price is fixed by supply and demand, and the minimum price is fixed by the cost of production.

And, *over the long run*, this may be true. But, as Keynes has said, over the long run we shall all be dead. And in practical economics and trade, it is what happens here and now that matters, not what may take place five years from now, when an entirely new set of factors may be present. I can recall when sugar and coffee sold far below the cost of production for over two years, between the fall of 1920 and the end of 1922. Growers kept on producing because it was better to harvest the coffee cherries on the trees and to cut and grind the cane and produce sugar than to get no income whatsoever during the year.

As to the difference between prices for staples and nonstaples being merely one of degree, one could say that the only difference between a man and a woman is the degree of development of certain organs. Or that the difference between a tabby cat and a tiger is only one of degree. But a cat and a tiger are really entirely different animals. And *market prices* and *cost plus profit prices* are also entirely different animals, subject to entirely different economic laws, and involving entirely different causes and consequences.

One economist of the New Deal era, Gardiner C. Means, wrote of prices for certain manufactured goods as "administrative prices." But his emphasis was on the theory that the free market, where prices are fixed by supply and demand, was distorted by the monopolistic practices of industry, with all the pejorative implications that this suggests. He did not go into the fundamental difference between prices fixed at the marketplace for primary products, and prices fixed at the factory by the producer on a cost-plus basis—a distinction that is natural, logical, inevitable and in no wise sinister.

Consequences of the Roosevelt devaluation

So what happened when Roosevelt debased the value of the dollar by raising the dollar price of gold? Take cotton, for example. Let us assume that the world price for cotton—the result of world supply and demand—is 4 pence in Liverpool or say 1 franc in Le Havre, and that this represents 6 cents in United States currency, as was approximately the case in March 1933.

Assume, then, that the price of gold in the United States is increased overnight by 50 percent. The world price would still be 4 pence or 1 franc, for there would be no overnight change in those currencies or in the world supply and demand for cotton. But the American exporter who gets the 4 pence or 1 franc for his cotton now finds that he is receiving 9 cents, not 6 cents. The change is instantaneous—simple arithmetic. You don't need to know beans about economics, just something about the facts of life in world trade, and the ABCs of arithmetic.

This is exactly what happened, and not for cotton alone, but for *every* commodity entering into international trade.

In a study of prices for world staple commodities in England, France and the United States from March 1933 to February 1934—not just a few selected commodities, but *every* commodity for which comparable prices could be found in the three markets, embracing 66.5 percent of all the international staples listed in the BLS index for 784 wholesale commodities—American prices rose 64 percent; European prices rose only 4 percent. The 69 percent increase in the dollar price of gold meant that American prices for the international staples rose 58 percent more than world prices.

The correlation would have been even closer had it not been for tariffs, quotas, and other barriers to trade. And each individual commodity in the comparison, month after month, revealed a similar gap between American prices in dollars and world prices in francs and sterling, not exactly the same percentages as the devaluation of the dollar, but, in the case of the commodities not burdened by tariffs or quotas, the correlation was so close that it was almost impossible to distinguish on my charts between the line showing the monthly rise in gold prices in the United States, and that for the difference between American and world prices.

I made similar studies in England, Sweden, Finland, Denmark, Norway and Argentina, after those countries, all in the "sterling bloc," went off the fixed gold standard in September 1931. The same results were observed. And in each of these countries, going off gold and devaluing their currencies broke the steady downward trend in the economy and started them on the way to immediate recovery.

For example, from September 1931 to February 1933, the Bank of England price index of primary products in England and the United States showed a drop in American prices of 22.6 percent, and a rise in English prices of 7 percent. In other words, the English primary product price index rose 38 percent compared with the index for American prices, during a period when the price of gold in England was raised 42 percent. The correlation would have been even closer, practically 100 percent, if the Bank of England had not used tea as one of the English list of commodities, and substituted coffee in the American list—gastronomically a sensible substitution considering how badly the English make coffee and the Americans make tea, but statistically unpardonable.

Now, let's go back to the United States. What happened to *domestic staple commodity* prices here from March 1933 to February 1934, when the 69 percent rise in the dollar price of gold produced a 64 percent increase in the American price of world staples?

Why, nothing—practically nothing. Their prices went up exactly 6.6 percent—a rise that may have been motivated by increasing demand, as President Roosevelt's heroic monetary measures brought the country out of the slough of economic despond into which it had fallen.

So far as the domestic staples were concerned—the products that are sold entirely, or almost entirely, in the domestic market—there was no reason why the farmer should charge any more for his hens, eggs or tomatoes, and no reason why the housewife should pay any more, just because the President had juggled the price of gold. The supply and demand for chickens, eggs and tomatoes in the United States were precisely the same before the rise in the dollar price of gold as they were after that event. And, from the viewpoint of the housewife and the farmer, a dollar was a dollar was a dollar.

These products were not exported in those days, and there was no Frenchman or Englishman standing ready to pay the farmer the same number of francs or shillings they paid "before the fall"—so prices in dollars remained unchanged. And that is exactly what happened.

So you can see why we have to make a distinction between the world staples and the domestic staples—the former were instantaneously, arithmetically, inevitably affected by the change in the price of gold; the latter paid no attention to it.

Now, how about the remaining items among the 784 commodities in the wholesale price index—the nonstaple goods? What happened to them?

They rose 15.1 percent. Why?

Well, the 1933 census of manufactures shows that, in the completed selling price of all manufactured products, 16.8 percent was made up of wages; 4.3 percent, salaries; 25.3 percent, overhead, profits, etc.;

and 53.6 percent, materials. Some of these materials were world staples, some domestic staples, and some semimanufactured products. Breaking this down, it was found that nearly 90 percent of the 15.1 percent rise in the price of manufactured goods was attributable to the increase in world staple prices. In other words, to the rise in the dollar price of gold.

Carrying the process back, and giving the proper weights to each of the components in the final selling price, it was found that while the BLS wholesale price index for the 784 commodities had risen 23.9 percent, 21.5 percentage points of that rise were attributable to the increase in the price of gold, and 2.4 percentage points were attributable to other, unascertainable causes.

Why the money managers can't control consumer prices

So we see that even so drastic a change as altering the gold content of the dollar can only directly affect the general price level to a limited extent—to the extent that the general index is made up of international staple commodities, whether directly or by reason of their incorporation in the manufactured goods included in the index. And we see, too, that, because a change in the dollar price of gold is linked mathematically, ineluctibly with changes in the dollar price for all the basic commodities of international trade, the money managers have it in their power, by changing the gold content of the dollar, not merely to raise or lower prices, but to keep the price level stable at all times, immediately and effectively—*but only if they use an international basic commodity price index as their guide.* For if they use any more comprehensive index—whether for wholesale prices or the cost of living—they would have to make a readjustment in the dollar price of gold many times the desired percentage readjustment in the total index, and this would wreak havoc with American prices for the international staples and wreck the economy of the country's farms and mining industries.

So when the money managers twice raised the price of gold during the Nixon Administration and announced to the world that this would not affect the cost of living, they simply didn't know what they were talking about, because they did not understand "the actual mechanics of money and prices" outlined in this chapter. The fact is that the rise in the price of gold immediately affected the cost of living to the extent that the price of world staples enters into that cost—and that is a very important extent indeed. And, ultimately, with a time lag of two to six years, the increase in the price of gold—the debasement of the dollar—affected practically all prices, although not all to the same degree.

The money managers were equally uninformed in their later pronouncements on the effect of the gold price change on American exports and imports. The fact is, as is clear from this analysis, that raising the dollar price of gold—i.e., a drop in the value of the dollar—has no effect whatsoever on the volume of sales of farm products and other basic commodities (for world supply and demand and world prices for those commodities in hard currency remained unchanged), even though it does mean higher prices for those products *in the United States* in terms of dollars.

On the other hand, with respect to exports of manufactured products, dollar prices are affected to only a minor extent by devaluation of the dollar. Hence, with the depreciation of the dollar, prices in marks, francs and other currencies will drop, and American exports of those articles will increase. There is no point in going into the effect of a change in the dollar price of gold on all the other entries in our balance of payments—it is easy enough to figure it out if one bears in mind the lessons of this chapter.

And President Nixon's, Ford's and Carter's economic advisers have been misguided in believing that the other tools of monetary management—raising interest rates, increasing bank reserve requirements so as to curb the lending powers of the commercial banks, or otherwise clamping down on credit—can keep prices down. They won't—unless those curbs are so drastic that they wreck the entire economy.

And unless wise monetary management is coupled with wise fiscal management—let's cut the usual polite jargon and call a spade a spade— unless the government cuts down drastically on its expenditures and balances the budget, the total budget with no bikini accounting and concealed federal agency expenditures, monetary measures alone can only serve to bury us in the pit that government profligacy has dug for us. (See Chapter 5 for the facts and fallacies involved in raising interest rates to curb inflation and attract foreign capital, and Chapter 13 for monetary measures under the Carter Administration.)

11. Are We Bankrupt?

We are troubled on every side, yet not distressed; we are perplexed, but not in despair.

II Corinthians 4:8

Saint Paul might well have been speaking of the tragic era when Franklin Roosevelt admonished us in one of his heartwarming fireside chats that the only thing we have to fear is fear itself. In 1933, when FDR devalued the dollar, we remained on the gold standard. The standard varied from time to time, sixty-four times in the course of a year, but at all times during that period the United States Treasury stood ready to buy and sell gold in unlimited amounts at whatever price it fixed as official.

It wouldn't sell to everyone, to be sure. Private individuals and companies were not allowed to buy or hoard gold except for bona fide numismatists and dealers in coins, and bona fide users such as dental suppliers, jewelers and manufacturers who needed gold in their business.

But the Treasury did sell freely to the Federal Reserve Banks, and these could buy and sell gold from and to central banks throughout the world, always at the official price, which eventually reached $35 an ounce. This sufficed to keep us on the gold standard in our international transactions, so that the dollar became known as a "hard" currency, the best in the world, because, with free trade in gold between the Fed and central banks abroad, other foreign banks, dealers and speculators could buy gold from United States gold stocks without limit.

The Treasury replenished its gold reserves through the Fed, and direct from American miners and others who had gold—the undertakers, for example, who salvage many thousands of dollars of gold from their crematories and seldom if ever turn over Grandpappy's tooth fillings to his heirs.

Abandonment of the gold standard

After the Nixon Administration officially fixed the price of gold in Washington at $42.2222 an ounce, in May 1972, the actual market price in

118

Zurich and London and other world markets rose to over $185 and has later Yo-Yoed back and forth between $130 and $282. And that was because we are no longer on a gold standard, and the difference between the $42 price and $130–$282 reflects world lack of confidence in the American dollar.

On August 15, 1971, after the April 1971 devaluation, the United States informed the International Monetary Fund that it would no longer buy and sell gold to settle our international transactions. This was made irrevocable—at least until we change our minds again—when the administration in May 1972 altered the dollar price of gold for the second time. We simply do not have enough gold to meet our obligations, considering how many billions of dollars are circulating in Europe and could be mobilized through the central banks and presented for payment at the official price of $42.2222. But we have served notice on the world that we are not going to meet our obligations at that price or at any other price.

Knowledgeable estimates of these foreign dollar holdings (Eurodollars and other demand liabilities) run between $250 and $700 billion, of which some $100 billion net is held by foreign governments and banks or reported by American banks. This latter figure is all that the Commerce Department or the Fed or the IMF are able to use in their summaries of our balance of payments, and it is the basis of computation used in Chart 5. The rest of our foreign exchange indebtedness is held by private persons, business firms and institutions.

The foreign central banks have not in the past attempted to mobilize and collect the dollar bills circulating in Europe or the Eurodollars due from American debtors—interbank and intercompany accounts—because they know that if they did the United States would be bankrupt or, rather, that the United States would either refuse to pay or would be forced to change the value of the dollar from 1/42 of an ounce of gold to a fraction of that amount. And now that the United States has not only declared that it has no intention of meeting its obligations in gold but has in effect devalued the dollar to less than 1/10 of its pre-Roosevelt parity by auctioning off a part of its gold reserves, our European and other creditors are stuck with paper money and accounts receivable that may eventually be worthless—or worth only as much or as little as the United States Government is willing to say they are worth.

So can you blame Germany, France, Japan, Switzerland and other countries—who have managed their own monetary affairs with prudence—for expressing their annoyance with the United States, whose profligacy has driven us to virtual bankruptcy, and now threatens the rest of the world with an economic crisis such as has not been experienced in this century?

We are bankrupt—as nearly as a sovereign nation can be said to be bankrupt—for we no longer have the capacity to pay our creditors, and we have served noticed that we won't pay them.

Our present fiat money
The dollar today is what is known as "fiat money," from the Latin for "let it be" or "let there be"—as in *fiat lux,* "let there be light." (This may explain to those who are not classical scholars why so many American universities use *"Fiat Lux"* as their motto, rather than a more American device such as "Buick Palmolive.")

The United States is saying, as other governments that have issued fiat money in the past have said: "Let this be money! Let this piece of money be $100—or $1,000—or $10,000."

There is nothing else behind it—just the say-so of the Treasury!

Sure, the piece of paper is good "for the payment of all debts, public and private." The Internal Revenue Service will accept it in payment of taxes, and the Post Office for postage stamps, or the automobile dealer will take it in payment of a car.

But there is nothing that says you can buy an automobile for *one piece of paper*—you may have to pay *a million pieces of paper.* And your taxes, which may now be $10,000 a year, may jump to $10 million. Not that I expect either of these things to happen. But, so far as fiat money is concerned, it is nothing but a piece of paper that says: "Let this be $1,000."

That is fine—until suddenly someone asks: "Sez who?"

Then the whole structure crumbles. Someone finds out that the Emperor really has no clothes. Because that is what happens when inflation gets out of control, when governments keep on spending beyond their means—and keep on and on until the bubble bursts. That is why no economist can predict, except by luck, just what is going to happen or when.

The crisis of confidence
Things go along fairly smoothly, with a 10 percent increase in the money supply and a 10 percent increase in prices, then a 20 percent increase, then 30 percent and so on—perhaps up to a 100 percent or even a 1,000 percent increase—and then, suddenly, panic sets in.

People are so used to thinking that a dollar is a dollar is a dollar that they keep on talking of a rise in prices—inflation—when what they ought to be talking of is the *debasement of the currency.*

That is what is occurring in the United States today. It is what happened in Germany, France, Brazil—every country that has had a 100 percent or a 1,000 percent or a billion- or trillionfold increase in prices. But at some point in the process, and no one can predict just when it will happen, someone will be given a piece of paper reading: "Let this be a dollar." And that someone will exclaim: "Sez who?"

That is the beginning of the end—the *crise de confiance*, as economists call it. A crisis of confidence—triggered perhaps by some trivial or wholly extraneous circumstance such as Watergate or an inopportune statement by someone in the administration or the Congress or the press. And then all hell breaks loose!

What is behind the dollar?
Oh, but you say, the dollar is not fiat money. It has behind it all the wealth and resources of the United States. The public debt of the United States is insignificant compared with all the wealth in this country—land, buildings, structures, goods, cash, everything—estimated at $5.7 trillion. One very estimable economist told me that very thing. And we could, with equal logic, add that the dollar has behind it not only the sum total of all its mines and factories and arms but the strength and courage of its people, the spirit of true patriotism that will never let us down.

Horsefeathers! Flag-waving won't help. Have you ever tried collecting on a mortgage of that kind? No, all that is behind the dollar is the simple precatory phrase: "Let this be money"—fiat currency, nothing more. There is nothing—*nothing*—behind the dollar. But the dollar is behind the eight ball. And so are we all.

The disappearance of our gold reserves
The gold reserves and net foreign exchange balances—which once backed our currency by being made freely available to the Federal Reserve System, and through the Fed to the rest of the world—have vanished into thin air, as is shown in Chart 5.

The $22.8 billion of gold (nearly 650 million ounces at $35 an ounce) at Fort Knox and at the Fed on December 31, 1950, less a net foreign exchange debit of $6.2 billion in current account, had dwindled to $12.6 billion in gold (less than 300 million ounces at $42.2222) by December 31, 1978, and a *minus* net balance of $96 billion in current account, as shown by the chart, *a net loss of $100 billion!*

The figures behind the chart through 1977 have been taken from the IMF *International Financial Statistics,* but, since March 1978, the International Monetary Fund has been unable to obtain from the United States Treasury any statistics for American "external liabilities" and

CHART 5—United States Gold and Foreign Exchange Reserves

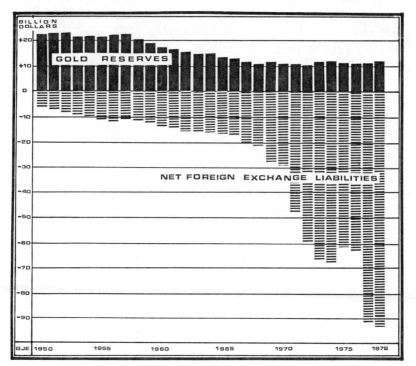

"external claims," nor are the figures elsewhere available in any published compilation—a further example of the bikini accounting prevalent over the past two years.

So the 1978 figure for our foreign exchange debit is an estimate and the space for the 1979 figures in the chart has had to be left in blank. But we can judge, from the administration's $30 billion emergency borrowing and its stepped-up sales of gold, that by mid-1979 our gold reserves must be around $10 billion—down from 650 million ounces to some 240 million ounces—and that our net foreign liabilities must be around $130 billion, which would make the graph line in the chart break through the bottom frame and into the text. No wonder the administration prefers to keep this evidence of its maladministration secret from the IMF and from the American public!

Truly, the American dollar and the American people have been "left naked to mine enemies," as Wolsey said when Anne Boleyn procured his downfall.

The chart does show, however, that the losses in our gold and foreign exchange reserves have continued to mount at an ever-increasing pace, i.e., at the rate of $1.3 billion a year from 1950 through 1961, attributable to foreign aid, and a loss of $3.6 billion a year from 1962 through 1976, a reflection of the Vietnam War plus continuing foreign aid, which together proved more than our economy could stand. This was followed by an estimated loss of $68 billion from January 1, 1977, to December 31, 1978 (and undoubtedly at an accelerated rate since then), which can only be attributed to our present foreign and domestic policies that have brought us to the current crisis.

The crisis is recent, immediate, economically more disastrous than the Vietnam War, but the events leading up to it have been developing ever since 1948. The drain on our gold and foreign exchange reserves began when we started handing out foreign aid at the rate of some $5 to $6 billion a year. And, as can be seen by the chart, by the time President Kennedy took office, and before he launched us on the Vietnam War, the Bay of Pigs, and the Alliance for Progress, our net reserves had already shrunk to $3.6 billion (the difference between our gold assets and the net foreign exchange debits on December 31, 1960; the chart shows the year-end status for each year). We have been in perpetual deficit ever since.

But to blame any one administration for the present situation, just because the crisis has now become acute, is much like the story of the chap who fell from the seventieth floor of the skyscraper and yelled out, as he passed the fifth floor: "It hasn't hurt yet!" Or like the profligate son who inherits $10 million and squanders $1 million a year—there is no pinch until the last million is gone. The blame lies with our American do-gooder complex which has led all administrations and all Congresses, from 1945 on, into believing that we Americans have a duty to impose our brand of "democracy" and our standard of living on all the world, through foreign aid, international denunciation and meddling and even armed intervention.

The chart, moreover, shows only the tip of the iceberg of our financial distress—the gold reserves and the *officially reported* net foreign exchange indebtedness to foreign governments and banks. The Federal Reserve Bulletin reports $320.4 billion of *selected* and *reported* liabilities against the dollar as of December 31, 1978, and claims of $177.2 billion against foreigners which, allowing for the $12.6 billion of gold reserves, would imply that our gold and foreign exchange reserves together were $130.6 billion in the red, not $83.4 billion, as shown in the chart. And I question whether we can safely use the net figure when, according to the officially reported figures, $41.5 billion out of $114.2 billion owing to American banks is owed by the underdeveloped, default-prone countries of Latin America, Asia and Africa, and the banks have even less chance of collecting most of that money than our European creditors have of collecting what we owe them, but are unable to pay because of our balance of payments deficits.

Unless, indeed, our government continues to bail out the banks by such largess as the $350 million aid promised to Panama in connection with the 1978 Canal treaties, and the $70 to $500 million a year or more promised under the sliding-scale commitments of those treaties. Or the $5 billion or so of aid promised to Egypt and Israel as an incentive to persuade them to agree to the peace that presumably they both desired.

Moreover, unofficial estimates reported total United States bank loan commitments abroad at $207 billion at the end of 1976, and it is reported that secret figures a year later for all Western banks combined, including American banks, which are the prime lenders, revealed $170 billion in "bad" loans, $250 billion in "endangered" loans. If these reports are correct, we may ask if they portend a replay of the Kreditanstalt failure which set off the 1931 debacle that gave the final fillip to the 1929 crash.

Conservatively, our net available gold and foreign exchange reserves at the present time must be put at a minus figure of at least $275 billion, and possibly as much as $700 billion, considering that only *selected, reported* liabilities are published by the Fed, and allowing for the more pessimistic estimates of Eurodollars outstanding. Even the lower estimate represents a deficit that no other nation has even remotely approached, not even Germany on the eve of her trillion to one debasement of the mark. We are on the brink of disaster, and only the most heroic measures can save us from chaos. This means, at the very least, the total cessation of foreign aid and of our overt and covert intervention in the affairs of other nations, and, at home, a balanced budget with no bikini accounting.

Lest you think that Chart 5 may exaggerate our gold and foreign exchange deficit, because the gold is valued at the official price of $42.222 an ounce and is obviously worth more than that, remember that the "Net Foreign Exchange Liabilities" shown on the chart record only the officially reported known amounts and should be increased by somewhere between $200 and $600 billion to take care of up to $170 billion in "bad loans," plus estimated, unreported and unknown Eurodollars and other liabilities. Whereas the value of the gold reserves might, at the most, be quadrupled, say to $168 an ounce, which would mean an increase of only $36 billion. For, if we tried to dispose of our entire gold reserves, as Professor Arthur Burns recommends(!), it is highly unlikely that we could get the peak price of over $280, and, at this writing, even $168 an ounce is optimistic.

This would make our net gold and foreign exchange deficit somewhere between $210 and $300 billion, or perhaps as high as $660 billion, if some estimates are accurate.

Unless, of course, Washington persists in its present policies and we reach trillion to one inflation, which would wipe out our entire foreign liabilities, except our debts in marks, francs, yen, etc., and make our gold reserves worth $42 trillion! And totally wreck our economy.

The international deficit and government spending

There is no one to blame for the present situation but the United States Government. The deficits in our balance of payments for 1977 and 1978 were $21 billion and $24.6 billion respectively. The deficit is concealed by a change in statistical method made in June 1978, when the Bureau of Economic Analysis of the Department of Commerce decided to include, as "receipts of income," the unremitted earnings of American-controlled corporations in foreign countries, much as if you, as individuals, had to report on your income tax returns, not just the dividends you may receive from your AT&T stock, but the earnings that AT&T retains and "plows back into the business."

But the unremitted earnings of these overseas subsidiary corporations are not "receipts of income" in the United States and may, in fact, never be received, particularly if we bear in mind the confiscations of American-owned companies and properties in so many countries of the world—Mexico, Bolivia, Argentina, Brazil and Venezuela, among others. And, aside from confiscations, retained earnings in foreign countries are not "received" in the United States, and should not be computed as "receipts" when measuring inflow and outflow.

This is not written in criticism of compilers of the statistics who do a superb job of estimating and tabulating the flow of funds in the balance of payments. And they are quite correct in adding these retained earnings of American-controlled corporations to the total of American investments abroad, which is in accordance with established accounting practices, and conforms to the uniform treatment recommended by the International Monetary Fund.

It is the misuse of these figures by the Council of Economic Advisers, and hence by other administration spokesmen, that is open to criticism, as they are thus able to minimize the dangers in our international balance of payments position by alluding to deficits in current account of $15.3 billion and $15.9 billion in 1977 and 1978, instead of the actual deficits, which are $21 billion and $24.6 billion, respectively.

The significance of the true balance of payments deficits, computed on the traditional, historical basis, lies in the fact that United States Government expenditures abroad—including the cost of maintaining our military bases, interest payments to the Saudis, Germans and others, but chiefly the cost of foreign aid—amounted to $21.2 billion in 1977 and $26.7 billion in 1978, practically identical to the true amounts of our balance of payments deficits.

The London *Economist* writes: "The outflow of gold and dollars is entirely attributable to the American Government's special payments." The explanation is simple. We, as individuals, as well as corporations and other private spenders, can only spend what we've got. There never would be any problem with the balance of payments if the flow of funds all came from and went to the private sector, as was the case, save for wartime, throughout most of our history. But the government can spend without limit—at home by debasement of the currency and abroad by draining the country of its resources and borrowing sums we are unable to repay from our present balance of payments—and can keep on spending until we are driven from our present position of domestic and international insolvency to one of complete bankruptcy. Such a situation seems assured by the administration's 1980 budget, which calls for $22 billion of foreign-aid authorizations and for $630 billion of total expenditures.

Forget what you have been told of foreign-aid "outlays" budgeted at $6 billion, and budget "authority" of $8.3 billion. Bikini accounting again—the actual total for the foreign-aid budget, concealed in various parts of the Budget Report, is $21,865,425,000, give or take a few billion dollars.

The drain of foreign aid

Oh, but foreign aid, you say—if you have been reading the papers or listening to the pontifications of our political pundits or the self-serving protestations of those who have played philanthropist with taxpayers' money—foreign aid doesn't mean that we actually send money abroad. Most of our foreign aid consists of the export of American goods, and exports help the American economy. And a large part of our aid is not in grants but loans, and these will be repaid. Balderdash!

The great bulk of our so-called loans to the less-developed nations will never be repaid, and such repayments as have been made have in nearly every case been effected solely out of the proceeds of further loans or of outright gifts—"budgetary assistance grants"—from AID.

And it is sheer hypocrisy to describe the "soft loans" of AID or of the World Bank or the Inter-American Development Bank—all of them subsidized by us—as "loans" when they are repayable, if at all, thirty or forty years hence at 1¼ percent interest or some other unrealistic rate. With inflation, these are negative rates of interest, and neither interest nor principal can be collected except with the consent of the "borrower."

And I know that these "soft loans" and the interest on them have only been repaid out of new loans, because I was on "the inside" in Bolivia, and learned what was going on there and in other parts of Latin America. On one occasion, for example, the Bolivian Government only agreed to resume payments on its defaulted debt to the Export-Import Bank because they were confident that by so doing they would get many times that amount from AID and the World Bank. And, after they got the new loans, they again reneged on their promises, and they are still in default to the Eximbank today—although Congress would never know it from the bikini accounting in the Annual Reports of the Eximbank to Congress.

I could cite similar examples in other countries, but it would be hearsay, not facts that I can vouch for on the basis of my own knowledge.

And to claim that foreign aid really doesn't cost the United States anything, but on the contrary benefits our economy because it is made up largely of shipments of American machinery, farm products, etc., is either blatant hypocrisy or crass ignorance of the nature of the balance of international payments.

When a grain exporter or a manufacturer exports his products in the usual course of business, *and is repaid by the foreign buyer,* there is indeed a gain to the economy. But if he is not repaid—a rare circumstance in normal commerce—there is obviously no gain but a loss, a loss of the grain or merchandise that was once a part of our national assets, our tangible wealth.

And when the United States *gives away* the grain or the merchandise, or "lends" the money for its purchase with an uncollectible loan for fifty years at 1¼ percent the operation is manifestly not a gain, but a direct loss to the American economy. And that loss is reflected in our balance of international payments and in the loss of our gold and foreign exchange reserves seen on Chart 5.

Yet the administration, in a blitz campaign to enlist support for foreign aid, has had the Departments of Agriculture and Commerce send out letters to key members of Congress to remind them of their states' dependence on the export sales of manufactured and agricultural products and the key role of foreign aid in making such sales possible, which has caused one senator, Russell Long of Louisiana, chairman of the Senate Finance Committee, to remark that reasoning of this nature "simply takes my breath away. . . . We have millions of Americans who'd love to buy American goods *if we gave them the money to do it with.*"

Reported foreign aid to date, since July 1945, including American contributions to the Inter-American Development Bank and to the World Bank and its "soft-loan" subsidiaries, has meant an aggregate loss to the American economy of $150 to $200 billion according to official statements, but actually at least double that figure if we can judge by the concealment of foreign-aid items in the 1979 and 1980 budget reports. We are some $200 to $400 billion poorer than we would have been had it not been for foreign aid—and don't let anyone tell you that it really didn't cost us anything because we didn't actually ship the money, we shipped goods, or because we really only "loaned" most of that money.

And this $200–$400 billion loss is a very large part of the reason why our dollar is worth only a fraction of what it was worth ten, twenty, thirty years ago. The other part of the reason is domestic deficit spending as shown in Chart 1, discussed in Chapter 6.

The Marshall Plan aid

This is not to condemn the foreign-aid program as having been wholly counterproductive. Certainly, the Marshall Plan aid was necessary, as, without it, Europe would literally have starved until their new crops could be planted and harvested after the war, and their shattered factories started running again on production for peace. And the governments in those countries, both friend and foe, were competent enough, and their civilian sectors experienced enough, to put the Marshall Plan aid to good use. So we may say without hesitation that the Marshall Plan aid and similar assistance to Japan were absolutely essential, and avoided international catastrophe on a scale that—even taking the most callous viewpoint—would have cost this country far more than the cost of this emergency assistance.

More fallacies in foreign aid

Whether or not the outward flow of aid subsequent to that time—chiefly to the "underdeveloped" nations—has benefited those countries to the same extent that it has impoverished us is another story that cannot be told within the compass of this book.

But it might be stated, for example, that it does seem rather pointless for us to have given so many billions of dollars of food aid to India when that country has 220 million head of cattle which the Hindus won't eat because of religious scruples, but which are eating up the crops and vegetation that could otherwise be put to human use. (For comparison, there are fewer than 122 million head of cattle in the United States.)

And when 100 million untouchables in India—a sixth of the population—are treated as subhuman outcasts and kept in perpetual poverty by the Indians themselves, can we be expected to feed and help that nation?

An analogous argument may be adduced in the case of other

underdeveloped countries that demand food for their starving masses in that their troubles are largely of their own making. And we have given away $25 billion of food, impoverishing ourselves, ruining the agriculture of the recipient countries and feeding a population boom in Latin America, Africa and Asia that presents the gravest danger confronting the world today.

It may be added—and this, too, is relevant to the subject matter of this book—that, so far as Latin America is concerned, the Alliance for Progress, despite all the ballyhoo and high-sounding promises that attended its birth, has been a costly and disastrous failure; that the gap between poverty there and progress here is greater than ever; that the Latin Americans are bitter with frustration, anger and resentment; and that their governments are now demanding *as a right* what Europe and Japan gratefully welcomed *as a boon.*

At the same time that we are handing out aid in the billions, governments and economists in Latin America, obsessed by the feeling of inferiority that is inevitable when a proud people become the objects of foreign charity, are proclaiming that in reality the United States is not giving aid to Latin America but is merely repaying a part of what we owe them because of the imbalance in the balance of payments—i.e., the Latin American countries buy around $1 billion a year more from the United States than we buy from them.

To argue that we "owe" foreign aid to Latin America because they buy our goods is like saying that we as individuals are entitled to charitable contributions from the supermarkets and department stores because we are their customers. Or that Japan and Malaysia have a duty to give us aid because the United States buys two to three times as much from those areas as they do from us.

But there is no limit to the fallacies in the arguments for foreign aid, such as the claims of certain Mexican economists that we don't give them aid—they give us aid, because their tourist expenditures in and imports from the United States outweigh our imports from Mexico and tourist outlays in that country, and because the interest and dividends we receive each year from our investments in Mexico exceed our annual new investments in that country—which is not surprising, considering that we have been investing in Mexico for over a hundred years and even a 2 percent return on the cumulative investment should be expected to exceed the new investment in any one year.

Aid to the underdeveloped nations

So long as we continue to pour out foreign assistance to the underdeveloped countries, we can expect these and other fallacies and animosities to continue to build up to the explosion point. There is no surer way to alienate even our true friends in Latin America—and there are no people on earth more *simpático,* more intelligent, and more deserving of our respect than the people of the Latin American republics—than for our government to continue doling out grants and so-called loans to the governments of those nations. Just as the surest way to make an implacable enemy out of an erstwhile good neighbor would be to shower extravagant gifts upon his spouse or in any way treat him as an object of charity.

Latin Americans, as well as those in other less-developed areas, are aware of the truth behind the warning of George Washington: "That it is folly in one nation to look for disinterested favors from another; that it must pay with a portion of its independence for whatever it may accept in that character.... There can be no greater error than to expect or calculate upon real favors from nation to nation."

So it is not surprising that many of the most influential writers in Latin America—not the politicos in office who reap the benefits of American aid—see our assistance policy as a Machiavellian plot to impose American "economic imperialism" on the impoverished countries of Latin America. Fuel has been added to the fire by the fact that we are devoting one sixth of all nonmilitary foreign assistance—$204.5 million out of a budget of $1.3 billion—to *sterilization, abortion* and *birth control* assistance. We have supplied (through September 1977) 1.7 billion condoms to nations in Latin America, Asia and Africa, and 18 billion contraceptive pills, plus abortion advice and sterilization services.

The zealous and well-intentioned directors of that phase of our foreign-aid program fail to see that many people in the third world—and not Catholics alone—see this as the most iniquitous side of our scheme for world domination.

The fact that there are many people in the third world who demand and receive these contraceptives and abortion-sterilization services should not blind us to the fact that there are many millions more who understandably resent our intrusion into the most sacred precincts of their family life. And the only proper solution is for our government to keep its cotton-picking fingers out of the affairs of other nations—to cease foreign aid and foreign intervention, and let each nation of the world manage its own internal affairs as it sees fit, without self-righteous criticism or meddling from Washington.

Because of AID and the activities of the Inter-American Development Bank and World Bank, we know that governments in Latin America neither having nor meriting the support of their people have been kept in power; that corruption has been fostered on a scale never heretofore imaginable, with crooked politicos and their friends pocketing a substantial part of our aid and depositing it in Switzerland or elsewhere; that we have financed, directly or through the international agencies, disastrously uneconomic industries and vast public works that, instead of benefiting the recipients of our assistance, will keep them impoverished for a generation to come—as, for example, a $50 million highway, so little needed and with so little truck traffic that annual interest and maintenance alone worked out at $200 a truck trip, with the result that the "loan" is in default, and the highway unusable for lack of maintenance.

This is only one out of hundreds of projects, even more anti-economic and vastly more expensive—running into billions of dollars—that have left Latin America more impoverished than ever and fuming with a resentment against the United States that froths over with increasing venom at every international conference—in Chile, Panama, Peru and here in the United States. Pan-American meetings seem to have only one purpose—to "pan" America!

And for that, we have paid our money and lost our gold reserves! Like they say, they expect more from America, and they get it!

Of course, it must be admitted that Latin America's troubles can also be largely attributed to the well-meaning and humanitarian efforts of the Rockefeller Institute, and of the United States public health authorities, which have helped to wipe out disease and reduce the infant mortality rate, thus increasing the population growth rate to such an extent that production of food, clothing and housing has barely kept up with population and, in many cases, has lagged behind.

The late Marxist President of Chile warned his countrymen that Chile is now too poor to import the food it needs, and that this is "the decade of hunger" for Latin America. Chile's rate of inflation has been 62 percent to 504 percent a year over the past five years. And in the good old days before United States food aid made farming unprofitable for many Latin American farmers, there was not a single country in that part of the world that did not produce all the food it required for its own needs plus a surplus for export.

Companions in misery
In short, to answer the question posed by this chapter head—"Are We Bankrupt?"—we are. And if it will give us any comfort, we are not alone in that predicament, for we share it with Burundi, Chad, Ghana, Lesotho and

Mali, with Burma, Jordan, Indonesia, Pakistan and Sri Lanka, with Bolivia, Chile and Uruguay, and with all the other ninety-four less-developed members of the IMF.

We also share it with England and Italy, the only major nations of the Western world, other than the United States, so dedicated to Keynesian economics or to a government-controlled economy that they have spent themselves into national bankruptcy. The Italians know they are bankrupt, for the flight of capital from that country into Switzerland in 1977 and 1978 was at the rate of *$50 billion a year!* (although the measures taken by Switzerland in 1978 may perhaps have tended to curb this flight). England is now in Phase IV of its succession of futile, frustrating wage and price control and "incomes" programs—a country that has been on welfare for so long that, after fifty years on the dole, the British workers have forgotten how to work. It takes ten British workers at the Ford plant in England to produce what four West German workers or five Belgian workers produce at the Ford plants in their countries, using identical machinery and with the same overall management.

The per capita production of the working age population in the United Kingdom is now below that of any other industrial country in Europe. And British labor costs—the cost per unit of output—are higher than in any of the other ten major industrial countries of the world, even though hourly wages in Great Britain are lower—lower even than in Japan, and half the estimated average hourly rates in the other nine countries.

Lord Rothschild, former chairman of the government's "think tank," has predicted that by 1985 Britain will be one of the poorest countries of Europe, with a gross per capita national product about equal to that of Italy and half that of France or Germany. "It seems to me," he has declared, "that unless we take a very strong pull at ourselves, and give up the idea that we are one of the wealthiest, most influential and important countries of the world—in other words, that Queen Victoria is still reigning—we are likely to find ourselves in serious trouble."

Other than Lord Rothschild, there appears to have been—until recently—only one major personality on the British political scene who knew what England's troubles were all about and who had the courage and impudence to tell them—that most highly intellectual of all political figures, the most hated, most admired, most brutally frank Member of Parliament: Mr. Enoch Powell.

"We are only humbugging ourselves," he claimed, in an attack on the government's economic policies, "when we pretend that we don't know the disease that is afflicting Britain, and that we don't know the remedy." The disease, he went on to say, is inflation. The cause is the excessive growth of government expenditure. And the remedy is to bring this expenditure safely back within the limits of the rate of growth of the economy.

In the past year, however, others on the British political scene seem to have reached the same conclusions on purely pragmatic grounds, although no one has as yet ventured to challenge the government deficit spending as simply unsound economics—which is scarcely surprising considering that British economists, like our own, are practically 100 percent Keynesians.

The price controls and wage agreements negotiated by the Wilson (Labour party) government in 1975 proved futile and finally blew up completely two years ago under the Callaghan (also Labour) government. But Prime Minister Callaghan himself had already seen the light prior to the defeat of his party in May 1979, as shown by his speech in May 1977 to the Labour Party Conference:

> We used to think that you could just spend your way out of a recession and increase employment by cutting taxes and boosting government spending. I tell you in all candour that that option no longer exists and that insofar as it ever did exist, it worked by injecting inflation into the economy. And each time that happened the average level of unemployment has risen. Higher inflation, followed by higher unemployment. That is the history of the last twenty years.

And, in the spring of 1978, Callaghan's son-in-law, Peter Jay, at that time the British ambassador to the United States, and formerly financial editor of *The Times,* referred to that speech as "throwing Keynes out of the window." A defenestration that, unfortunately, had not yet come to pass. But the ambassador has come out with some strongly expressed views of his own that tally completely with the ideas expressed in this book—with reference, of course, solely to the situation in the United Kingdom, and tactfully refraining from any comments on parallel developments in the United States.

Mrs. Margaret Thatcher, the leader of the Conservative party and, since May 1979, the Prime Minister, has long held anti-Keynesian views, as set forth in her election campaign pamphlet, *The Conservative Manifesto.* So there may be room for hope that England will eventually see the error of its ways and go back to the free-market economy that was once England's pride and is now Germany's joy. But the hope must be faint, as England has been a welfare state for half a century and it will not be easy to return to freedom. Unless, indeed, the United States should lead the way by adopting the policies set forth in Chapters 15 and 16 of this book, and demonstrate the true path to economic freedom by its own dramatic recovery from inflation and stagnation.

A pity that there is no Rothschild or Powell or Callaghan or Jay or Thatcher in this country to bring us back to reality from the cloud-cuckoo land of President Nixon's Phases III and IV and their economist-ridden aftermath, although the present administration may eventually attempt to head in that direction when it realizes that, as a consequence of its deficit spending program, both inflation and the flight of capital have been greater over the past two and a half years than ever before. Let us hope so.

Meanwhile, it should give us pause to realize that Italy, the United Kingdom and the United States are the only industrial nations in the world in their present parlous state of affairs, and that Japan, Germany and Switzerland, with no oil resources of their own, have managed to recover from the temporary squeeze engendered by the world petroleum crisis and are now enjoying the prosperity that has resulted from their attempts to maintain a free-market economy. And that, in common with the ninety-four less-developed countries in the IMF, it is the United States that is primarily responsible for the present worldwide inflation. That it is only the patience and forbearance of our creditors that save us and the world from total bankruptcy.

12. The Balance of International Payments

The only direct advantage of foreign commerce consists in the imports. A country obtains things which it either could not have produced at all, or which it must have produced at a greater expense of capital and labor than the cost of the things it exports to pay for them.
John Stuart Mill (1848)

The proof of the wisdom of Mill's dictum is to be found in a study of the balance of international payments, even though the idea of such a balance was only scantily developed in his time.

The balance of international payments is really a very simple concept, although most writers on the subject would seem to veil it in mystery, with the exception of the great master of the art, Dr. Ray Ovid Hall, whose brilliant work at the Commerce Department nearly fifty years ago led to his dismissal—his investigations tended to show that all was not going as well as it should have in Hoover's glorious reign, and that prosperity was not just around the corner.

The concept is simple enough but, on the other hand, the actual compilation of the figures is a very complex task indeed, calling for detective and deductive abilities that would have been envied by the late Sherlock Holmes himself.

Today there are at least seven different definitions of the balance of payments—what items ought to be included or not—and economists will never cease to debate exactly which compilation of figures is meaningful or meaningless. But if we were to go into that question in detail, this book would have to be twice as long and ten times as confusing.

The debits and credits

It is perhaps easiest to understand the balance of international payments if we go back to the days when practically the whole world was on a gold standard basis, and if we visualize each transaction as though we actually

135

had to pay out gold for everything we buy from abroad, and received gold for everything we sold abroad. Our exports are listed in the balance as credits—someone has to pay us gold—and our imports as debits—we have to pay gold to some foreign country.

Now then, when an American corporation or individual makes an investment abroad, you can see that he has to ship gold. So that, so far as the balance of payments is concerned, an investment is just like an import—a debit. And when the individual or corporation receives interest or dividends from abroad, someone has to ship gold here—so it is like an export, a credit.

Just think always in terms of which direction the gold has to be shipped, and all the mysteries of a balance of payments vanish. It is a valid approach, too, as, even though the United States is not now on a gold basis, the unpaid balances in the international accounts must eventually be settled in gold—or defaulted.

Exports and imports

Now, the merchandise items in the balance of payments—the imports and exports—give us what is called "the balance of trade." And years ago, the "mercantilists," led by French Finance Minister Jean Baptiste Colbert (1619–83), and his disciples in France, Holland and England—a century before the days of Adam Smith, used to think that a "favorable"' balance of trade was the *summum bonum* of a nation's existence. Exports were good; they made a country rich and great. Imports were bad; they drained a nation's resources—gold.

And, of course, these countries did need the gold they got from exports to wage the wars they were always fighting among themselves, as well as to buy the few luxury goods they wanted from abroad. But the imports were a luxury, the exports a necessity—or so the mercantilists saw it. And Colbert himself was a genius, no doubt about it. He was the one who defined the science of taxation as the art of plucking the most feathers with the least squawk.

England, and most countries of Europe, are still greatly dependent upon export trade to buy the things they need from abroad. And so is Latin America, as well as such prosperous countries as Australia and New Zealand—much more dependent than the United States or Russia or China, for example.

In this country, exports account for only a small fraction of what we produce, between 4 and 5 percent. If we didn't export a single dollar's worth of goods, it would scarcely affect anyone in this country—*directly*, that is.

But *indirectly* it would affect everyone, and very much indeed, because the vital importance of exports is the gold we get from them—we are still talking in gold standard terms—and with that gold we can buy the imports that are absolutely essential if we wish to maintain our present standard of living.

Manganese, tin, chromium, cobalt, rubber, quinine, cocaine, iodine, tagua, carnauba, babassu nuts, are among the many things we simply must import from abroad because we don't produce them here. Coffee, tea, cacao, bananas, are among the many amenities of life that, likewise, are not produced in this country, at least not in commercial quantities.

Then there are other products that, although produced here, are not produced in the quantities we need, such as sugar, bauxite (aluminum ore), mercury, nickel, lead and cowhides. Yes, cowhides—because each bull, steer, cow and calf has only one hide apiece, and we don't consume enough meat to satisfy our needs for leather. So we have to import cowhides from Argentina and Uruguay where they consume an enormous amount of beef and, although their gauchos use a great many boots and saddles, they do have surplus hides. For cowhides are used for hundreds of industrial purposes, quite aside from the principle use of the cowhide, which is, of course, to hold the cow together.

But it would be a mistake to think that exports are the only way we can pay for imports. And it is just as great a mistake to pair off any one item in the balance of payments against any other item, and speak of the "net balance of trade" or "net tourist payments" or "net" anything. American tourists don't get the money they need for their travels from foreign tourists who come to this country. There are no "net" items in the balance of payments. All of our exports, visible and invisible, all the transactions that bring gold into this country, pay for all of our imports, visible and invisible, and all the transactions that take gold out of this country.

Composition of the balance of payments

The "visibles" are, of course, the tangible items—the merchandise exports and imports. The "invisibles" are such things as the expenditures of American tourists abroad and of foreign tourists in this country. These offer no difficulty to understand because, whether we import a case of Löwenbräu for our future enjoyment or consume it on the spot in Munich, we are going to have to pay for it in gold.

And so on, through the entire list of invisible items—foreign aid, gifts by immigrants to their relatives abroad (such entries being known as "unilateral transfers"), purchases of Hiroshige prints by Japanese collectors in New York, interest payments in both directions, travel expenses, royalties, the maintenance of American bases overseas and hundreds of other items that take all the skills of our statisticians in the Commerce Department to ferret out and evaluate.

The aggregate of all those items—imports and exports of goods and services, foreign aid and private gifts—is known by the Commerce Department as the "balance on current account" and is generally referred to as the "deficit" or "surplus" in our balance of payments, a graphic portrayal of how we are doing in our international transactions.

Then, in addition to these current account items, we come to what are known as the "capital accounts," the changes in the total of U.S. assets abroad and of foreign assets in the United States. These include the long-term and short-term foreign loans and investments (in former years, the changes in short-term balances were regarded as a balancing item, not as a part of the capital accounts), whether made by individuals, banks or corporations, plus government "loans" which, to the extent that they are not really loans but gifts, overstate our solvency without, however, altering their impact on the balance of payments.

These capital accounts are a bit tricky to understand, but again, if we think of actual gold, then it is clear that when we lend money abroad we must ship gold, so it goes down in the balance of payments as a *debit,* just like an *import.* And when the loan is repaid, or when we borrow from abroad, someone must ship us gold, so it is like an *export*—a *credit.*

Traditionally, when the United States was on a gold standard, gold currency and bullion shipments were not included in the merchandise trade, but were regarded as a balancing transfer, which in fact they were. And, as in all double-entry accounting, the two sides of the balance sheet must always balance. But, of course, it is not really a balance sheet, but more like a corporation income account or flow-of-funds statement, a statement of the operations during the course of the year, not a statement of assets and liabilities at the end of the year.

And the surpluses or deficits—with one exception, we have been in a deficit position every year since 1949—are therefore balanced and must be paid for by: (a) actual shipments of gold, imported or exported, plus (2) "errors and omissions."

Actual figures in the balance of payments
Now, let's get down to actual figures, so we can see just what has been happening to our balance of payments over the past three decades. For this will tell us what the present inflation is all about—this plus the deficit spending at home.

And let us turn first to the balancing entries that are generally overlooked in discussions of the balance of payments. The first balancing item—the actual shipments of gold and changes in gold reserves held for foreign account—would normally be an insignificant entry in a nation's balance of payments, whether the world is on a gold standard or not. Just as in domestic operations, when every bank had gold coins or bullion in its vaults, it was only occasionally that one bank had to transfer gold to another bank or to the Fed. The vast bulk of transactions was handled through accounting debits or credits interbank or in the clearinghouse or in the Fed, and it was only when the flow had been too great in one direction or another that actual gold was trucked from place to place.

The same was true internationally under the gold standard. Nations were able to move billions of dollars in trade, services and investments with only relatively minor "settling" operations in gold. But in recent times, after more than thirty years of foreign aid and over ten years of war in Indonesia, plus the flight of capital from the United States, it has been another story. There has been a steady erosion of our gold reserves year after year, with no significant exceptions, from 1949 through 1972. In 1973 we prohibited all further gold exports—we had only $11 billion left—which is why our foreign exchange deficit has continued to grow and why, in the past several years, it has taken from $130 to $282 to buy one ounce of gold in the world gold markets, and why gold futures have been traded in New York and Chicago at up to $329 an ounce.

The second balancing entry—"errors and omissions"—is the most revealing of all. Prior to World War II, this item was without significance, representing nothing but the inevitable inability, despite the best detective and statistical work possible, to ascertain the exact amounts of all the entries in the balance of payments. Under a worldwide gold standard, when nations could not spend more than they had, it was truly an errors and omissions account. And perhaps some of you are old enough to remember when accountants always used to end their statements with "E&OE"—errors and omissions excepted.

The flight of capital

From 1945 to 1949—the years of the so-called dollar shortage in Europe and Latin America—the errors and omissions entry became ominously large. Analysts of the balance of payments, both within and without the government, agreed that the plus figure in the errors and omissions column represented for the most part the flight of capital from Europe and Latin America to the United States because of qualms among the people of those countries as to the stability of their currencies and because the American dollar was considered the soundest in all the world. This movement averaged over $500 million a year!

Since 1960, however, the errors and omissions entry has also been ominously large, but in the opposite direction. It represented for the most part, *a flight of capital from the United States to foreign countries—at the average rate of $443 million a year from 1960 through 1968 ($3,987 million), and $3 billion a year from 1969 through 1974 ($17.8 billion)!!* Yet no analyst, so far as I know, within the government or out, has dared to alarm the public by pointing out the implications of the minus figures in the errors and omissions column. The New York Federal Reserve Bank analyst calls them "unrecorded capital items . . . representing unrecorded outflows." The Commerce Department calls them "statistical discrepancies."

In 1975 and 1976, perhaps because of a change in the political situation in the United States, worldwide confidence in the dollar seems to have revived temporarily, and the figures indicate an inward flow of flight capital (possibly a return of U.S. flight capital) of $5.4 billion and $9.3 billion respectively. The outward flow of capital flight from the United States resumed in 1977 at the rate of $927 million a year, followed by an inward flow of $11.4 billion (est.) in 1978 that might be explained by flight capital from Iran in anticipation of the revolution, and from other OPEC countries.

If your reaction to the flight of capital from the United States is one of horror or indignation, if you conclude that the speculators, or managers of multinational corporations, who must be guilty of this state of affairs ought to be jailed, your reaction is perfectly normal. And at many times in history and in many countries of the world, this has been the outraged reaction of legislators and presidents who have enacted laws or decrees prohibiting the flight of capital, with the most dire punishments that human ingenuity could devise.

And such laws and decrees have inevitably proved futile. In fact, the enactment of such legislation served only to press the panic button that marked the beginning of the end. There has never been a government capable of plugging all the leaks that make possible a flight of capital. And before you rush to condemn those "guilty" of participating in a capital flight, think of those Jews in Nazi Germany who had the foresight, courage and ingenuity to evade their persecutors and escape not only with their lives but with some small part of their possessions.

So reserve your indignation, not for those people who have had the prescience to salvage what they could of their life savings, and vent it instead on the interventionist administrations in the United States that have been so profligate with taxpayers' money in Vietnam and foreign aid that they have brought us to international bankruptcy.

As to the multinational companies, it is unlikely that they have engaged in a *flight of capital* from the United States. What is more probable—and I am not unacquainted with their practices—is that management, being fearful of further dollar depreciation and unwilling to subject their foreign profits to double taxation, decided not to press the overseas subsidiaries to remit to the United States the last penny of profits, but to leave a nest egg for future investments abroad.

The Commerce Department estimates that these retained earnings of American-controlled corporations abroad amounted to $7.3 billion in 1977 and $10.1 billion (est.) in 1978 while accumulated retained earnings held abroad by the multinational companies have been variously estimated at between $130 billion and $270 billion, a range that shows how little we really know of the facts affecting the stability of the dollar. Of course the bulk of these assets consists of inventories, accounts receivable and working capital needed in the operation of the business. But at least $25 billion is in cash or the equivalent, and perhaps half of that amount can be considered as unremitted balances that could and normally would be remitted to the parent companies were it not for fear of the continuing debasement of the dollar.

While, of course, the action taken by any one multinational company in keeping its balances abroad is perfectly legitimate, it may well be disastrous if all American companies with overseas investments pursue a like policy. And this does not imply any hint of collusion—merely an instance where the "fallacy of composition" is indeed an apt commentary. What is good policy for each individual company may be disastrous if that policy is pursued by all.

Congress or the administration may decided to impose income tax or even criminal penalties to discourage this form of capital flight. But it would be unfortunate if present resentment against the actions of a *few* multinational corporations were used for political purposes to condemn *all* multinational corporations for having pursued foreign exchange policies that have been prudent and legitimate, and only inimical to the interests of the United States because the United States Government itself has recklessly squandered the nation's gold and foreign exchange resources.

So far as the flight of capital is concerned, I doubt the effectiveness of any legislative or executive measures that could be taken to thwart American individuals and corporations from maintaining and increasing balances and investments abroad. When not even the death penalty in Germany or other drastic sanctions by the most dictatorial governments of Latin America have ever been able to block the flight of capital, it would be naïve to believe that any prohibitive measures could be effective in a free America. In fact, any attempt to curb the flight of capital—other than putting a stop to government spending abroad—would intensify the flight and mark the beginning of the end for the American dollar.

President Kennedy imposed a 16 percent surtax on foreign income precisely to deter the outflow of capital by Americans investing abroad. President Johnson decreed the most drastic—and unjust—balance of payments curbs in American history, announced in his famous January 1, 1968, address to the nation. And capital flight since those two events has been greater than ever before. In every country of the world where the government has attempted to stay the flight of capital, instead of putting a stop to its own profligacy, the consequence has been total catastrophe.

Misuse of the balance of payments figures

The minimizing of the balance of payments deficits in current account by the President's Council of Economic Advisers has already been discussed in this and in the previous chapters. But there is another element of obfuscation in our international transactions, not so much with respect to the balance of payments compiled by the Bureau of Economic Analysis of the Department of Commerce, but with respect to one of the items in that compilation—the export and import trade figures that are published each month well in advance of the date that the balance of payments estimates are issued.

Briefly, when the main purpose of such figures should be to determine the surplus or deficit in a nation's international position, does it make sense to include in our exports such items as the shipment of several billions of dollars of goods each year, required for the sustenance and military support of American soldiers abroad or the many more billions in foreign military aid, or in economic aid to the third world, practically none of which will ever be repaid except out of the proceeds of uncollectible "loans"? Of course not!

If it did make sense, then we could easily solve all the problems of our unfavorable trade balance by giving away more billions of dollars of goods, moving the rest of our army abroad, and transposing the entire Washington bureaucracy to the Bahamas, where we would pay them, establish commissaries and provide for their sustenance precisely as we now do for our troops abroad and for the swarming bureacracy of the Foreign Service, USAID and others who cram our embassies overseas in close to two hundred countries of the world. The Commerce Department balance of trade and balance of payments figures would then all be in balance. But would we be any more solvent? Would our true deficit position be improved by such juggling? Of course not!

And there are many other misleading entries in the crude Commerce Department figures for the balance of trade (merchandise exports and imports) and balance of payments (all credits and debits, including invisibles and financial movements) which were not misleading in the good old days before the United States started playing Santa Claus to the world, but which are now just another example of the government's hypocritical bikini accounting today.

But government officials delight in citing the crude export-import figures without waiting for the analytical presentation of the balance of payments, thus attempting to show that things are not as bleak as one might think. Not that those in government are incurably dishonest, but that so many of our officials are too new in office, too unsophisticated to know the facts of life in government accounting and where to look for Catch-22.

In fact, some three years ago, President Ford's closest economic consultant actually quoted to me the just-published raw export-import figures for 1974—a favorable trade balance of $11.5 billion—as evidence that there was no further cause for worry as to the outlook for the dollar, leaving me speechless—or as close to that condition as one of my temperament can be. (The foreign aid included among our exports amounted to $11 billion.) Yet this official—one of the most competent advisers the President could have enlisted for his inner council—was not to be faulted for citing misleading statistics when he was compelled to rely for his information on a permanent bureaucracy, some of whom are incompetent while others are extremely reluctant to change their ways and outlook with the advent of each new administration.

As a commentary on the latter phenomenon, which will illustrate the obstacles each new administration faces, a year after President Eisenhower assumed office, one of the most capable officials who has ever served in the Treasury Department told me that trying to get trustworthy information from the permanent staff, and particularly any attempt to get them to implement the policies laid down by the new administration, was like trying to sweep feathers out of the room with a broom—there was no tangible resistance, but no matter how hard one swept there were just as many feathers left in the room as when one started.

Yet Treasury is and always has been by all odds the most efficient and least politicized of government departments, and the Secretary of the Treasury at that time was the best we have ever had since Alexander Hamilton, with a staff of under and assistant secretaries to match. The present administration is still too new in the saddle and too overwhelmed by the pressure of events to know where to turn for reliable information in the face of a reluctant and sometimes hostile staff of civil servants.

Civil service reform

It may be that it was frustration of this kind that prompted the present administration to propose civil service reform legislation and to give "top priority" to its enactment. The President's initial justification for his proposal was that he found it impossible, because of civil service rules, to dismiss superfluous or ineffective employees and thus reorganize the bureaucracy for greater efficiency.

The 1978 act not only provides new rules for dismissal but has made it possible for replacements to be appointed, not from the top three available candidates as formerly, but from the top seven, and has also established a new super-category of about nine thousand managerial-rank civil servants at higher salaries but subject to dismissal.

It is impossible to fathom, and certainly one cannot impugn the motives behind this legislation, for, as Lord Coke once said: "The Devil himself knoweth not what lieth in a man's mind." But it may be pointed out that an unscrupulous President might find that his loyal friends from his home state, or from the home states of loyal congressmen, were not quite bright enough to reach the top-three rank and that increasing the available candidates to the top seven, while dismissing as many as necessary of the existing bureaucracy, would give him greater leeway for political patronage, with the super-managerial salaries as an additional incentive.

If so, this would directly affect inflation, for any criterion other than merit alone in the appointment of government employees increases the cost of government and hence the burden of taxation or of printing-press inflation.

The balance of payments cover-up

Getting back to the balance of payments, our representatives in Washington seemingly do not even *want* to know the facts. In February 1968, a month after President Johnson's Draconian balance of payment measures, one of the ablest of our congressmen held a public "Balance of Payments Seminar" to which he invited some of the most distinguished academic economists in the country, and qualified observers and questioners from the major newspapers, the AFL-CIO, U. S. Chamber of Commerce and National Association of Manufacturers. And, in the course of the question-and-answer period, it turned out that, to avoid any appearance of partisan political bias, the speakers had been expressly requested not to discuss the budget deficit or the Vietnam War! The alpha and omega of all our problems!

Can we still compete in foreign trade?

However, the major factor in our balance of payments deficits in recent years has not been foreign aid and the Vietnam War, but the unfavorable merchandise trade balance—$31 billion in 1977 and a record $34 billion in 1978.

Some would be inclined to blame this trade deficit on oil alone, inasmuch as petroleum imports amounted to $42.3 billion in 1977 and $39 billion in 1978, and these imports should certainly be cut in half. Oil imports would, in fact, be cut if Washington had the courage to stimulate domestic production by removing all price and other controls and imposing a tariff equivalent to say 25 cents a gallon on all petroleum imports (i.e., approximately $12 per barrel of crude), plus a sales tax on all petroleum products, domestic or foreign, equivalent to another 25 cents a gallon—the figures are arbitrary, perhaps wholly unrealistic and given purely by way of example.

For comparison, gasoline excise taxes are far higher in Europe: 89 cents in Belgium, 79 cents in France, 82 cents in Germany, $1.14 in Italy, 90 cents in the Netherlands, 65 cents in Sweden and 71 cents in the United Kingdom. The rest of the world is convinced that the United States is upsetting the economies of the whole world by its recklessly wasteful demand for oil—a limited natural resource—and other countries will never believe we are sincere in preaching cooperation until we make an honest effort to cut down on our petroleum consumption.

But to blame the trade deficit on oil alone when our total balance of payments debits amount to some $350 billion (the reported totals include some netted figures) is like saying that a person who spends $35,000 a year and runs a deficit of $3,000 a year can properly blame that deficit entirely on college costs of say $4,000 a year, when perhaps extravagant vacations or entertainment really account for the shortfall.

Basically, the blame for our trade deficit lies with the fact that the United States is no longer competitive in many lines of production in which we once ruled supreme, and that our exports therefore no longer suffice to pay for our imports.

Prior to World War II, American automobiles were without peer. Some 85 percent of all the automobiles sold in international trade came from the United States. A few Rolls-Royce, Mercedes-Benz and Hispano-Suiza cars were sold worldwide, and perhaps a score of less prestigious, unhyphenated makes. But the great bulk of the international demand for automobiles was for American cars.

In quality and price, and in that combination of quality and price that determines value, American cars were virtually beyond competition. But, since then, higher wages, the lack of adequate quality controls, union interference with efficient production practices, theft in the factories, the whole gamut of inhibiting forces listed in Chapter 14 and, above all, the burden of excessive taxation and regulation have raised American production costs to such an extent that, in many lines of production, *we can no longer compete in the markets of the world.*

In 1978 we imported $20.6 billion of foreign automobiles and automotive products; exported $13.2 billion, of which a good percentage doubtless went to American soldiers and Foreign Service officials abroad.

In 1928, when I was chief of the Latin American Section of the U. S. Bureau of Foreign & Domestic Commerce, I led a delegation of Latin American engineers through the Ford, Chevrolet, Buick, Packard and Studebaker plants, and the thing that impressed them most was the constant supervision by the foremen and the strict quality controls at every stage of production, with the rejection of any parts or assemblies that were not up to the standard.

In 1967, as chairman at The University of Michigan of an international organization of students of business administration, I led a group of European business students through the factory of one of the leading producers of "quality" cars in the United States, and was amazed to see at one of the presses that every piece turned out was obviously defective, with the press stamping each steel sheet three times and off-center, whether because of the carelessness of the operator or maladjustment of the machine. As the pieces were not rejected but placed on the assembly line, I questioned the engineer who was guiding us through the plant, and was told that the part in question was the bottom plate so that the defect made no difference (!), and that, if the foreman tried to impose strict quality controls, there would certainly be a work stoppage, with the National Labor Relations Board inevitably supporting the labor union if it came to a showdown. The economist of another major automobile manufacturer confirmed that the situation was the same in his company.

The recall of 22 million defective cars in 1977 and 1978 may be, in part, a reflection of this decline in American automotive workmanship, although it would seem that most of the blame must lie with management, perhaps in emphasizing appearance rather than engineering.

By contrast, later that same year (1967), on a tour of the Mercedes-Benz plant in Germany, it so happened that ahead of me in the line of visitors was a University of Michigan engineering graduate, similarly engaged in picking up a car previously ordered in the United States. And we were both impressed by the exceptional quality controls, far stricter than those observed by that young man in any Michigan plant, and even superior to those I had seen at the Packard plant in 1928.

That is one explanation for the drop in America's standing in international trade between 1928 and 1978—the decline in quality controls. And it holds true in many lines of production, although manifestly not with respect to the manufacture of computers, airplanes, photocopiers and other articles where American invention, capital investment and innovation, coupled with quality control, have overcome the high cost and declining work standards of American labor.

The ailing steel industry

Another explanation of the decline in America's ability to compete in world markets is that much of our industrial plant has fallen seriously behind that of Europe and Japan and is largely obsolete or obsolescent. To avoid any imputation of bias—that I might be trying to "prove a point"—the following discussion of the crisis in the American steel industry is taken from the monthly review of the Swiss Bank Corporation:

> *The steel industry of the U.S.A. has fallen seriously behind in international competition in recent years, because of its outmoded production structure. While the fundamental importance of the industry is undisputed, precisely that fact is one of the reasons the government has imposed more or less stringent price controls for the past 15 years or so; as a result, the steel companies were unable to accumulate the earnings in boom years necessary to weather below-average margins during the recession and undertake urgent restructuring. So they were in no position to modify production plant to suit modern technology, introduce energy-saving processes or improve productivity to any extent. Nor were they able to implement the latest theories on optimal mill location. Some of the mills date from the industry's early days around the turn of the century. Only one new medium-size steel mill has been erected in the past 15 years. Another unmistakable sign of this slide is the fact that a listing of the 92 biggest and most efficient furnaces in the world includes only five in the U.S.A. The country has fallen even further behind Japan lately in spite of the inordinately risen wage costs there. In 1976 output per worker was 460 tons of steel in Japan, only 275 tons in the U.S.A. The labor cost advantage amounts to $65 per ton. On average, the Japanese produce at about 30% lower costs than their competitors in the U.S.A.*

It was not until September 1978 that the first modern blast furnace in the United States was completed (by Bethlehem Steel), the first such plant that is as advanced technologically as any in Japan or Germany. Plus a new steel plate mill and a steel bar mill that are the most modern installations of their kind anywhere in the world.

And, as further evidence that it is not American technology or management that is lacking, when the People's Republic of China called for worldwide bids for the construction of a $1 billion iron ore processing complex, United States Steel won the contract award in competition against the leading European and Japanese suppliers, and Bethlehem Steel was awarded a similarly competitive contract for construction of a $100 million processing plant. It seems probable that American companies would have been awarded at least a part of the $2.3 billion Chinese steel mill contract entered into with Japan in 1977, if the United States had not stubbornly refused to recognize the existence of the People's Republic of China at that time.

The only possible explanation of the technological lag in the American steel industry is that the United States Government has, over nearly two decades, by threats of reprisals and other political pressures, prevented American steel companies from raising prices sufficiently to attract the new capital necessary to install new steel complexes, notwithstanding which the industry has made every effort to bring its plants up to date by cutting dividends to the bone and ploughing back profits into plant as set forth in the following chapter.

Farmers to the rescue

In fact, if it were not for the efficiency of the American farmer—whether in grain or soybeans or chickens or peanuts—American exports would be only a fraction of what they are today and our international balance of payments position would be even more disastrous than it is. Agricultural exports, which averaged $5.5 billion from 1956 through 1970, have amounted to over $22 billion in each of the past five years, rising to a record $23.7 billion in 1977, and a new record of $29.4 billion in 1978.

In further proof that it is largely the American farmer who is supporting the American economy, in 1933 it took 14 weeks and 18 pounds of feed to produce one 3½-pound frying chicken; today, our chicken and egg factories take only 8 weeks and 7½ pounds of feed for the same result. European chicken farmers simply cannot compete despite the good old-fashioned flavor of their farm-grown hens. And the Common Market countries have had to raise their tariff barriers again and again to shut out American competition.

The output per man-hour in American agriculture in general has increased at a rate of nearly 6 percent a year from 1950 to 1975, meaning that production per man has *quadrupled* during that period! In 1950 the United States had 9.9 million people working on farms; by 1975 the number had dropped to 4.3 million. Each farmer today is producing enough food and other agricultural products to feed and clothe forty-nine people at home and provide a substantial surplus for export, compared to 1950 when there was one farmer for every fifteen people and our farm exports were a quarter as large as they are today. If the American automobile manufacturers had been able to increase their efficiency in the same ratio, we would have Fords and Chevies running out of our ears, and the Japanese and Germans would go back to making toys. The American farmer is providing 85 percent of all the giveaway food relief in the world today.

Thank God for the American farmer who would neither need nor want any welfare from Washington if the government would stop providing welfare to a billion people at home and abroad, thereby debasing the American dollar and adding to the cost of everything the American farmer has to buy.

Conclusions

It is small comfort to be told that, in the past year or the past five years, prices have risen less here than in England or Japan and very little more than in Germany. That may very well be, but in the field of automobiles, motorcycles, cameras, radio-TV equipment and many other goods, American wares have been priced out of the market increasingly over the past twenty-five years—*and there is no present indication of any reversal of that trend.* Nor can we expect a complete turnaround in this state of affairs unless and until we adopt the drastic remedial measures set forth in Chapter 15.

Must we lose confidence in America's future? Are we headed on the irreversible downward slope that, according to Oswald Spengler's *Decline of the West,* has been the fate of every one of the world's great civilizations?

Not in my book, we're not! In the first place, I don't regard the remedies proposed in Chapters 15 and 16 as an impossible dream. And, in the second place, if you examine the list of American exports over the past fifty years, you will find that over 50 percent of those exports in any year consists of products that simply did not exist twenty years earlier or, if they did exist, were of such minor importance that they hardly had a place in our international statistics.

American genius, invention and innovation in manufacturing processes, plus capital investment, account for more than half the products exported from this country in any given year. Computers, instant cameras, xerographic copiers, were all developed in this country, and have practically no competition in the world's markets.

And, before those exports, there were automobiles, electric refrigerators, air conditioners, airplanes and countless other products, either invented by Americans or produced by Americans better or cheaper than in any other country of the world.

And if the consumerists and environmentalists—the fanatics—don't drive American exports out of the world markets altogether with their insistence on impossible standards of perfection that other nations do not impose, American exports can be counted upon to rectify our balance of payments position as they have always done in the past. Perhaps to raise our exports to 10 percent of GNP, as was the case prior to 1930, instead of the 4–5 percent we have today.

Provided, of course, that our government stops financing German, Japanese and other exports to Latin America (and probably elsewhere in the world) under bilateral and multilateral agreements that make it impossible for American exporters to even enter a competitive bid. And provided we take effective steps to put a stop to the discriminatory practices directed against United States exports by the very nations that are beneficiaries of American aid.

Am I implying that the United States has actually been financing the exports of Germany, Japan and other countries in deals that discriminate against the United States? Yes, dear reader, that is exactly what I mean—either directly through nonearmarked aid or "loans" which foreign governments use to buy imports from our competitors under barter or other deals which preclude American suppliers from competing, or indirectly through the World Bank or the Inter-American, Asian or African Development Banks. Washington has been so timorous of antagonizing the underdeveloped nations, for fear of losing voting support in the United Nations or the Organization of American States, that we have failed to take effective steps to put a stop to these abuses. Or even let the American public know what's going on. Never underestimate the total incompetency of our foreign-aid bureaucracy.

We have even participated in a world coffee cartel which has been largely responsible for raising the retail price of coffee from 50 cents or less a pound to $3 or more, of which a large portion represents a tax paid by the American consumer to a foreign government, such as the 44 cents a pound tax that Brazil levies on green coffee exports, 85 cents on instant coffee. There have been cartels before—international, government-sponsored monopolies in restraint of trade—but this is the first time in my memory that any importing country has officially connived with an export monopoly to raise the price of the commodities that its consumers must buy. Or, as our government and theirs euphemistically (and hypocritically) phrase it, to "stabilize prices."

Furthermore, the United States has at times aided foreign cartels by laying up "stockpiles" of various metals, supposedly for national defense purposes. We have stockpiled enough tin, for example, to more than equal thirteen years of Bolivian tin exports, which should certainly suffice for the longest war in American history.

And, late in 1977, we signed an international sugar agreement in Geneva with seventy-one other countries, aimed at increasing world sugar prices from about 7 cents a pound wholesale to 11 cents a pound in 1978 and up to 21 cents in later years. Adding transportation charges and duties, a world price of 11 cents a pound means approximately 14½ cents wholesale in the United States. But even that level was not sufficient to satisfy the Democrat senator from Idaho and his counterparts in the House and, in 1979, Congress passed, and the administration approved, a sugar bill that will add a further 11½ cents to the consumer price of a five-pound bag of sugar, rising to an additional 60 cents or more by 1982. Each cent a pound increase means a rise of $224 million in retail sugar costs. A bonanza for Communist Cuba and a further kick in the behind for the American housewife. I ask you—how many American housewives have read in the papers or heard over the networks that they were being thus indecently assaulted by their own government? Or will they blame the supermarkets for the higher prices?

To cap the climax, in November 1978, the United States acceded to the demands of the so-called Group of 77, negotiating on behalf of the third world countries—i.e., the most backward, underdeveloped nations which are the chief recipients of American foreign aid—and has agreed to contribute to a $6 billion fund that those nations are demanding to "stabilize" the prices of eighteen additional commodities we purchase from them. The actual amount of the United States contribution is hazy—perhaps an initial fund of $500 million, with the United States contributing 25 percent, but, whatever the eventual cost may be, we may be sure that it will be concealed from Congress and from the American consumer through the usual bikini accounting.

Someday, I trust, the American people will awaken to the situation, and Washington will be forced to make it possible for American consumers to buy without being held up by foreign cartels, and for American manufacturers and farmers to compete freely in the world's markets without subsidies but without discrimination. So don't sell America short!

13. Incomes Policy and Price Controls

...not old-style liberalism ... which is identified with economic laissez-faire, [but] neo-liberalism in which the positive role of the state [is limited to] establishing the juridical, competitive and monetary framework necessary to a viable market economy. ...

Wilhelm Röpke (1963)

Röpke's formula, carried out by his former pupil, the late Ludwig Erhard, expounds the basis on which Germany's phenomenal economic recovery over the past thirty years was built. But not even the most thriving economies, such as those of Germany, Japan, France, Switzerland and Spain, have managed to avoid the problem of higher prices, of wage increases outpacing the increase in productivity. In fact, in recent years, inflation has been worse in Japan and Spain than here. The problem of inflation is universal and will probably always constitute a threat against which all nations must ever be on guard. What we can hope for is that our government will eventually see the wisdom of the Röpke-Erhard approach in which government intervention in the economy is limited to that essential to ensure a free market, so that it will no longer be the government itself that is the cause of inflation.

The "incomes policy" approach
In Sweden and the Netherlands, they were relatively successful for a number of years in bringing employers and labor unions together in order to determine from time to time mutually acceptable increases in wages and other income (interest rates, rents, profits, fees, etc.), with a view to maintaining full employment and reasonable stability in prices. This approach is known as an "incomes policy."

But the Dutch and Swedish efforts have both gone down to failure. In Sweden particularly, the welfare policies of the government—Sweden's

"Middle Way" between capitalism and communism, much touted in the early days of our own New Deal—have pushed labor costs so high as to price many Swedish products out of the international market altogether. Aside from the fact that labor union pressures antagonistic to quality controls—in the Volvo plant, for example—tended to damage the Swedish reputation for quality as compared with German and Japanese competitors. The present coalition government seems as completely committed to the idea of a welfare state as was the predecessor Socialist government, and Volvo and other manufacturers are now compelled to pay workers 85 percent of their normal pay even when their plants are shut down, the shutdowns being largely the consequence of the drop in exports. And the labor unions are demanding 100 percent pay for idle time. Swedish taxes take 53.3 percent of the gross national product, compared with 47.4 percent in Norway, 46.7 percent in the Netherlands and 45.0 percent in Denmark—the welfare states.

In England, where they follow the "Muddle Way" rather than Sweden's "Middle Way," they have been trying to establish an "incomes policy" since the early 1960s, but have been decidedly less successful than the Swedes or Dutch for reasons that are obvious. In the Netherlands and Sweden, the employers' associations and the labor unions are strong, united and, in general, highly responsible. They have usually been adversaries only in the sense that the employees naturally want the highest possible wages, and the employers the highest possible profits.

But both sides have until recently realized that the prosperity of the whole nation depends largely upon foreign commerce, and that their country's ability to compete in international trade depends upon its success in keeping price increases within reasonable bounds. Both countries are extremely law-abiding, accustomed to obeying the rules—at least such rules as are laid down by democratic processes. And in neither country are strikes or mass unemployment the problem that they are in England or in the United States.

None of these conditions applies in England. The English (not to mention the Scots, Irish and Welsh) are much too individualistic to accept whatever compromise their leaders might reach, and the leaders know that, if they were reasonable, they would soon be leaders with no followers. So strikes and unemployment are, and for many years have been, serious indeed. Nonetheless, at least up to the spring of 1979, England has been determined to make a go of its incomes policy, or the "social contract" system, as it has been called by the Labour government. But labor's violations of their agreements were even more frequent under the Labour party than under the Conservatives, and in November 1978 the British

Trade Union's Council flatly turned down the government's proposal for moderation in its wage demands. However, whether under a Labour or a Conservative government, it may be that the country will eventually "muddle through" as it has always been proud of doing.

So when a socialist economist such as John Kenneth Galbraith insists that we should adopt an incomes policy in the United States as a cure for inflation, we may suspect that he is either pulling our legs or else being outrageously political. Two English writers, after a careful study of the incomes policies pursued in England, Sweden, the Netherlands, the U.S.S.R. and Nazi Germany, conclude that such policies are a harmful trap that does not cure inflation, makes unemployment worse, increases the preponderant political power of the labor unions and leads either to economic impoverishment or to the "serfdom of totalitarian government." And Gunnar Myrdal, the Swedish socialist economist and Nobel laureate, has proclaimed that the Social Democrat program has turned the Swedes into a "gang of hustlers."

The economists again

Can you imagine what would happen in this country if the government were to try to *force* the labor unions and employers to get together on wage increases low enough to ensure price stability? Aside from the fact that, in the United States as in England, the real problem is not wage-push inflation, but demand-pull inflation motivated by excessive government spending.

In an incredible TV discussion on the Merv Griffin show between the learned and witty Professor Galbraith and Carroll O'Connor—who has never sounded more like Archie Bunker than he did on that show— Galbraith "proved" that an incomes policy was the answer to our inflationary problems by pointing out that those countries that have an effective incomes policy have the least inflation. Like saying that those countries where prices have risen the least have the least problem with inflation. The good professor kept his tongue so conspicuously in his cheek during Archie Bunker's comments—a characteristic of Galbraith's TV delivery—that it is hard to say whether he intended his remarks as humor or as economics.

Professor Samuelson, less flamboyant but no less learned than his Harvard compeer, keeps his feet closer to the ground—and the rest of him, too (Galbraith is 6' 8" or, as he puts it, 5' 20"). So, while he gives space in his textbook to a discussion of incomes policy, he refrains from presenting it as a panacea for all our ills.

And Samuelson has become increasingly conservative with the

passage of time, conceding, as I have already pointed out, that 2 percent per annum is the maximum acceptable rate of inflation, not 5 percent as he formerly held. And now—miracle of miracles for a man who more than anyone else in America is responsible for indoctrinating the last two generations of economists in Keynesian theory—he presents his ninth and tenth editions of *Economics* as a *"post-Keynesian neoclassical synthesis."* So apparently his views are no longer so far apart from those of Dr. Wilhelm Röpke, the mentor of the German economic recovery, who speaks of an "anachronistic Keynesianism," or of Dr. Otmar Emminger, the new president of West Germany's central bank (the Deutsche Bundesbank), who, despite his London School of Economics education, considers Keynesian theory no longer "relevant." Perhaps with the mellowing of time, Professor Samuelson may even come around to agreeing with that old war-horse of classical economics, the late Sumner Schlicter, who, over twenty years ago, wrote an essay, "The Passing of Keynesian Economics," and will admit that a dollar of reasonably stable purchasing power should be our goal.

And, so long as we are on the subject of economists and you, dear reader, may wonder what weight you should give to the pronouncements of this or that exponent of the dismal science, you might bear in mind that, by and large, the professors of economics in the graduate schools of business—many of them directors or consultants of banks and business firms—are, in general, apt to have a somewhat more realistic grasp of the facts of economic life than their compeers in the colleges of arts and sciences.

The truth is that the outstanding university economists of whatever branch do have an amazingly broad and deep knowledge of the past and present course of economic events in this country and only go astray when they attempt to predict the future on the basis of their theoretical training or when they are placed in a position to dictate practical political policies and make decisions in reliance on their untested pet economic theories. For this is where Orwell's and Keynes's admonitions with respect to intellectuals are most pertinent—"their resources for self-deception are greater" than those of the common herd, and that "it is astounding what foolish things one can believe if one thinks too long alone, particularly in economics."

Even the greatest of the pre-Keynesian economists were woefully wrong in their predictions on a new, limitless "plateau of prosperity" on the very eve of the 1929 crash, viz.: Joseph Davis (Stanford), Edmund Day (Michigan), Charles Dice (Ohio State), Irving Fisher (Yale), David Friday (Michigan), Edwin Kemmerer (Princeton), Willford King (NYU), Joseph Lawrence (Princeton).

And today's economists are equally misguided in their predictions and advice. As when an international group of "experts" met a year ago at a Common Market conference in Paris and endorsed a "slow but steady" approach to the problem of inflation (although the only approach that has ever worked is the "miracle" of instantaneous stabilization); predicted an average collective rate of economic growth for the world of 5.25 percent a year (when past predictions, even for a single country, have almost invariably proved inaccurate); and recommended that all industrial countries should follow the American example and set themselves firm guidelines for the growth of their money supply and for budgetary policy.

The American example, indeed! The United States has completely messed up its own economy and threatens to wreck the economy of the rest of the world, and Germany, Japan and Switzerland have given us such striking examples of monetary strength and economic growth by following policies diametrically opposed to those that have brought the United States to the very brink of disaster.

By and large, you may put somewhat greater faith in the pronouncements of members of the National Association of Business Economists than in those emanating from members of the more prestigious, highly academic American Economic Association (to which I belong). Most of the former, you will find, prefer not to flaunt their Ph.D.s in their business occupations. Perhaps because they recall the story of the young man who was given a job in Washington in the early days of the New Deal when the city was flooded with Ph.D.s from Harvard and other mental institutions. And he was puzzled by the name of his boss on the office door, embellished with the mysterious letters: "B.S., M.S., Ph.D." But the young man's senator, who had gotten him the job, explained in a voice redolent of corn pone: "Well, son, you know what 'B.S.' stands for. And 'M.S.' means more of the same, while 'Ph.D.' means piled higher and deeper."

And, finally, there are those economists who occupy high executive positions in the great financial, industrial and commercial corporations—not just as economic advisers who may yet retain some traces of the bloom of economic innocence, but in top managerial posts where the hard facts of business life have taught them to put aside such childish toys and teaching tools as Phillips curves and econometric models and get down to the nitty-gritty of real-life situations.

There are hundreds of such economists throughout the country, fully qualified Ph.D.s with the invaluable background that a study of economic history and theory provides. Yet they are practically unknown to the public at large for the simple reason that they have little time to write popular books or book reviews or make extravagant but newsworthy statements to the press, nor do reporters habitually interview them for their views on the economic events of the day—men such as Emilio Collado of Exxon (retired in January 1979), Walter Hoadley of Bank of America, James Burrows of Charles River Associates, G. A. Costanzo of Citibank and Gabriel Hauge, chairman of Manufacturers Hanover Trust (retired in April 1979) and his fine staff of economist vice-presidents, Tilford Gaines, Irwin Kellner and Dimitri Balatsos, as well as scores of other economists better known in business circles than in academic.

These are the economists, dear reader, whose views are truly worth listening to, men on whose advice our government should rely, who should represent our country at its international monetary and economic conferences and who, upon retirement, should be appointed to the highest posts in government or named as members of the Council of Economic Advisers, governors of the Federal Reserve Board, or directors of the regional Federal Reserve Banks. Not academic professors of economics or other theoretical economists with no practical financial experience, such as those now on the Board of the Fed and elsewhere in Washington.

The true money experts

But perhaps it may occur to someone in the present administration to turn for advice, not to the professors of economics—Republican or Democrat, left wing, right wing or socialist—whose advice got us into the present mess. And to solicit the counsel of those whose business in the practical world of affairs is *money*—in other words, the bankers.

Not just any li'l ol' country banker—although small-town and country bankers are often among the wisest and most honorable of men, and one of the best books ever written on economic matters was titled *The Country Banker* (George Rae, 1885). But a banker with vast experience and understanding in both domestic and worldwide finance, investment and business, a man to whom foreign exchange and international commodity trading are neither mysteries nor arcane economic phenomena, but the very bread and butter of one's daily business existence.

I am referring to such men as the late W. Randolph Burgess, whose Ph.D. in economics shone as brilliantly as that of any of the professorial economists, and who served as vice-chairman of the First National City Bank of New York and for many years thereafter as Undersecretary of the Treasury, one who could claim the further merit of having had his views on economics denounced as "damned nonsense" by one of the outstanding chairmen of the President's Council of Economic Advisers. Practically a Medal of Honor under present circumstances.

And if this slim volume is referred to as "damned nonsense" by the fifty best known academic economists in the country, I could wish for no higher accolade, although I would be disappointed if it were so described by a majority of the fifty leading bankers in the country. And I would not be chagrined if one or two of the university professors—perhaps remembering the views of the late Professor Edwin W. Kemmerer—admitted that there might be something of value concealed in the crudities of its style. Nor would I be astonished if a substantial number of the fifty most eminent bankers took issue with one chapter or another of this book, deploring that it scares hell out of them. Which is what it is intended to do. This is a time for evoking action, not for pussyfooting.

There must be at least a half a dozen bankers in the country today as well qualified as was Dr. Burgess to advise the administration on the present problem, and if this book persuades the President to turn to one of those to guide him through this critical period, it will have served a useful purpose.

The "guidelines" approach and "jawboning"

But, to get back to the subject of "incomes policy," unless its advocates can find some magic, workable means of persuading labor leaders and management to meet together in peace like the wolf and the lamb in the promised Kingdom of David, it is clear that such a policy is no cure-all for our present ills. Although it should indeed be our long-term goal.

But, as the political genius of Lyndon Johnson saw clearly that an incomes policy was not a workable solution, he accepted the advice of his economic magus, Dr. Walter Heller, and resorted to wage and price "guideposts," to be enforced by evidence of administration displeasure.

Unfortunately, as Professor Samuelson has said of those guidelines, "scowls by the President" cannot solve the dilemma. This proved true despite the fact that no other President has ever possessed a scowl of such high potency as President Johnson.

In the end, it was found that industry was generally intimidated by the scowls, and kept prices down to the point where profits in some industries almost reached the vanishing point, thus deterring the new investment that might have reduced shortages and solved the problem.

But not even President Johnson dared outscowl Mr. Meany, nor risk losing the labor vote in the coming elections. So wage increases went on merrily, guidelines or no guidelines. They didn't work.

And the same may be said of "jawboning," presumably so called in memory of Samson, who used such a weapon to slay the Philistines.

President Kennedy's most celebrated jawboning confrontation

was when U. S. Steel raised prices in 1962, and the President remarked that his dad had warned him that "all businessmen are sons of bitches"—a conclusion presumably reached by introspection rather than by observation. Kennedy's threats—and there is so much a President can do to harass any business, what with antitrust action, costly tax investigations and public denunciation—forced Bethlehem Steel to hold its prices down, and U. S. Steel was then compelled, because of market competition, to follow suit. But wage increases went on undeterred, for there has never been a President, since Franklin Roosevelt blasted John L. Lewis, who has dared to raise his voice against that of organized labor.

So eventually steel prices had to go up and the only tangible result of presidential jawboning and the consequent profit squeeze was to curtail further investment in the expansion and modernization of plant until the advent of an administration less hostile to American business. And that, as previously pointed out, has made our steel industry increasingly obsolete and unable to compete in the world market. Despite which, over the past ten years, the steel companies have invested many billions of dollars in new plant, and in September 1978 a pioneer mill, the equal of any in the world, started production—this in the face of foreign competition, rising costs and burdensome government-imposed environmental controls.

The present administration has likewise been engaged in a jawboning confrontation with the steel industry from July 1977 to date, the jawbone being chiefly that of the chairman of the Council of Economic Advisers, with only an occasional assist from the President himself.

But again neither the President nor his advisers have dared to outshout or outthreaten the belligerent and redoubtable George Meany. And the head of the President's Council on Wage and Price Stability, who had angered Mr. Meany by criticizing wage contract increases exceeding the guidelines, has been publicly told that he must no longer determine policy nor speak out without authorization. So jawboning and guideposts and "incomes policy" are manifestly not the answer, at least in this country.

The price control approach
Early in the Nixon Administration, the President bowed to the pressures of an opposition Congress and of anti-Republican labor leaders, and reluctantly, halfheartedly, turned to price controls.

He knew, because his economic counselors so advised him, that they would not work, that they had never worked in any country of the world at any time in recorded history.

Gaius Aurelius Valerius Diocletianus (A.D. 245–313) was one of the greatest of the Roman Emperors, respected and beloved not only over the twenty-one years of his reign (284–305) but during the eight years from his retirement to his death. The only black marks that history has written against his name are his attempt to enforce mandatory price and wage controls and that he was mean to the Christians.

In A.D. 301 he issued the famous or infamous Edict of Diocletian that decreed maximum prices for all goods and services (wages), set forth in such detail that they listed eighty-four different kinds of woolen goods and over two thousand articles of linen. The edict had behind it the full force and power of the Roman Empire, with the penalty of death for violation or evasion.

Yet, despite the dire sanctions, prices continued to rise and the Roman currency, the denarius, which in A.D. 301 was quoted at 50,000 d. to the golden £, dropped to 120,000 d. to the £ by 305 and continued to fall in value until by 450 it was quoted at 504,000 d. to the £ (does this remind you of the American dollar in the present era?). And the denarius, which, prior to Diocletian, was made of silver, was thereafter minted in bronze covered with a wash of silver (is this reminiscent of Johnson's fake silver, nickel-copper coinage?). And, by 450, even that pretense was abandoned and the denarius became an unabashed bronze coin which decreased in size and weight year after year until finally it was no bigger than a nailhead and was popularly known as a *minissimus* (are you reminded of our newly minted undersized fake silver dollar?). Prices, of course, rose commensurately with the decline in the value of the currency.

In other words, price controls did not work. And they have never worked anywhere in the world, except perhaps for the wartime controls in England, when that indomitable country was fighting for its very existence. Under those desperate circumstances, any attempt at black-marketing, at evading the controls on prices or on the one egg a week allotment that was permitted to everyone, would have brought down the wrath of all good British subjects upon the transgressor. So, briefly, under the blitz of Nazi bombs and rockets, the controls did work.

After Diocletian

Despite this almost universal history of failure, President Nixon felt compelled to initiate price controls for fear that Congress and labor and public pressure might force him to take even more desperate measures. So he announced that the controls would be temporary—Phase 1 of a new economic policy.

And Phase 1, as we know, was followed by Phases 2 and 3 and 3½ and 4. And, at long last, after still another shift in economic advisers, with the administration running around like a chicken with its head chopped off, even Phase 4 was phased out, save for the few halfhearted restrictions which still continue to plague the economy.

We were phased and fazed to a fare-thee-well. But it didn't work any more than denunciation and jawboning and guideposts did under Presidents Kennedy and Johnson, when wholesale prices rose 27 percent. Or than President Truman's complete and mandatory price controls did, when wholesale prices rose 60 percent in the first five and a half years of his administration, and 74 percent by the end of the sixth year.

In five and a half years under President Nixon, through July 1974, wholesale prices rose 55 percent, then a further 18 percent in two and a half years under President Ford, and 27 percent (est.) in the first two and a half years under President Carter. And, if you are beguiled into thinking that we survived the Kennedy-Johnson and Nixon-Ford inflations and the record-breaking Truman inflation, remember that we were not yet bankrupt in Truman's time, while we are bankrupt now. And that inflation must be stopped instanter if we are to avoid an economic disaster of the dimensions of the 1929–32 crash here or the 1923–24 catastrophe in Germany.

It is clear in retrospect—and should have been clear in prospect—that price controls, whether voluntary or mandatory, do not work and will not work. All that price controls have ever accomplished in any country in which they have been tried has been to reduce production. Agriculture, industry and commerce are discouraged by controls, and a drop in the rate of increase in the gross national product has inevitably followed. But people's memories are short, and it is probable that a majority vote today would favor compulsory price controls, oblivious to the fact that the last time we had wide-range mandatory price controls in this country was under President Truman who gave us our first taste of 100 percent inflation (see Chart 4 and discussion in Chapter 7). President Nixon's limited mandatory controls, of course, proved completely futile.

When President Ford first took office, his economic advisers knew that price controls were doomed to failure, so they seriously recommended, as a cure for all our ills, a $15 billion cut in a $304 billion spending budget. This is like a family that spends $30,000 a year when it can only afford to spend $15,000, and then thinking that a $1,500 cut will save the day. A 5 percent cut in government spending, or even a 20 percent cut, would be no more than a Band-Aid, when what is needed is a surgical operation.

Then, when President Ford's plea for a balanced budget and the proposed 5 percent spending cut fell on deaf ears in Congress, and his other semi-anal plans, including the advertising agency approach of "Win Inflation Now" buttons, failed to win popular support, he jumped on the Keynesian bandwagon and advocated a $16 billion cut in taxes, a $349 billion spending budget, and a $52 billion deficit, meaning that in calendar year 1975 the government had to borrow $93 billion, apparently including some $24 billion for the nonbudgetary federal agencies. This program completely overlooked the fact that such Keynesian nostrums got us into the mess we are now in, and have been responsible for the even more desperate economic and social situation in England and in the ninety-four underdeveloped nations that are members of the IMF.

The 1978 wage and price program

Repeatedly over the first year and a half of his administration, President Carter asserted that he was firmly opposed to price or wage controls, and there is every reason to believe that this determination represents a deep-rooted conviction that such controls are futile and contraproductive.

But apparently he failed to realize that practically the sole cause of inflation in the country was deficit spending by the federal government, the creation of printing-press money by the Federal Reserve System in exchange for the Treasury's IOUs. And not one of his economic advisers was qualified, by actual experience in having put a stop to inflation anywhere in the world, to advise him what had to be done.

So when all the predictions of all his economic advisers that the rise in prices would slow down proved to be false, and inflation went on at an ever-accelerating rate, political and public pressure at last compelled him to do what he knew was wrong. And exactly two weeks before the November 1978 election, he announced, with all the fanfare worthy of a nobler cause, a wage and price program no better but probably no worse than the failed programs of his four predecessors.

He recognized that inflation "is our most serious domestic problem," and his promises to "hold down government spending, reduce the budget deficit, and eliminate government waste"; to "slash federal hiring and cut the federal workforce"; to "eliminate needless regulations"; and to "oppose any further reduction in federal income taxes" are eminently sound.

But they are promises only, and his Secretary of Health, Education and Welfare uses his chauffeur so frequently for nighttime and weekend trips that the chauffeur's overtime pay amounted to $23,538 plus his regular salary of $14,047, all at the taxpayers' expense. While the program itself is as footless as any that has been proclaimed over the past twenty years. And apparently the President knew it, for his preamble to the program is tentative, hesitating: "We have tried to control it [inflation] but we have not been successful. . . . I do not have all the answers. Nobody does." But, of course, somebody *does* have the answers—not his economic advisers, obviously, but the authors of the successful anti-inflation programs in Germany (twice), France, Japan, Greece, Peru, Colombia, Chile, Ecuador and Bolivia (twice), referred to in Chapters 6 and 7.

He continues in the same hesitant and reluctant strain: "If there is one thing I have learned beyond any doubt, it is that there is no single solution for inflation" (but, of course, there is, as this book shows); "What we have, instead, is a number of partial remedies" (but the proposed "remedies" will not work and the promises remain promises).

And then, with a bow to California's Proposition 13 and to the people who "are simply sick and tired of wasteful Federal spending and the inflation it brings with it," he announces: "We have brought the deficit down by one-third since I ran for President—from more than $66 billion in fiscal year 1976, to about $40 billion in fiscal year 1979—a reduction of more than $25 billion in just three years."

But the administration's own 1979 Budget Message to Congress reported a budget deficit of $45 billion for the 1976–77 fiscal year (actual), and $60.6 billion for the 1978–79 fiscal year, while his 1979–80 budget, which purportedly shows a deficit of $29 billion, actually proposes authorizations that will give a deficit of $127 billion. And remember that the government's budget and expenditure figures are all of them bikini accounting, concealing from the public view the essential figures of the nonbudgetary expenditures, losses and deficits.

When the President comes to discussing the actual proposed "remedies," the wage and price "standards" (he avoids the use of the term "controls" or "guidelines," which have been thoroughly discredited), he is even more hesitant: "If tomorrow, or next week, or next month, you ridicule them, ignore them, pick them apart before they have a chance to work, you will have reduced their chance of succeeding."

Except for that anguished plea, and the timing of it just a fortnight before the elections, the administration program is no more "ridiculous" than that of his predecessors, and this book does not propose to ridicule it, but merely to point out that, like all prior plans, from that of President Kennedy on, it cracks down on business but not on labor—on prices, not on wages.

For labor, the President asks that workers limit their total wage increases to 7 percent per annum. But, with elections looming, he exempts the "lowest paid workers" and he assures all others that, if inflation exceeds 7 percent (which it undoubtedly will), he will give them tax rebates equivalent to the excess. Which will require a mechanism more complex and more costly than any other aspect of our already costly income tax procedures and will increase the government deficit by many billions of dollars—a sure road to ever-escalating inflation.

For business, his "target," "goal" and "standard" is a price increase not to exceed 5¾ percent per annum, and although this limitation is not "mandatory," it is accompanied by the threat to crack down on business with all the power that the government can muster including, specifically, the denial of government purchases amounting to $80 billion a year from any firm that fails to meet this standard. Which will call for accounting procedures and enforcement machinery more complicated than any that have ever previously been devised. The following is the "Price Compliance Formula" contained in the *White House Fact Book on Wage/Price Standards* that businesses must follow—if they can:

$$P\,(t) = \sum_i \left[P_i\,(t) \times \frac{R_i}{\Sigma_j R_j} \right]$$

Imagine trying to apply that formula to any business that manufactures or sells hundreds or thousands of different items. And because of the uncertainties and complexities of enforcement, and the peculiar "productivity" provisions and other loopholes in the wage/price standards, business firms will face constant harassment from the enforcers and will be compelled to play ball with the proper politicians and political fundraising committees from now until the 1980 elections.

But as the President so earnestly begs Americans to support his proposals and not to "pick them apart," the only commentary on the validity or futility of the administration program will be to point out that, in just the first ten days from the time that the President divulged the substance of his plan, i.e., from October 19 to 29, the Dow Industrials index fell 35 points, the value of the dollar dropped 12 percent in terms of gold and the dollar price of gold continued to rise in London and on the Chicago and New York futures markets. This represented the collective practical judgment of thousands of investors in this country and throughout the world, of people far more knowledgeable than any of the President's theoretical economic advisers, and who—unlike the economists—are "putting their money where their mouth is."

Unfortunately, when it becomes apparent over the course of the coming months that the "voluntary" anti-inflation program is nothing but an exercise in futility, the pressure of the politicians, the press and the public is such that the administration will almost certainly be driven to mandatory price controls, and to foreign exchange measures even more Draconian than those enacted by President Kennedy in 1963 and President Johnson in January 1968, when the dollar was still a "hard" currency and the dollar price of gold was still $35 an ounce.

If one had to assign a date for the beginning of our current inflationary woes, it would either be 1961, when Kennedy launched us into the Vietnam War followed by his surtax on foreign income to save the dollar, or 1964, when Johnson started the present welfare "explosion," followed by his futile and counterproductive attempt in 1968 to stop the flight from the dollar, for it is from that latter date that worldwide lack of confidence in the American dollar began to accelerate, and the inflationary spiral started on its present precipitate climb.

And if President Carter is driven, by political pressure or by frustration, to emulate President Kennedy's ill-advised 16 percent surtax on foreign income, or President Johnson's disastrous attempt at foreign exchange and dollar flight controls, we shall then know that we are headed on the same road as Germany in the years leading up to its trillion to one inflation, when price controls and the prohibitions on capital flight carried fines and criminal penalties that included the death sentence. "Mandatory" controls indeed—but they didn't work any better than President Truman's mandatory price controls or President Johnson's mandatory restrictions on the flight from the dollar. Or Diocletian's edict of A.D. 301.

The desperate hours

Appropriately, on the night of October 31—the Witches' Sabbath—President Carter gave the final go-ahead to a plan, conceived in desperation, that had been formulated four days earlier by his Secretary of the Treasury and the chairman of his Council of Economic Advisers to cope with the disastrous worldwide reaction to his wage and price program.

In a frantic flurry of local and international telephone calls, the Treasury and the Federal Reserve arranged for the United States to borrow immediately from the International Monetary Fund $2 billion in German marks and Japanese yen, with a further $1 billion to be borrowed later; plus the immediate sale to the IMF of $2 billion in special drawing rights (the international "printing-press money" referred to in Chapter 8); plus "swap credits" of $6 billion from Germany's Bundesbank, $5 billion from the Bank of Japan, and $4 billion from the Swiss National Bank (the "swap" is purely to save face, for, as pointed out in Chapter 9, we have nothing left to swap—it is purely a "Save the U.S.A." deal); plus the promise that the Treasury will issue up to $10 billion in obligations payable in foreign currencies (a confession of total lack of confidence in the U.S. dollar); plus a fivefold step-up of sales from our gold reserves from 300,000 ounces a month to 1.5 million ounces a month, or say some $5 billion a year at current gold prices.

As was to have been expected, this sudden mobilization of $30 billion in borrowed marks, yen and Swiss francs, plus the promise of the sale of some $5 billion a year from our diminishing gold assets, turned the markets sharply around, and things began to look brighter by the time of the President's State of the Union message with its promise of a "New Foundation."

So far as that slogan is concerned, one might say that the First Lady, always attractive, never looked lovelier. But, in fact, the expression was borrowed from the first stanza of the Communist "Internationale," as pointed out by Senator Daniel Moynihan (Dem.-N.Y.), precisely as President Johnson's "Great Society" slogan was taken from a book of that name by the English Socialist Graham Wallas. Which is not to say that either slogan is representative of the ideologies of either President, but rather of their speech-writing, policy-making staffs.

But borrowed money has to be repaid and our balance of payments is already in deficit to the tune of over $20 billion a year, so we simply do not have the means to pay back what we borrow. And Deutsche Bundesbank officials have warned that they cannot continue indefinitely to support the dollar at the rate of $50 billion a year, as they did in 1978, with a reported loss of $6 billion.

The sale of our gold reserves, already depleted by more than half, and with foreign exchange debts ten times the amount of our remaining gold reserves, will leave us monetarily defenseless.

To anyone who remembers at close hand the disastrous trillion to one inflation in Germany in the early 1920s, it is disheartening to see that we are following that precedent almost to the letter—the unworkable price controls, the soaring interest rates, the depletion of the gold stocks and accretion of a huge foreign indebtedness with no possibility of repayment from any available surplus in the international balance of payments, and the continued government deficits financed by printing-press money, central bank credits and new issues of government debt, the only difference being that in Germany the increase in the money supply was chiefly in printed currency—which, at least, is interest-free—while in the United States it is chiefly in printed Government IOUs. But in economics that is a distinction without a difference; it represents an increase in the money supply in either case and is equally inflationary.

Unless the President makes a radical shift away from all his present policies, programs and promises, and follows in the footsteps of Schacht, Kemmerer, Erhard, Rueff, Ikeda and the other monetary stabilizers who brought the "miracle of stabilization" in each of the eleven instances cited—an instantaneous end to inflation, with no "austerity" except in government spending, and no economic slowdown—unless this happens, we are well on our way to an inflationary crisis such as that which spelled the doom of Germany's well-intentioned Weimar Republic.

The rise in interest rates

And, of course, as in the case of the Weimar Republic when the mark was climbing to its trillion to one climax, the Federal Reserve has raised the discount rate as part of the administration's Halloween crisis strategy. In September 1978 the Fed had raised the rate to 8 percent. The last previous time it had raised the rate to that level was in April 1974 in the midst of a severe credit crunch; its action was followed by the worst recession this country has ever had since the Great Depression of 1929–32. But, on November 1, in desperation, they hiked the rate up once again—to a record 9½ percent, the seventh increase in a single year.

The Keynesian economists of the administration and the Fed are still operating under the delusion that the Fed's direct action on discount rates, and its target of pushing up the market interest rate on federal funds, will curb inflation and help the balance of payments by attracting foreign capital to invest in high interest rate bonds in this country. As pointed out in Chapter 5, under Facts and Fallacies, high interest rates and other monetary measures are the wrong weapons for stopping inflation. Like using a shotgun to kill a fly, the peripheral damage exceeds the objective.

The money managers themselves admit that high interest rates will cause a recession, but they insist that a mild recession is the only way to "cool off" an inflated economy. This simply is not true, as is proven in the eleven instances cited in this book where nine countries have put a stop to rampant inflation practically overnight, without recession and without "austerity."

Moreover, high interest rates do *not* attract capital unless there is confidence in the reasonable stability of the currency. And confidence in the value of the dollar is lacking today, both here and abroad. Capital is fleeing from the United States, where one can get 9 percent interest or more on a bond, to Switzerland, where 4 percent is the norm. And in every country of Latin America where inflation has been rampant and interest rates run to 36 percent per annum or higher, capital flight to Switzerland and other havens has been endemic over the past thirty years.

But the economists close their eyes to these facts as, if they opened them, they would have to confess that everything they have ever learned, and taught to their pupils, is as false as the fallacy of the Phillips curve—the exploded theory that stopping inflation means unemployment, that there is a necessary "trade-off" between inflation and employment. There isn't.

14. Why We Have Inflation

What is necessary to make us a happy and prosperous people? A wise and frugal government, which shall restrain men from injuring one another, which shall leave them otherwise free to regulate their own pursuits of industry and improvement, and shall not take from the mouth of labor the bread it has earned.

Thomas Jefferson (1801)

How are we to go about following Jefferson's advice? Simply by insisting that our government carry out the only policies that have ever—in any country and at any time—served to stop and reverse an inflationary tide.

Namely, retrenchment in government to the point where expenditures are paid for in full from current government revenues. Plus a cutback in the government's overseas expenditures to the point where we can once again start rebuilding our gold and foreign exchange reserves.

Contributing factors in the present inflation

Let's make a list of some of the things that have contributed to the rise in prices over the past decade, and to the mess we are in today. But bear in mind that government deficit spending and printing-press money far outweigh all other factors combined—that if it were not for deficit spending, we could easily handle the other factors contributing to inflation, and that there would be no mess. And bear in mind, too, that this list contains many sacred cows, that you may be furious and outraged at having them labeled inflationary. But, to be honest, you will have to admit that they all do contribute to an increase in the cost of living. It is a matter of choice, and you—and I—may be willing to put up with some inflationary pressures in a worthy cause.

Why prices are high and going higher.

Motherhood: Nobody ever says anything against Motherhood. Well, it's high time that someone did. Were it not for Motherhood, there would be no crime on the streets, no juvenile delinquency, rape, murder, kidnapping, war. All the ills that have beset mankind, *including inflation*, can be attributed to Motherhood. It is Motherhood that has doubled the population of this country over the past fifty years. And with 220 million people looking for a plot of land on which to build a farm or factory or home, when only the same 3.5 million square miles of land are available, is it any wonder that land prices are higher than they were? The population squeeze is now beginning to be felt in this country, which was not true one hundred years ago. And higher prices for land—the one major economic input whose supply is not unlimited—mean higher production costs for everything. And higher wages, too, because labor must strive to keep abreast of the cost of living. So Motherhood—too much of it—is a basic cause of high living costs today.

Waste: Waste is the besetting sin of the American way of life—new automobile models every year; new fashions for women four times a year; giant-size servings in restaurants and full garbage pails at home; expensive throwaway wrappings, boxes, bottles, cans; the acquisition of new things before the old are worn out—all these things add to the cost of living.

Protective tariffs: If tariffs were for revenue only, say a tax of 5 or 10 percent on *all* imports, even those that are now duty-free, they could replace other more burdensome taxes and in that case would not add to the cost of living. But the majority of our customs duties are protective tariffs, so high as to bar many potential imports and thus produce no revenue. And tariffs add substantially to the cost of goods that do enter the country, and make it possible for manufacturers to maintain high prices on goods produced in the United States. There can be no doubt that if our protective tariff system were abolished the cost of living would be substantially reduced. Whether or not this would totally wreck our economy is another question that cannot be answered within the scope of this book.

Monopolies: Politicians and economists like to blame the iniquity of big business—the monopolies and oligopolies—for higher prices. In actual fact, however, thanks to our antitrust legislation, collusive price-raising is the rare exception. Violations are widely publicized and denounced, which accounts for an exaggerated idea of their prevalence. General Motors, Ford, Chrysler—the typical examples of oligopoly (i.e., domination of the market by a relatively few firms)—keep their selling prices as close as possible to their estimated costs. The industry is highly competitive and knows that a 10 percent price increase means approximately a 10 percent decrease in sales and hence lower profits. The only really wide gaps between prices and costs are found, not among the monopolies and oligopolies, but among the thousands of manufacturers of cosmetics, women's dresses and similar products, and among the thousands of neighborhood delicatessens, boutiques and small stores where there are neither oligopolies nor monopolies. The buying public is aware of this fact, even though the economists and politicians continue to blame big business for high prices. Actually, big business, whether on the farms or in the factories or supermarkets, is one of the greatest forces in this country making for *lower prices* through innovation and efficient management practices.

The cost of dying: The cost of dying is another thing that adds to the cost of living. Aside from the pomp and expense of funeral services, the medical profession adds greatly to the cost of hospital and medical services by keeping alive persons who can continue living only in agony and humiliation. Were doctors to heed the injunction: "Thou shalt not kill, yet need not strive officiously to keep alive," it would reduce the cost of living and of dying.

Restrictions on production: When labor unions impose limitations on how many bricks a mason may lay in a day, or prescribe maximum widths for the brushes a house painter may use, or when government places limits on agricultural production and pays farmers for *not* producing (a system happily ended with the 1973 farm act), prices are bound to be higher.

Unnecessary labor: When labor unions require newspapers to set type for advertisements already set in type, or places of amusement to employ live musicians who sit idle while canned music is being played, or when the federal government requires businessmen to spend 36 million man-hours a year filling out government reports and in other superfluous paper work, this adds to production costs and makes for higher prices. According to a government estimate, federal regulation costs consumers $130 billion a year, and adds $666 to the present average cost of an automobile. And between now and 1985, the automobile manufacturers will have to invest $78.5 billion in new plant just to meet the government's fuel economy standards, a drain on the capital market that could otherwise be channeled into new productive capacity in that or other industries, with corresponding benefits in the shape of higher employment, lower prices and increased economic activity.

High wages: No, high wages do not mean high prices so long as labor works as hard and as well as it can and so long as wage increases do not outstrip the innovation, invention, good management and capital investment that add to labor's productivity. To a large extent, wage increases have been the *consequence* and not the *cause* of today's inflation.

High profits: Nor are high profits the cause of the present inflation. Net profits of all corporations (1977) averaged 3.74 cents on each dollar of sales, and of this only 42 percent went to the owners in the form of dividends, the rest being plowed back into the business. For the department stores and five-and-tens, net profits represent less than 3 percent on sales, for the food chains less than 1 percent. The great oil companies have been more consistent as profit-makers, averaging approximately 3½ percent on sales, which works out at about 1½ cents per gallon of gasoline. Compare this with the approximately 14 cents a gallon you pay in federal, state and local taxes. If the oil companies made no profits at all, you *might* be able to save 1½ cents at the gas tank but, if there were no profits, there would be 630,000 employees out of work at Exxon, Gulf, Mobil and Texaco alone, and no new capital to finance the exploration, research and development which the nation needs. So when politicians or political commentators tell you of the billions of dollars in profits made by this or that corporation or group of corporations, ask yourself what that means in terms of a reasonable return on the present value of the investment, or in cents per dollar of sales, and you will conclude that profits are not the clue to rising prices. Quite the contrary, they are essential as a stimulus to investment in new and more modern plant and hence a major factor in keeping down the cost of living.

Minimum wages: When government fixes minimum wages, this makes for higher prices and creates unemployment which in turn means higher taxes to care for the needlessly unemployed, again adding to the cost of living. See Chapter 6.

Technological improvement: No, technological improvement does not make for unemployment and higher costs for the economy, except temporarily and in isolated instances until readjustments can be made. To the contrary, it is the greatest force for maintaining full employment and *lowering* prices. As John L. Lewis, of blessed and hated memory, used to say: "Any labor leader who opposes technological improvement must have a hole in his head; it is the only thing that can give us higher *real* wages and lower prices."

Ecology: While a clean and healthful environment is essential to human well-being, and those constructive environmentalists who are working in that direction are to be applauded, the *extremists* who insist upon 100 percent perfection *immediately* are contributing to higher costs and threatening to wreck the economy. The major source of pollution, by weight, is reported to be more a matter of pulverized rubber dust in the air than of the toxic lead and other gasoline pollutants from car exhausts, and thus the only solution would be to ban rubber tires or automobiles. Some of the ecological *extremists* would apparently have us regress to the horse and buggy stage, forgetting that a horse and buggy pollutes all day long, whether it is used or not, and contributes far more pollution to the environment than the most flatulent automobile. Inasmuch as pollutants are harmful solely through their ingestion, the test is—which would you rather sprinkle on your breakfast cereal, the gaseous emanations from an automobile tailpipe, or the solid and liquid emanations from the tailpipes of the old gray mare? But, quite aside from ecological fanaticism, even the presently enforced measures for the protection of the environment cost an estimated $18 billion in 1975 and will cost $40 billion by 1981, which will add two or three times that amount to our family budget and make it increasingly difficult for American products to compete in the world markets. In ecology as in everything else, we cannot get something for nothing, and we must weigh costs as well as benefits. But did you know that, in the fight for Senator Muskie's 1976 "Clean Air Act," the Clean Air Coalition, embracing lobbyists for the Friends of the Earth, the Sierra Club and the Ralph Nader organization, was supported by a $5 billion a year corporation which manufactures the platinum catalytic converters used to reduce noxious automobile tailpipe emissions, and that the Washington lobbyist for that corporation, according to *The New York Times*, is a close friend and luncheon companion of the lobbyists for those three "public-interest" groups? Or that the pine needles in American forests produce half as much air pollution as all the automobile tailpipe emissions combined?

    Consumerism: Akin to the ecological extremists are the consumerist *fanatics* who, in Orwellian Big-Brother fashion, insist upon protecting us fools from our own follies by demanding prohibitively costly standards of excellence. Or insisting on squawking seat belts or exploding air bags that, regardless of their alleged desirability, will add another $400–$500 to the cost of living. Or telling us that saccharin causes cancer in rats if they consume it at a rate equivalent to a human drinking eight hundred bottles of diet cola a day. And trying to prevent us from consuming such poisons for our own good. They have already succeeded in prohibiting us from using cyclamate sweeteners which, strangely enough, are permitted in Canada, where saccharin is barred. Must be a difference in the climate. In any event, "consumerism" adds to the cost of living at the rate of over $100 billion a year, according to the Office of Management and Budget, and the consumer advocates are lobbying unceasingly for a new Agency for Consumer Protection—we already have 33 federal agencies and some 400 bureaus and subagencies operating more than 1,000 consumer-oriented programs. And if anyone thinks that a new bureau will eliminate the old, he is not familiar with the ways of government.

Crime: Organized crime, in drug-pushing, prostitution and other rackets, adds to the cost of government at all levels, as well as to the corruption of government officials that is reflected in a lowering of moral standards in all walks of life and increased costs in business as well as government. Individual crime—the crimes of violence and even more directly the nonviolent crimes of shoplifting and employee theft—increases the cost of everything we buy. The last two categories of crime alone add an estimated $23 billion a year to the family budget. In all, white-collar crime costs $44 billion a year and crime in all categories over $125 billion. Of this total, the Mafia takes in a gross of at least $48 billion, meaning a net, *untaxed* profit of $25 billion. Compare this with Exxon, the largest industrial corporation in the United States, with sales of $65 billion and net profits of $2.8 billion. It is hypocritical to contend that "so long as we have the social diseases of poverty and human displacement we will have crime." The United States, one of the richest countries, is the crime capital of the world, the leader in murder and other violent crime of all the great nations; this was not true fifty years ago when we were poor. Spain, one of the poorest countries in Europe, has the least number of murders (one murder per million of population) and less than one-fiftieth the amount of violent crime (rape, murder, robbery, aggravated assault) that we have in the District of Columbia alone, where there are 1,481 *reported* cases of violent crime a year, per 100,000 population. A debased moral standard, not poverty, is the cause of crime, but crime is indeed one of the major elements in the high cost of living in this country.

Racism: The moral or ethical aspects of racism are not germane to the subject of this book. But the economic consequences of racism clearly are pertinent. When preferences are accorded to persons of one race or nationality over those of another race or nationality in job-seeking or promotion, or in business or educational opportunities, this definitely adds to the cost of goods or services; it is one of the factors adding to inflation. And this is true whether the racism manifests itself in discriminating against persons of minority races, or in giving preference to persons of such races, which means discriminating against the majority. Quite aside from the unconstitutionality of discrimination based on race or sex or national origin—which is irrelevant to this discussion—the fact is that any criterion other than merit means inefficiency in producing the goods and services we need, and thus adds to the cost of living.

Fair-trade laws: Fair-trade laws and other market-restrictive legislation add substantially to the cost of living as may be seen by the lower prices for liquor and other products in states that do not have such laws. For example, a pair of eyeglasses that costs $20 in Texas costs between $60 and $70 in California, where retailers are prohibited from advertising prices. It is too early to see whether or not recently enacted legislation will be effective in eliminating these so-called fair-trade practices. But there are other fields where restrictive laws add to consumer costs. For instance, federal law has long prohibited the sale of TV sets that do not receive UHF as well as VHF frequencies, and now radio receivers are required to receive FM as well as AM channels, which will add some $50 to the cost of most automobiles. The heavily subsidized "public broadcasting" stations lobbied this legislation through Congress regardless of the public interest, thus contributing to inflation to an extent far in excess of the $180 million a year they receive in subsidies, or the $1.2 billion they are now demanding.

Taxation: Taxation at all levels of the government—federal, state, county and municipal—takes over 50 percent of our national income; in other words, half of our cost of living is made up of taxes, most of which are taken from us by stealth, not openly as in the case with the income tax, property tax, etc.

Corporate income tax: This tax adds directly to the cost of practically everything we buy, as well as indirectly through its encouragement of government-subsidized extravagance in business. See Chapter 15.

Deficit financing: Even more of a burden than taxation, although invisible, is the deficit financing of the federal government which is the direct cause of inflation and higher prices. See Chapter 6.

Compulsory spending: When Congress decries the "impounding" of funds by the administration, and insists that every last cent appropriated be spent, it adds to taxation and inflation-creating deficits. If the administration manages to erect a government building for $5 million when $6 million has been appropriated, what is it to do—spend another million in ruffles around the top? An appropriation should not be viewed as a command to disburse every last cent appropriated, but as a limitation on the amount that may be spent. All that the Constitution provides is that: "No Money shall be drawn from the Treasury but in Consequence of Appropriations made by Law." The conflict appears to have been disposed of for the time being by the Congressional Budget and Impoundment Control Act of 1974, which requires the President, perhaps unconstitutionally, to request permission of Congress on every decision to economize. Not that the administration has ever been backward in spending every last cent it could lay its hands on. From my service on the government payroll in 1956–57, I learned that it was then "SOP" (standard operating procedure) in the State and Defense Departments to warn all bureaus and offices each May to spend every penny of their available funds before June 30, else they might find their budgets cut in the coming fiscal year. I have since learned that the practice prevails in every department and agency of the government, except that the deadline has been moved forward to coincide with the new October 1 fiscal year. Early in the present administration, the Secretary of the Treasury and the then director of the Office of Management and Budget were "perplexed" and "baffled" to discover that the government had a little item of *$7.6 billion* which it had underspent, as compared with the budget, and which they were completely unable to account for. The administration has since been able to reduce this "shortfall" to $6 billion. But this incident goes to show that the government's bikini accounting can be as amazing to those in the government as the bikinis themselves are to all of us who go to the beaches and watch the young women breast the waves and vice versa.

Welfare: When government seeks to do what we as individuals should do, with charity in our hearts, this is the chief cause of our higher taxes, budget deficits and inflation.

Medicare: Medicare and welfare medical payments for the indigent (Medicaid) are a contributing factor in the skyrocketing cost of medical care. Fee schedules have been turned into a racket by a few irresponsible members of the profession, making for a shortage of facilities and nursing care for everyone and adding to hospital and medical costs for all.

Foreign aid: The $150 to $400 billion we have contributed to foreign aid is one of the causes of our monetary debasement and a major cause of the loss of our gold and foreign exchange reserves and the present precarious position of the dollar. The continuation of such aid means the perpetuation of these consequences. See Chapter 10.

War: Last but not least, the cost and waste of war itself and interest on the public debt to pay for past wars are two of the major forces—second only to welfare expenditures at home and abroad—behind the government deficits and the high cost of living today. When government fails to take those measures that are essential to keep us out of war, when politicians recklessly attempt to get the support of immigrant or racial minorities at home by attacking the internal policies of foreign governments, and when people perversely vote for candidates of the very party whose Presidents have never failed to go over the brink of war in this century, then we can scarcely expect any substantial reduction in the cost of living. If military expenditures have not been given greater stress in this exposition, it is because the entire outlay for national defense has dropped from 43 percent of the total budget in fiscal 1969, the last budget enacted under the Johnson Administration, to 23.8 percent of the total in fiscal 1977, the last Ford budget, and to 21.9 percent in the Carter budget for fiscal 1980. Which is not to say that our defense expenditures should not be cut, nor that they are not a significant factor in our current inflation. They are, and they should be cut—to the extent that they can be trimmed without jeopardizing our military strength. But the very necessity of maintaining our military might over the next year or more of negotiation for a permanent peace in the Mideast and elsewhere only adds emphasis to the need to put an immediate end to the current inflation through the drastic economic measures advocated in this and the following chapters. For an economic catastrophe in the United States, toward which we are now inevitably headed if inflation proceeds apace, would be as disastrous to our influence as a mediator for peace as the disintegration of our military power.

In sum, if you support any of the things listed above that have contributed and are still contributing to the high cost of living, then you should stop complaining about higher prices. For you, dear reader, are part of the problem.

Of course, you may suspect that parts of the foregoing list, and even of the remainder of the book, may have been written with tongue in cheek. Yet, as all the matters inveighed against in this list of culprits do indeed contribute to raising the cost of living, then, to the extent to which any of the more novel suggestions may have been made in jest, I too am part of the problem. But, to quote Horace, *ridentum dicere verum quid vetat*? (yet may not truth in laughing guise be dressed?).

For the truth is that we are not ants but human beings. We do not live by bread alone. A primrose on the river brim is truly something more than a riparian *primula vulgaris*. And a rise in the cost of living, if attributable to wise objectives—such as decent wages, adequate leisure and a country free from the pollution of filth and crime—is *the price we pay for civilization.*

The rise in government spending
As it is the government that is responsible for the present mess, only Congress and the President, working in cooperation and not at cross-purposes, can get us out of it.

Private citizens and corporations cannot, like government, spend more than they possess, and banks will not unstintingly give them credit to squander beyond their means either at home or abroad.

The overextension of credit in the private sector can be and at times has been—in 1928–29, for example—the forerunner of disaster, but never on the scale of the catastrophe attributable to government profligacy. And, at the present time, the problem and the crisis must be laid almost exclusively at the doorstep of the government.

Not to the Nixon Administration alone, which had the misfortune of coming into the picture at a time when our gold and foreign exchange reserves were already at a minus figure of over $16 billion. Not solely to President Johnson, who entered the scene when those reserves were in the red to the tune of nearly $1 billion. But to a whole chain of policies initiated and carried out by well-meaning but misguided men, from 1950 on, that served to reduce our gold and foreign exchange stock from the impressive total of nearly $17 billion to the catastrophic minus figure of over $80 billion. And a deficit of $200 to $620 billion more than that if we include the Eurodollars and other reported and unreported foreign exchange debits listed in Chapter 11.

And to a whole chain of policies, equally well intentioned and equally misguided, dating from President Franklin Roosevelt's New Deal, that have brought our federal government expenditures up from $3.3 billion in 1927—only 3.3 percent of our national income at that time—to over $629 billion for the 1979–80 fiscal year, which will represent 36.4 percent of our national income. And even that figure errs on the side of conservatism, for, as has been pointed out, there are many government outlays that are concealed in the expenditures and losses of government guaranties and government-sponsored agencies.

Every workingman in this country spends on the average over 36 percent of his time working for the federal government and a further 14.5 percent of his time working for the state, county and municipal governments (after eliminating the duplication of federal grants to the states and cities). The expenditures of state and local governments have risen from $7.8 billion in 1927 to $300 billion in 1978, with the burden varying from $494 per capita in Arkansas to $1,252 in New York and $2,296 in Alaska.

State and municipal spending

At least the states, counties and cities cannot be blamed for the $275 billion deficit in our gold and foreign exchange reserves, nor can they print money or compel the Fed to buy their bonds and notes. The state and local bond issues are purchased voluntarily and generally for investment, so that they are not "monetized"—i.e., they do not add directly to the printing-press money with which we are plagued, and hence are not a major factor in our present inflation.

Except to the extent that the U. S. Treasury—with no apparent constitutional authority—contributes to the state and local budgets through "revenue sharing" "fiscal assistance" and "interest subsidies," or comes to the rescue of municipalities such as New York, which, through their own profligacy in pensions and payouts, have come to the brink of bankruptcy.

Not solely on constitutional grounds, but pragmatically as the only way the federal government can escape the vicious cycle of deficit spending and inflation, Washington must put a stop to its state and municipal subsidies and bond guaranties. In fiscal 1977 the Treasury gave $5 billion to New York State alone for welfare and local public works, and in July 1978 Congress voted to guaranty $1.65 billion in New York City bonds, an amount not included in the federal budget. If the cessation of aid means the bankruptcy of New York City, so much the better, as only through bankruptcy can its citizens cut down the city payrolls and escape the consequences of its outrageously high pension plans. Retirement benefits (pension plus Social Security) of the typical New York City employee (taking a person retiring at age sixty-five with a final year salary of $14,000, and a living spouse) range from 119 percent to 129 percent of the final year's pay. Retirement on disability increases these pensions, *which are then tax-free,* and the percentage of alleged "disability" retirements is increasing every year, although still falling far short of Washington, D.C., where some 82 percent of the retired policemen and firemen are drawing disability benefits, largely at the expense of taxpayers nationwide, as the federal government subsidizes the District with grants of $317 million, plus loans of $159 million (1980 budget).

Despite New York City's default in 1975 and Cleveland's in 1978, Washington may well be the worst managed and most highly subsidized city in the country. In September 1978 Congress voted to grant the city an additional $1.6 billion subsidy—vetoed by presidential "pocket veto"— just to take care of its pension program, which has no funds set aside to meet the more than $2 billion in benefits that an incompetent and improvident city administration has obligated the city to pay to its retirees.

Municipal bankruptcies are nothing new in American history. And, although the bankruptcy of so large a city as New York would be opposed vociferously, perhaps violently, by an unholy alliance of city employees, politicians, bond dealers and bankers (who hold many of the city's bonds), it is the only way to avoid national insolvency. For the federal government cannot very well bail out New York City, with cash or guaranties, and refuse to do the same for hundreds of other municipalities which would be encouraged to emulate the irresponsible profligacy of New York and Washington. It is estimated that, out of some 15,000 banks in the nation, only 79—for the most part, small banks scattered throughout the country—would be in danger of insolvency in the case of a New York City default and, even though the large city banks would be very unhappy, to say the least, and could be expected to lobby frantically against a cessation of federal aid, this would be a small price to pay as a safeguard against national disaster. Depositors in the banks would, of course, be protected by FDIC.

Fortunately, as an aftermath of the California Proposition 13 referendum, Congress in August 1978 voted to postpone indefinitely consideration of the administration bill to provide $1 billion a year in "supplementary fiscal assistance" to insolvent municipalities. The "Antirecession Fiscal Assistance Program," which has been channeling $1.3 billion a year to localities with high unemployment—the "countercyclical aid plain"—expired on September 30, 1978. But, with all the political promises given in anticipation of the November elections, it is hardly realistic to believe that the subsidy will not be reenacted—or increased—before the end of the 1978–79 fiscal year—a good argument against the new October 1 to September 30 fiscal year; calendar year or June 30 budgets might be less subject to Election Day pressures.

Welfare and the federal budget

Eliminating government "charity" with taxpayers' money would in all likelihood call for an end to all subsidies to farmers and businessmen, for example, the $600 million a year subsidy to the merchant marine, which amounts to $12,000 a year for each of the 50,000 persons employed in the industry. (I have doubtless stepped on some well-heeled toes in selecting this one example arbitrarily out of the thousands that could be cited and can only say that, out of all the subventions granted by our government, this is the one that I personally would most like to see continued.) And it would certainly put an end to all federal welfare spending, with millions of people on relief of one kind or another, many of them second- and third-generation welfare recipients.

Why should those who work be compelled to pay federal taxes to support those growing millions of people who do not work? Why should three generations of welfare recipients be allowed to procreate still another generation, double the size, of still more welfare recipients, a large proportion of them mentally defective or, as we are told nowadays, culturally deprived. Plus an army of bureaucrats to handle the handouts. For example, in the District of Columbia, the Department of Human Resources, which is the city's largest agency, paid out $228 million in welfare in 1978, but it took a total operating budget of $423 million to handle those payouts, including the salaries of over 8,000 staff members. Most of this money comes from the federal government, in other words, from taxpayers all over the United States.

A study made some five years ago at New York's New School for Social Research—a decidedly left-wing, prowelfare institution—shows that the average welfare family was then receiving in welfare payments and food coupons the equivalent of $7,000 gross income a year, and that payments could run as high as the equivalent of $11,500 gross income before tax.

Budget appropriations, classified by "function and agency," show that authorizations for the "welfare" agencies added up to $262 billion in the 1977 fiscal year, or 56 percent of the total official budget, and $302 billion in the 1978–79 budget, or 53 percent of the total. But these figures included the entire allotments for "Income Security," "Health," etc., and certainly the Public Health Service budget falls within the constitutional "general welfare" provisions, as distinguished from Medicaid and other health services that represent "welfare" for the individual, not the general welfare. An estimated 39 percent of the "Income Security" payments represent Social Security benefits paid for on an actuarial basis by wage earners and employers, and only the unpaid portion of such payments can properly be regarded as "welfare."

Going through the entire 1979 budget report, item by item, I found thirty-seven appropriations, scattered among nineteen agencies, that clearly represent "welfare" for individual recipients (including 61 percent of Social Security authorizations), rather than general welfare. Those handouts added up to $189.6 billion in 1977 (40.5 percent of the total budget authorizations) and $201.5 billion in the 1979 budget (35.5 percent of the total). The list is doubtless incomplete, but it is all that could be gleaned from the printed budget report.

In the 1980 budget report, however, the table that used to show budget authorizations by "function and agency" has been suppressed, and only budgeted "outlays" by function and agency are shown, which minimizes the aggregates by 13.5 percent. Of course, any expenditures "authorized" will undoubtedly be spent, and probably exceeded, even if some of the "outlays" may drag on into the next fiscal year. So if the public is to be properly informed as to what it can expect in the way of government spending and deficits, it is entitled to know the total amounts the President is asking the Congress to authorize for each function of government.

But in all of the administration's public statements on the budget, and in the report of the Council of Economic Advisers, reference is made solely to estimated "outlays" eliminating, moreover, the nonbudgetary agencies, and comparing those minimized totals with gross national product, not with national income, which is the logical basis for comparison. So, with that devious bikini accounting, the administration and the CEA are able to come up with a proposed 1980 budget of $531.6 billion, which they point out is only equal to 19.3 percent of GNP, and gives a deficit of only $29 billion. Not a single item is labeled "welfare," the only use made of that perhaps disparaging term being in the name of the Department of Health, Education and Welfare itself. So, instead of using the word "welfare," which everyone can understand, the budget disguises the expenditures under the terms "transfer payments," "human resources programs," "grants in aid," etc., which no one can understand, and scatters these items throughout scores of places in the budget report so that it is impossible to determine just how much or how little the government is spending on welfare.

In fact, having plowed through the four-volume, 2,205-page 1980 budget report and the 306-page report of the President's Council of Economic Advisers, I might say that I used to use that kind of material in my garden, although I never spread it on so thick. For I find that total budget authorizations, including the off-budget agencies, amount to $629.6 billion, not the "austere" $531.6 billion, as the President and his Council tell us; that this will equal 35.4 percent of national income and not just 19.3 percent of GNP; and that the predicted deficit will be $127 billion, not $29 billion. And even on the basis of "outlays," not budget "authorizations," the deficit will come to $59.7 billion, as shown in the budget report itself, but not in the administration pronouncements. And even these figures fail to reveal the true burden of federal expenditures because they do not include the unrevealed total of federal guaranties, the defaults on guaranteed loans, and the deficits and borrowing of government-sponsored agencies.

Thus there was no way in which I could arrive at a reliable total for federal welfare in the 1980 budget. All that could be gleaned from the budget authorizations "by agency and account," not "by function and agency," was that welfare authorizations, *to the extent they can be determined,* will aggregate at least $191.8 billion, or 31.1 percent of the total.

The impact of welfare
Based on figures included in the report of the Council of Economic Advisers, there are some 49 million people in the United States living

"below the poverty level"—although in almost any other country of the world two thirds of these people would be accounted well-to-do, what with their automobiles, television sets, electric refrigerators and extravagant consumption of junk food.

So, from the totals budgeted for welfare, it can be seen that federal welfare for the poor must amount to over $3,900 per person, say $19,600 per welfare family of five—and this is the federal expenditure alone, not counting over $34 billion of welfare expenditures by the states and municipalities, which would bring total government welfare outlays to over $24,000 per family, not including, of course, private charity.

But does the average poor family get this $24,000 or more? No, of course not. The great bulk of this money, contributed by the American taxpayer and by inflation-generating printing-press money, goes to the support of the bureaucracy that is needed to dole out this huge amount of money, from the Secretaries of HEW and HUD on down to the lowest levels of the rank and file in federal and local governments, and to the construction and maintenance of the monumental government buildings needed to house this great bureaucracy, the building costs being laden with graft and waste in the General Services Administration, and the payroll costs burdened with salaries, pensions and perquisites far higher than those same employees could earn in private life.

Together with the $21.9 billion in foreign aid projected for the 1980 budget, our domestic and foreign federal welfare authorizations, so far as can be determined, will add up to at least $213.7 billion, 50 percent more than the $139.2 billion authorized for national defense. And, as is pointed out in Chapter 11, some foreign aid is concealed in the defense budget.

When President Eisenhower left office, there were some 45 federal welfare programs in operation in the federal government. By the time Lyndon Johnson left office, there were 435 such programs. What the total is now is anybody's guess and President Carter has not yet been able to steer his new expanded welfare system—at an additional cost of $17.4 billion—through a balky Congress. But, however the reorganization plans pan out, the total cost of welfare can be expected to go up and up unless Congress abolishes federal welfare once and for all as *unconstitutional* (see following chapter).

Some relevant items: The food stamp program, which began with a budget of $66 million and 367,000 recipients, now has a caseload of some 20 million people and an outlay of $7.3 billion (this is for the 1977 fiscal year; it is undoubtedly higher today). Some 929,000 *people received food stamps to which they were not entitled by law, while another 1.8 million received more stamps than they were entitled to.*

ITEM: The administration has proposed classifying families of four earning up to $14,200 as "in need of relief," and larger families with incomes up to $20,000. Which would add some 8.3 million families to the welfare rolls. How many people and how many votes would be represented by 8.3 million families is uncertain.

ITEM: A "liberal" Boston newspaper reports that a welfare mother with six children is receiving tax-free welfare of various kinds equivalent in all to an annual earned income of $20,000 a year.

ITEM: The GLACC (Greater Los Angeles Community Action Agency) has been receiving half a billion dollars a year in federal funds to handle the city's poverty programs, chiefly for the relief of "minority" families. A federal investigation has revealed that the agency is overrun with embezzlement and corruption, that 90 percent of its expenditures were tainted with noncompliance and irregularities, as a consequence of which the agency was scheduled to be shut down as of January 1, 1979, by presidential order. The expenditures are being continued, of course, but under different management.

ITEM: The administration has sponsored, and Congress has approved, a four-year extention of the Comprehensive Employment and Training Act at an estimated cost of $46 billion, despite the fact that CETA has a record of mismanagement, corruption and political intervention unsurpassed among all the federal welfare schemes. But, with the November elections looming, the overriding consideration was that, since its inception in 1973, CETA has provided 8 million Americans with jobs and training—at a cost to the taxpayer of $3,000 for each of the 8 million beneficiaries, exclusive of their annual salaries ranging up to $10,000—and that in the 1978–79 fiscal year CETA is scheduled to make available 725,000 federally funded public service jobs, give job training to 1 million applicants, and summer jobs to thousands of "minority" young people. Quite a lot of votes if one includes the families of those recipients.

ITEM: Between 6 and 12 million illegal immigrants in the United States, half of them from Mexico, are receiving so much in wages and Social Security payments that they are remitting from $3 to $10 billion each year to their families at home—i.e., the United States is paying welfare to indigents abroad in addition to our foreign aid to *their government, with dire consequences for our balance of international payments. And these illegal immigrants have taken 4 to 6 million jobs, many of which could otherwise have been filled by American workers. It would be a simple matter to round up and deport practically all the illegal immigrants if the United States properly policed the issuance of photographed, fingerprinted, plastic-encased Social Security cards, inasmuch as all employers are required to pay Social Security taxes for all their employees. Instead of which, the administration is considering a general amnesty which would surely constitute an unconstitutional extension of the President's power to pardon individual criminals, for it means the nullification of the criminal law.*

Perhaps it is high time that we Americans return to the ways of the founding fathers, abolish federal welfare, and heed the injunction of St. Paul: "... if any would not work, neither should he eat" (II Thessalonians 3:10). This is not to say that Americans should abolish charity from their hearts. Far from it! But is it charity, is it right, for those in government to give away other people's money?

Let the people of the United States, individually or through their churches and in the spirit of true charity, donate a tithe of their available income to charitable and philanthropic causes. And let the state and local governments and churches establish houses where old people, and others who cannot work and are not supported by their children, can live out their days in such comfort as the taxpayers and parishioners are willing to provide. Where it costs the federal government $20,000 a year to care for each welfare family, the county poorhouse could do the job for $4,000 for each individual who needs to be on welfare, and the indigent's family could handle it for $1,100, based on government figures for the cost of maintaining one additional person in a family in the top "poverty-line" bracket. And it is on the family that the primary responsibility lies.

A county poorhouse, such as we used to have in prewelfare days, would be far less demeaning and humiliating than the red tape and bureaucratic runaround to which welfare applicants are subjected, as portrayed in a harrowing television documentary shown on the public broadcasting stations. A documentary that, incidentally, offers conclusive evidence that none of the welfare recipients and applicants shown is mentally or educationally capable of handling the welfare payments.

It is unconscionable to shift the burden of taking care of the aged or disabled poor from the family to the taxpayer. And it is against the principles of the Constitution to shift the burden from the states and local governments to the federal government. As well as financially impossible, for this nation cannot afford to continue spending $200 billion a year for the waste and profligacy of federal welfare.

The budget report lists welfare among the "uncontrollable" outlays, meaning merely that it cannot be cut *unless the law is changed*, while the worldly-wise, the faint of heart, say that welfare is "untouchable." It can't be cut—politically. There would be *revolution*! "Rioting in the streets," as President Ford's closest economic adviser told me some three years ago.

Well, if the worldly-wise would rather wreck this nation than take a chance of losing the votes of those who have been living on the taxpayers' bounty, when the Constitution itself, as interpreted by the Supreme Court, requires that "welfare" for individuals, as distinguished from the "general welfare," be "reserved to the States, respectively, or to the People," then let the revolution come now while the taxpayers and those who work for a living still outnumber the bureaucrats and those on welfare, and while the total cost of government is still only around 50 percent of national income.

National health insurance

But seemingly we may be about to embark on one more fantastic addition to our federal welfare program—a new "National Health Insurance" scheme. One such bill submitted to Congress during the Ford Administration would have meant an aggregate estimated cost of $102.7 billion a year, the burden of which would have fallen exclusively on the working and taxpaying classes. And at least 70,000 employees in the Department of Health, Education and Welfare to administer the program—more than double the number of those who now manage and mismanage the present Medicare and Medicaid programs

These were merely estimates prepared by HEW, a department that through six administrations, and under various names, has maintained a consistently high standard of incompetence, perhaps nowhere better illustrated than in their contention (until Congress intervened) that the Civil Rights Act, which bans sex discrimination in any organization that receives government support means that the Girl Scouts must accept boy members, and the Boy Scouts girls. Which would certainly have called for intensive application of the Scout motto: "Be Prepared!"

Only recently, an HEW regional office refused to pay an $850,000 subsidy to the Belleview, Washington, school district on the ground of sex discrimination, because it found that under the state's disciplinary program only two girls had been spanked as compared with thirty boys—

a determination that was not reversed until the district's congressman took matters in hand.

In the case of the current "social services" programs, which HEW originally estimated would cost $40 *million* a year, actual appropriations listed in the 1979 budget, including federal grants to the states, are placed at $13.7 *billion*, more than three hundred times the original estimate. By this time, you will be aware of the fact that you cannot rely on *any* statements made by the federal government with its hypocritical bikini accounting. But when any spokesman for HEW or HUD or one of the other welfare agencies makes a statement, you will know that you must bear in mind the words of the Apostle John: "He is a liar and the truth is not in him."

Sad to relate, the same warning must now apply to statements made by the present Council of Economic Advisers. For when the President had to demonstrate that a national emergency existed in order to obtain a back-to-work order under the Taft-Hartley Act to end the 1978 coal strike, the Council of Economic Advisers came up with supporting statistics that the General Accounting Office—the Controller General—has found "questionable," stating that they "did not present a fair assessment of the situation to the public." And the White House then invoked "executive privilege" to deter Congress from investigating the "questionable" statistical methods of the CEA.

The warning as to credibility may likewise apply to the "Ten Principles" laid down by the administration for HEW—probably drafted by HEW itself—as a guide to developing a program for National Health Insurance, including such fine-sounding, self-serving admonitions as:

> *The plan must support our efforts to control inflation ... by reducing unnecessary health care spending. The plan should include aggressive cost containment measures and ... should be designed so that additional public and private expenditures for improved health benefits and coverage will be substantially offset by savings from greater efficiency in the health care system. The plan will involve no additional spending until fiscal year 1983, because of tight fiscal constraints and the need for careful planning and implementation.*

But perhaps the White House intended the last sentence as a clue to the whole set of principles which should be translated: "We don't have the money, but this should keep the Health Insurance lobbyists quiet until 1983, and then, *après moi le déluge*."

The National Health Insurance plans now being considered—or being deferred—by HEW are far more ample in scope than the $102.7 billion bill submitted during the Ford Administration. But—typical of all welfare estimates—the politicians who are sponsoring the scheme have cut the cost estimates to $80 billion if the plan is enacted *in toto*—which seems unlikely in the wake of the California tax revolt—one may be sure that health insurance will ultimately absorb more than the total present cost of our entire budget, over $600 billion a year.

Welfare lobbyists in this country are fond of pointing to the "success" of the British national health insurance plan—health care for everyone who wants it, and free of charge. Well, the cost of medical care in England is higher than in any other major nation in the world with the exception of the United States. But it is paid for, not by the patient, but by the taxpayer and, even worse, by the deficit financing and printing-press money that lie at the root of all England's troubles today. National Health Service certainly is not "free"— "there is no such thing as a free lunch."

And in the United States where medical and hospital costs have risen far out of proportion to the costs of other goods and services, the chief reason for that disproportionate rise is Medicare, Medicaid and, even before that, the Blue Cross, Blue Shield and other prepaid health services. Where patients do not have to worry about doctor and hospital bills, there is no natural supply and demand pressure to keep costs down; hypochondriacs go back to their physicians and care centers again and again for incurable imaginary ailments that—if such services had to be paid for—would have been taken care of by the time-tested remedies of grumbling and griping. That has been the case in England and would certainly prove to be the case in this country if Medicare, Medicaid and Blue Cross–Blue Shield are replaced by National Health Insurance. To avoid misinterpretation, I should add that I strongly favor Blue Cross–Blue Shield and other privately financed health services, which are better managed and less costly than the government-managed services, but *any* prepaid service is bound to engender abuse and higher costs, just as automobile damage insurance—while necessary—does increase the cost of automobile repairs. You can't repeal human nature.

So, if National Health Insurance becomes a fact—and people in this country are saying, as they do in England: "Isn't it wonderful? Free medical and hospital care for anyone who needs it!"—we may be sure that the *cost* of health care will be ten times as high as it is today. But it will be financed, not by the patient, but by ever-increasing taxes and printing-press inflation without end.

Except that, long before that catastrophe could come to pass, let us hope that there would indeed be a revolution, not by the welfare recipients and lobbyists, but by the farmers, labor unions and workers, the taxpayers who will have to foot the bill. Let us hope that, if that time comes, the workers and taxpayers will still outnumber the welfare pan-handlers.

Social Security
When Social Security was first introduced into this country from New Zealand, it was one of the most meritorious innovations of the New Deal with a total tax rate of 2 percent on the first $3,000 of wages, split equally between employee and employer—a maximum tax of $60 a year. The tax has since been raised step by step until, by December 1977, it reached 11.7 percent on the first $16,500 of taxable income for a total of $1,930. In December 1977 Congress passed and the President signed a new law raising the 1978 tax to 12.1 percent for a maximum of $2,140, with the rates rising to 14.3 percent, maximum $5,748, by 1986—nearly one hundred times the New Deal level. When the legislators returned home for their Christmas vacations, however, they were intimidated by the outcry of outraged constituents and have since then been trying to agree on a tax rollback, with the deficit made up from special taxes, such as a tax on crude oil, or from general revenues—oblivious of the fact that *there are no general revenues available*; the budget is already in deficit to the tune of $60–130 billion.

The problem is that Social Security has become a welfare scheme and is in deficit for between *$4 and $5 trillion*. Add that to the more than $4.6 trillion in unfunded, assumed liabilities on government pensions—i.e., pensions the government has obligated itself for but has no funds to pay—and there is a *total deficit in unfunded liabilities of over $9 trillion*.

And you need only turn to Chart 4 and accompanying comment to see what even 1 trillion means—equivalent to 85 trips to the moon and back. *The government is bankrupt!*

Or at least it would be bankrupt if it had to meet its obligations as people and states and municipalities must do. But governments do not go bankrupt; they just print paper money to meet their obligations or resort to the modern method of creating bank deposits out of thin air, out of the hot air of government IOUs. And it is easy to see that the United States is not just on its way to catastrophe, but that it already has on its books uncovered obligations sufficient to drive us to the trillion to one inflation Germany went through in 1923.

What with Medicaid and disability pension legislation, and old-age pension benefits tied to the cost of living index, Social Security is no longer a viable insurance plan. To take the disability aspect alone, when Congress pushed through a plan some twenty years ago to allow disabled workers to retire at age fifty instead of sixty-five, the sponsors of the legislation announced that the total additional cost would be about $860 million and that there would only be 1 million workers on the disability rolls.

The age fifty limitation was removed in 1960, and today there are nearly 5 million "workers" or their dependents on the disability benefit rolls at a cost of $12 billion a year. Ten years from now it will be 7 million people and $33 billion, *assuming that there is no more inflation*. But, at 7 percent annual inflation, it will be double that amount.

And these "workers," once they get on the disability payroll, practically never get off it. Out of nearly 5 million people on the rolls, only about 35,000 have been "rehabilitated" each year. Why should they work when a worker in his early twenties can pay Social Security taxes for as little as eighteen months and get disability benefits for the rest of his or her life? And when those benefits for a "worker" with one child can reach as high as $12,600 *tax-free* income a year for life, plus free Medicaid?

One voice of reason has been raised to stay the demand for a Social Security tax rollback—you guessed it—that of Senator Russell Long, chairman of the Senate Finance Committee: "If Congress wants to cut payroll taxes it should trim Social Security benefits."

And, thus far, this powerful voice has persuaded enough senators to prevent a rollback, which would, of course, merely mean that the deficit would be hidden elsewhere in the budget and would do nothing to prevent a possible, eventual trillion to one inflation. But the legislature and the administration seem to have been so terrified by the 1978 California taxpayers' revolt that it seems doubtful whether Senator Long and his Republican and Southern Democrat supporters can hold the line much longer.

The California referendum, although a perfectly natural rebellion against high taxes, meant tackling the problem from the wrong end. The problem is government profligacy, and it is government spending that should be cut, as Senator Long has said—and cut back so sharply that taxes, too, can be reduced—instead of taking out the taxpayers' resentment on the teachers, policemen and firemen, as is almost certain to occur in California even though the voters themselves have indicated in the polls that what they want to cut is welfare.

The balanced-budget amendment

Another analogous proposal—a constitutional amendment to compel Congress to pass a balanced budget—also means tackling a problem from the wrong end. What budget? The 1979 and 1980 type of budget, with its bikini accounting and so many important expenditures omitted and no mention of the totals of government-guarantied loans, many of which must be paid by the government. How far does a budget budge? No administration and no Congress, no matter how well intentioned, can guaranty that actual revenues will come up to budgetary expectations or that actual expenditures will not exceed budgetary authorizations. And I doubt very much that Congress is likely to put real teeth into any budget-balancing amendment, or that a constitutional convention—if that route is adopted—would be capable of doing so.

The problem is not with the budget, but with the expenditures, and it should not be too difficult for Congress (not a convention) to write an amendment that would prohibit the administration or any governmental agency from spending more money in any month than it has collected in revenues during that month or in unexpended funds from the previous months of the fiscal year, using generally accepted accounting principles to cover depreciation, bad debts, funding of pension and Social Security obligations, etc. And prohibiting any borrowing by the government or any governmental agency, save in time of war or national emergency, declared and terminable by Act of Congress.

Misconceptions with respect to Social Security

Incidentally, when politicians speak of Social Security taxes, they almost invariably refer solely to the 6.13 percent rate (1979) paid by the employee, and this is the figure picked up by the media and by the outraged workers. But the actual rate is 12.26 percent, and the fact that half the tax is paid by the employer does not diminish the burden on the payroll by one iota. It merely means that the employer has 6.13 percent less that he could otherwise use in paying higher wages. So the workers—all of us—pay the 12.26 percent tax in one way or another. While the analogous "self-employment tax," when applied to workers over the age of sixty-five who cannot possibly expect to derive any benefits whatsoever from the tax, is robbery pure and simple—an outrageous addition to the normal income tax that these "senior citizens" must also pay on their income.

In all of this drift from Social Security insurance to welfare for some people and extortion for the rest, and the mounting pressure to have the worker pay less than half the cost and the employer the remainder, we have merely been copying the Latin American example, precisely as we have done in our double-budget bikini system of government accounts with its growing share of expenditures not appearing in the published budget at all. And we can see what this has done to inflation in South America—a billion to one in Brazil in my lifetime, a million to one in Chile, and the Colombian and Argentine pesos, once each worth 97 cents U.S., and now quoted at 38 pesos to the dollar and 1,000 pesos to the dollar respectively.

Many Latin American nations—once progressive, "liberal" little

Uruguay among them—have been ruined and taken over by military or communist dictatorships as a consequence of economic disaster engendered by social security and welfare costs in excess of the nation's economic capacity. The question is: Have we already exceeded ours?

With an automatic increase in Social Security benefits tied to the cost of living, a kid of fifteen who gets his Social Security number with his first summer job, and whose salary increases by the time he is sixty-five to the presently legislated taxable limit of $5,748 a year, will receive benefits of $4,200 *a month*, assuming only a 4 percent annual increase in the cost of living, which is far below current rates and is what some economists consider harmless. At 8 percent inflation, he would receive $27,600 a month—more than $330,000 a year! This is the inflationary dynamite we already have in our laws today! Except that, long before that fifteen-year-old kid retires, the dollar bill would not be worth the paper it is printed on, for inflation of the magnitude of 4 percent or 8 percent per annum can never be held down within that limit. And this country, too, will have exploded into trillion to one inflation and, at best, chaos, at worst, a communist or other dictatorship. At worst, because chaos is eventually brought under control, whereas dictatorship can only be ended by bloodshed.

A side effect of Social Security is that at least 500,000 voluntary private business pension plans—about 30 percent of the total number—have been driven out of business since 1974 when Congress, under pressure from "consumer-protection" lobbyists, passed an Employee Retirement Income Security Act to "protect" the rights of workers under private pension plans by compelling employers to make the plans fully funded instead of being paid for out of current income. The private plans had been established by far-seeing, public-spirited businessmen, long before there had been any talk of government Social Security—most notably in the case of AT&T. And later, in 1950, General Motors led the way to a new generation of business-financed private pension plans until there were some 1.6 million such private plans in operation. Many of these plans, such as the nationwide college faculty plan, permit employee contributions of up to 15 percent of income with matching contributions by the employer, and under such plans the employee can retire at age sixty-five or seventy, after thirty years of service, with an income as high as 70–100 percent of salary. But with the 1974 act, many businesses found they were about to be overwhelmed by government regulations and could not afford to change their pension structure from one where benefits were paid from current income to fully funded plans. So the pension plans were dropped, to the dismay and prejudice of all concerned—which is a good example of what happens when the government attempts to meddle with the economy.

Government pensions

Most of the controversy about government pensions has centered around military pensions, with widespread criticism of "double-dipping." The military (including the Navy and Air Force) can retire after twenty years service, regardless of age, and *half of the military retirees are in their late thirties and forties*, meaning that most of them are available for other jobs, and that some 150,000 retirees have moved into the civil service— "double-dipping" out of the Federal budget.

The problem is aggravated by the fact that those who retire on a "disability" status can get increased benefits, *tax-free*. "Disability" can mean anything from flat feet on up. (I was retired at age eighteen after two years' service in World War I and could have claimed a lifetime flat-foot pension, but refrained; and I was not too disabled to volunteer in World War II at the age of forty, nor am I disabled now, but I neither get nor want an Army pension.)

In all, the cost of Defense Department pensions for some 2 million retirees has grown to $11.5 billion in the 1979–80 budget, plus accrued pension rights of more than $7 billion for those still on active duty. For comparison, the entire Army payroll is $9.8 billion, Navy $6.9 billion, Marine Corps $2.1 billion, Air Force $7.9 billion. The entire Air Force budget for aircraft and missiles is only $7.9 billion; the entire Navy budget for building ships is only $6.2 billion. Let me repeat—the Defense Department must pay 40 percent as much for pensions as it pays for all the uniformed personnel on active service in the Army, Navy, Air Force and Marines combined. And, at the present rate of inflation, with the sliding scale of pension increases, it will be paying double that figure by 1987.

The Defense Department pensions are noncontributory. The taxpayer foots the entire bill. Or worse, the bill is paid with printing-press money to meet the federal deficits—and that means more inflation.

But it is not the military pension system alone that is at fault. The entire civil service pension system is practically noncontributory. In fiscal 1977, for each dollar of civilian salaries paid by the federal government, 29.3 cents was paid out for pensions. And of this the retirees paid 7 cents and the taxpayer 22.3 cents! A total tax bill for the civil service of $15 billion—some 67 percent more than the pensions paid to the military in that year. But, since the Vietnam War, the media have been so down on the Army and the Defense Department in general that all we ever read about or hear about are the military pensions.

All federal government pensions, military and civilian alike, have been hitched, like Social Security, to a cost of living index. There have been fifteen cost of living hikes in the past ten years, ever since this inflation linkage was enacted into law. The sum of the percentage increases thus far is over 78 percent but, as the increases are compounded, the actual increase has been over 112 percent and most employees who retired more than ten years ago are now receiving pensions in excess of their highest active-duty pay.

It is not as though federal employees were underpaid and had to be compensated by free or almost free pension plans far in excess of Social Security or any private pension plans. A recent, authoritative study, loudly denounced by the National Federation of Federal Employees, shows that federal employees receive salaries that exceed by 13 percent to 20 percent the salaries those same employees could receive in private employment, particularly in the lower brackets. This does not refer to those officials at cabinet or sub-cabinet levels who have taken substantial cuts in income on entering government service; on the other hand, there are many officials at top levels who "never had it so good." The study refers to salary only, and does not take into account the pension rights, long vacations, liberal sick leave and other benefits well in excess of those found in the private sector.

A 1978 investigation by the Civil Service Commission shows that 11.49 percent of federal employees are overgraded, and hence are overpaid even by the liberal federal salary standards, while only 3.28 percent are undergraded and underpaid—a report that has, of course, been attacked by the American Federation of Government Employees, which is even more vocal than the NFFE.

On the other hand, the head of the American Federation of State, County and Municipal Employees, the largest union in the AFL-CIO with a membership of over 1 million, has admitted that the munificent pensions, early-retirement privileges and abuse of tax-free disability payments are indefensible, an admission that would apply particularly in the case of municipal employees.

And the pensions as well as the salaries paid by the international agencies—the United Nations, World Bank, IMF, IADB, OAS, etc.—toward which the United States pays more than any other nation, are much higher than we pay our own civilian and military personnel. Probably the most fantastically overremunerated bureaucracy to be found anywhere in the world, perhaps with the exception of the top officials in the oil-rich Arab states.

Summing up, there is no reason why pension rights in the public sector should be noncontributory or exceed those in the private sector. The solution to the problem of "double-dipping," and to the inflation problem arising from this $4.6 trillion government pension fund liability, is simple. No government employee, civilian or military, should be entitled to retire on pension before age sixty-five, unless truly disabled, nor to any more than the regular, actuarial Social Security benefits divested of all welfare components, and with no cost of living increases. And he or she should pay for those benefits at the same rate as the entire working population of the country.

There should be one, welfare-free, actuarial Social Security system for all. Period.

The costs of big government

Remember that *anything* that the government does or that the government finances—whether it is running the Postal System or the welfare and health schemes, or lending money to home builders or small businesses, or even contracting for the construction of highways and government buildings—is going to cost the economy from one to two hundred times as much as it would cost if the programs and projects were carried on by private enterprise. And that you as taxpayers will have to foot the bill.

The General Accounting Office—an agency of the legislative branch of government which supervises the expenditures of the executive—has for the first time published a list of the "overruns" on federal construction projects handled by the government's civilian agencies.

Overruns in Defense Department purchases have for years been the subject of discussion and angry criticism, but we now know that they are far overshadowed by even greater overruns in the civilian branch. On 59 nonmilitary construction projects, the GAO reported that actual costs *exceeded the original estimates by two to nearly nine times, for a total overrun of $46 billion*, and that total overruns in the 269 civilian projects surveyed exceeded $57 billion.

The GAO further reports that the major reason for these overruns was *not* inflation, but engineering changes in the projects, authorized after the project was approved. And if any reader is innocent enough to believe that these engineering changes were necessary or inevitable or unpredictable, he or she is simply not familiar with the government's way of doing business.

What happens is that when the Postal System or any other agency or branch of the government calls for bids on a project—whether it is a building or a highway or whatever—one bidder with exceptional political connections will submit a bid so far below the competition that acceptance of the bid is virtually ensured. Then come the engineering changes—and that is where the successful bidder makes his profits, with total costs running two to nine times the amount of the original estimate.

One of the investigators of the multibillion-dollar scandal that cropped up in the General Services Administration—the agency that controls the purchases, building programs and rentals of the entire government—reported that corruption and waste were not confined to GSA alone, but existed in every department and agency of the government, and that fraud, graft and waste cost the taxpayer at least $25 billion a year.

Perhaps the only good thing we can say about this situation is that at least we know where our money is going.

Yet underestimates, fraud, graft and waste on specific purchases and projects pale into insignificance in comparison with underestimates, graft and waste on general programs such as Social Security, Medicaid, agencies like the Postal System, the REA, TVA, the regulatory and lending agencies and so forth. For, in those cases, there are no engineering estimates, and estimated costs are based on nothing more reliable than the zeal of those who are lobbying to get the program adopted, while actual costs can soar into the wild blue yonder.

And until criminal penalties are enacted for every federal program and project that exceeds the original cost estimates by more than 100 percent—which would have put in jail practically all our cabinet officers and budgeteers over the past forty years—there is no way of preventing the federal bureaucratic camel from putting its nose under the tent of our national economy.

Federal interest payments

In addition to welfare, Social Security and government pensions, there is another item in the federal budget that should be drastically trimmed—namely, interest on the public debt, some $44 billion in 1978 and $57 billion budgeted for 1980, which this generation of taxpayers must pay because they and their predecessors allowed the government to live for so long beyond its means.

The budgeteers tell us that interest is an "uncontrollable" expenditure that cannot be reduced no matter how they try to economize. Nonsense! If the government once again balanced its budget and repaid each issue of the public debt as it became due—and kept the hell out of the capital market—lower interest rates would almost immediately prevail for home mortgages and business and personal loans as well as for the government. And the interest burden in the budget could be cut in half. Three percent is a normal, reasonable interest rate for the government to pay, not 10 percent plus as the Treasury has been forced to pay in recent months.

If ever again the administration and Congress raise the debt ceiling—as they have done again and again and are still doing—the citizens should raise the roof! What blatant hypocrisy to state in the budget report: "The statutory debt limit is permanently established at $400 billion" when in reality the ceiling is raised whenever the architects of our fiscal policy ask for it—to $836 billion for September 1979. And when the actual public debt on that date, according to the 1979–80 budget, will be $899 billion, not counting some $130 billion of off-budgetary debt and various other forms of debt and debt guaranties which are exempt from that ceiling—a shocking example of bikini accounting.

15. The Way Out

This government is acknowledged by all to be one of enumerated powers. The principle that it can exercise only the powers granted to it would seem too apparent to have required to be enforced by all those arguments which its enlightened friends ... found it necessary to urge. ... Should Congress, under the pretext of executing its powers, pass laws for the accomplishment of objects not intrusted to the government, it would become the painful duty of this tribunal ... to say that such an act was not the law of the land.

John Marshall (1819)

Of all our Supreme Court justices, Chief Justice Marshall was the one who did most to expand the powers of the federal government against the opposition of the "strict constructionists" who contended that the Constitution did not empower Congress to carry out even its enumerated powers except by such *means* as were expressly set forth in the Constitution or were "necessary and proper," giving the most restricted sense to the term "necessary." So that when Marshall, in his opinion in *McCulloch* v. *Maryland* quoted above, emphasizes that Congress may not "pass laws for the accomplishment of objects not intrusted to the government," it is clear that *the powers of Congress must be "strictly construed,"* even though it may have wide latitude in the choice of appropriate means to achieve a legitimate end *"within the scope of the Constitution."*

And the simplest way out of our present dilemma, as will be seen below, may lie in our questioning the legitimacy of any laws enacted "for the accomplishment of objects not intrusted to the government."

The last, best hope

What with Watergate and its painful aftermath, and the overt hostility that developed between Congress and President Nixon, extending over to his successor—on partisan not personal grounds—it would have been unrealistic to have expected the two branches of government to work together in harmony during the pre-Carter years. Yet without that cooperation there was no way that we could have hoped to change our long-standing policies of government overspending at home and abroad. *And the economy cannot now endure two more years of national bankruptcy and continuing debasement of the dollar.*

With the advent of a Democrat as President and a Congress overwhelmingly of the same party, there may be at least a possibility of some degree of cooperation between the legislature and the executive. And it may be hoped that this little book, or some more able, more persuasive, more powerful voice will convince the administration and a sufficient number of our representatives and senators that Charts 1 and 5 mean what they say.

That, bankrupt as we are internationally—some $275 to $800 billion in the red, and refusing to meet our international obligations in gold—we can no longer afford to act as policeman for the world or to subsidize the corrupt and incompetent governments of the more than one hundred underdeveloped countries which are increasing their populations at such a rate that there is nothing we can do to help them. That, in ten more years, the self-supporting nations will be overwhelmed. And three quarters of the world's population will *demand* that they be supported by us and the other industrial nations—demands that they will thrust on us with the same truculent mendicity and unabashed mendacity with which we are now assailed by the millions of people on our domestic and foreign welfare rolls.

The world's population is now over 3.5 billion; in another thirty years it will be double that figure! And the increase will be entirely among the improvident countries that are screaming for welfare—from us. As one economist has observed with particular reference to Mexico, the population of the underdeveloped nations is growing by leaps and bounds. Certainly a graphic description of the procreative process! And this pullulating population increase, and the ever-augmenting cries for aid, are bound to escalate *ad infinitum, ad nauseam* and *ad absurdum.*

Unless God, in His infinite Wisdom and Mercy, shall send the Four Horsemen of the Apocalypse—Famine, Pestilence, War and Death—

to undo the damage that men have done. For surely those dread horsemen are more merciful than the men and women who bring children into this world to starve and to breed new generations that will starve in turn.

The quandary

In the first place, the executive and legislative branches of our government must recognize that the steady rise in the money supply is a reflection of the cumulative deficits of the national government, and that creating government bank deposits with the sale of printed IOUs is simply a modern substitute for the currency printing press; that freedom of the press was never intended to embrace the right of the government to print all the money it wanted nor to substitute some sophisticated subterfuge to the same end; and that it is these deficits that are virtually the sole cause of the continuing rise in consumer and wholesale prices. That we must therefore cut down drastically on our government spending, not 10 percent, not 20 percent, but at least 50 percent and preferably more. The ultimate goal should be the 3.76 percent of national income that was once our standard or, at the very most, the 10 percent in taxes that Benjamin Franklin said would be the mark of an oppressive government. And the sooner and the closer we come to that goal, the better.

Congress and the administration must also recognize that welfare at home and abroad is the principal cause of the present imbalance in the federal budget, that in the 1979–80 budget they add up to nearly double the projected expenditure for national defense—and that they must be *eliminated!* How to do it?

The Tenth Amendment

How can we continue to ignore the clear provisions of the Constitution? There is *nothing* in the Constitution, express or implied, that gives the United States Government the right to take money from some of its citizens and give that money to other citizens and to foreign governments except in payment of goods or services. And yet this is what federal welfare payments and foreign aid mean.

There are fuzzy-minded people who attempt to justify federal welfare (and even foreign aid) by the "general welfare clause." But they forget that the Constitution refers to "the *common* Defence and *general* Welfare," not to the welfare of any single individual or group of persons.

The Preamble states that "WE THE PEOPLE . . . in Order to . . . establish Justice, insure domestic Tranquility, provide for the common Defence, promote the general Welfare, . . . do ordain and establish this Constitution. . . ."

And, for the purposes outlined in the Preamble, the Constitution vests certain specified powers in Congress (Article I), among others, "To lay and collect Taxes, Duties, Imposts and Excises, to pay the Debts and provide for the common Defence and general Welfare of the United States. . . ." Again, *general* welfare—and it is only the confusion motivated by present-day loose usage of language that makes people believe that the "general Welfare of the United States" is synonymous with handouts or doles or charity to individuals. A variation on the theme that what's good for me is good for the U.S.A.

The Supreme Court, in *United States* v. *Butler* (1935), quotes with approval Justice Story (*Commentaries on the Constitution*):

> *The Constitution was, from its very origin, contemplated to be the frame of a national government, of special and enumerated powers, and not of general and unlimited powers. . . . A power to lay taxes for the common defence and general welfare of the United States is not in common sense a general power. It is limited to those objects. It cannot constitutionally transcend them.*

And in *Helvering* v. *Davis* (1936) the Court reaffirms the principles laid down by Story and states that "the line must still be drawn between one welfare and another, between particular and general." The discretion in drawing the line between the *general* welfare and the *particular* welfare— i.e., "welfare" in the current, modern sense, for the benefit of particular individuals or groups—belongs to the Congress, "*unless the choice is clearly wrong,* a display of arbitrary power not an exercise of judgment."

Again, in *United States* v. *Butler*, the Court states:

> *From the accepted doctrine that the United States is a government of delegated powers, it follows that those not expressly granted, or reasonably to be implied from such as are conferred, are reserved to the states or to the people. To forestall any suggestion to the contrary, the Tenth Amendment was adopted. The same proposition, otherwise stated, is that powers not granted are prohibited.*

For the Tenth Amendment, which is part of the original Bill of Rights, states: "*The powers not delegated to the United States by the Constitution, nor prohibited by it to the States, are reserved to the States respectively, or to the People.*"

Quoting again from the Supreme Court in *United States* v. *Butler*:

> *A tax, in the general understanding of the term, and as used in the Constitution, signifies an exaction for the support of the Government. The word has never been thought to connote the expropriation of*

> *money from one group for the benefit of another. . . . The question is not what power the federal Government ought to have but what powers in fact have been given by the people. . . . The federal union is a government of delegated powers. It has only such as are expressly conferred upon it and such as are reasonably to be implied from those granted. . . . The view that the [welfare] clause grants power to provide for the general welfare, independent of the taxing power, has never been authoritatively accepted. Mr. Justice Story points out that if it were adopted "it is obvious that under color of the generality of the words 'to provide for the common defence and general welfare' the government [of the United States] would be in reality a government of general and unlimited powers."*

If the Congress or the President were empowered to ignore the Tenth Amendment, and exceed the powers expressly vested in them, contending that the Preamble and the tax clause give them *carte blanche* to do anything they wish if in their opinions it will "insure domestic Tranquility" or "promote the general Welfare," then their powers would be absolutely unlimited. For there is nothing that they could not find some pretext for doing if they could interpret those two clauses according to their views of social or political expediency without the restraining inhibition of the Tenth Amendment. But ours—to quote John Marshall—is a Constitution of strictly enumerated powers, and any law enacted "for the accomplishments of objects not intrusted to the government" is "not the law of the land."

Fortunately, the very fact that "welfare" disbursements, foreign aid, and many other costly expenditures of the federal government are almost certainly unconstitutional and in violation of the Tenth Amendment provides us with a way out—certainly the simplest way out—of our present quandary.

For what President or legislator can be expected to vote for the total elimination of such expenditures, if he can possibly avoid such a difficult choice, when the "first duty of every politician is to get re-elected?" And—to take that cynical commentary in its least pejorative sense—if the true statesmen among our legislators and the administration refuse to bend to the will of at least some of the pressure groups confronting them, our government will be left wholly at the mercy of the demagogues.

No political figure can afford recklessly to antagonize even the less influential pressure groups, such as those that have raised the subsidies of the National Endowments for the Arts and for the Humanities from $5 million each in their first budgets to $154 million and $150 million respectively, in their 1980 budgets, and the National Science Foundation to over $1 billion. Yet where in the Constitution can we find any authority for using taxpayers' money to give a $5,000 subsidy to finance a book dedicated to extolling the pleasures of what the author so elegantly describes as "the zipless fuck"? Or authority for any of the thousands of other equally far-fetched taxpayer-supported ventures to which Senator Proxmire has awarded the Order of the Golden Fleece? Such as a $97,000 grant for a firsthand, on-the-spot study of the brothels of Cuzco, Peru, by a sociologist who happens to be the author of *Academic Gamesmanship,* a book that coaches professors on how to wangle money out of the federal government.

The simplest way out of the quandary
What, then, is the simple solution that would enable the administration and the Congress to reduce government expenditures by 50 percent or more—and most of our representatives in Washington "know in their hearts that this would be right"—and yet enable the statesmen among them to continue to serve the public and not be eliminated by the rabble-rousers?

Congress should pass, and the President sign, a bill creating an *ad hoc,* temporary legislative investigatory body, roughly similar in concept to the General Accounting Office (the office headed by the Controller General), and charged with the function of going through with a fine comb every activity and every expenditure of all the government departments and agencies, with a view to weeding out—the "fine-comb" metaphor calls for the word "delousing," but "weeding out" is gentler—any activity or expenditure that is in violation of the Tenth Amendment or any other provision of the Constitution. Appeal should be solely to a three- or five-man court appointed especially for that purpose, and composed of judges sworn to uphold the Constitution regardless of their personal views as to the desirability or otherwise of such activities and expenditures. These judges should be "strict constructionists" who can be counted upon to exercise "judicial restraint" and not usurp the powers of Congress or of the President or of the States, and mindful of George Washington's warning:

> *If in the opinion of the people the distribution or modification of the constitutional powers be in any particular wrong, let it be corrected by an amendment in the way which the Constitution designates. But*

let there be no change by usurpation; for though this in one instance may be the instrument of good, it is the customary weapon by which free governments are destroyed.

And the decisions of that court should by law be made immediately effective or, in the court's discretion, subject at the most to a six-month delay to allow for an appeal by writ of certiorari in those few and isolated cases where the Supreme Court may be willing to grant an appeal—and the Supreme Court should be granted a special appropriation to help it to deal with the additional burden.

But, to prevent the creation and growth of yet another mushrooming bureaucracy, the judges should have the qualifications and status of federal appellate judges and, after this special three- or five-man court has completed its task, they should be assigned to one of the circuit courts which are sadly in need of additional judges. And the investigatory agency, which would carry the main burden of winnowing out the improper functions of government, should be empowered to recruit outside consultants on a short-term or occasional basis for terms of not over one year, plus a temporary working staff of graduate accountants and lawyers from the leading law schools and graduate schools of business administration, as well as staff supervisors comprised of professors or retired professors from such schools. At the conclusion of the initial period of intensive investigation and decision-making, which should not exceed a three-to-six month period, some of the remaining members of the staff could be absorbed by the General Accounting Office as a permanent watchdog for the Tenth Amendment.

The "General Welfare" and "particular welfare"

As a lawyer, I am aware of the changing composition and temper of the Supreme Court, from the "Warren Court," which supported or rejected legislation according to the personal views of the justices as to the social, political or economic desirability of its objectives, to the "Burger Court," which has reverted to a policy of judicial restraint with the majority of the justices using as their governing criterion a determination of whether or not the legislation is authorized or prohibited by the Constitution, regardless of their personal views as to its desirability or expediency. Hence I would not dare predict precisely what present activities of government would be found by the proposed investigatory agency and appellate court to be in violation of Tenth Amendment limitations.

But, so far as the "arts," "humanities," and "sciences" are concerned, I might point out that the Constitution gives Congress the power "to promote the Progress of Science and the Useful Arts, by securing for limited Times to Authors and Inventors the exclusive Right to their respective Writings and Discoveries"—the patent and copyright clause. That provision is a *limitation* on the powers of Congress. Congress can promote the *useful* arts and sciences by granting patents and copyrights—*and in no other way*. There is no power, so far as I can see in the Constitution, to take taxpayers' money and give it to out-of-work poets, artists, tap dancers or frustrated potential inventors. Then, too, as Senator Moynihan tells us, "the best way to promote art is to make it illegal!"

And I have been hard put to find among the powers entrusted by the states to the federal government any authority whatsoever for subsidizing the construction and operation of an opera house, a theater and a music hall where the affluent public is permitted to buy tickets at prices running as high as $27 a seat. I say this despite the fact that I very much enjoy attending the plays and other spectacles put on at the Kennedy Center. But the Center is not even a modern version of the "bread and circuses" provided to keep the Roman masses happy, but a form of subsidized "cake and concerts" for the wealthy.

And now the trustees of the Kennedy Center, having managed their Trust in such a way that the Center is insolvent and with its roof and basement caving in and leaking, are asking that its $600,000 a year maintenance costs be paid by the National Park Service, and that Congress waive the $500,000 annual interest on the $20.4 million, fifty-year 2½ percent bonds that the government purchased as part of its contribution to the construction of the Center. At that rate of interest, virtually an outright subsidy, in addition to the $23 million in direct government grants—welfare for the well-to-do!

The question is not what I personally, or anyone else, may regard as a desirable function of government, but what functions the Constitution expressly delegates to the federal government, all else being reserved to the States or to the people. The *United States* v. *Butler, supra.*

Social Security

With respect to Social Security, the Supreme Court, in *Helvering* v. *Davis, supra,* has emphatically upheld the original Social Security plan enacted under Franklin D. Roosevelt, where the accruals to the "Old Age Reserve Account" were "determined on a reserve basis in accordance with accepted actuarial principles."

The Court left open the question as to whether or not the tax provisions and the benefit provisions of the Social Security Act are separable, petitioner Helvering (the Commissioner of Internal Revenue) arguing that the tax is not "earmarked" and that therefore Congress can spend the proceeds as it wishes, while respondent Davis (a stockholder of Edison Electric of Boston suing to enjoin the company from making payments or deductions under the act) argued that the two titles of the act "dovetailed" and that Congress would not have passed one title without the other, which is undoubtedly true. But, in any event, the benefits under the original Social Security Act were proportionate to the taxpayers' contributions on an actuarial basis. Thus they did not represent "welfare" but were comparable, at least in the minds of the public and of Congress, to life insurance benefits and premiums.

The Court expressly held that payment of those benefits, *under the original actuarially computed plan*, were "not in contravention of the Tenth Amendment." But there appears to be nothing in the Constitution or in the Supreme Court decision cited above that would empower Congress to so change the Social Security structure that at least 50 percent of the Social Security and Medicaid benefits are now distributed as "welfare" with no regard to contributions, actuarially computed or otherwise. Thus taking money from some taxpayers, either in Social Security taxes or from general revenues, and giving it to other people who may not even be taxpayers—"the expropriation of money from one group for the benefit of another" which is barred by *United States* v. *Butler, supra.*

En passant, it is a perversion of the truth when lobbyists for lower Social Security taxes and higher benefits argue that Social Security is the most regressive of taxes, on the ground that a person whose salary is $22,900 or less must pay 6.13 percent of that salary in tax while one whose salary is $100,000 pays only 1.4 percent in tax. The fact is that both taxpayers pay 6.13 percent on all salary up to $22,900, and that the benefits each taxpayer ultimately receives are proportionate to his or her contributions. While, in the lowest brackets, the beneficiaries receive additional amounts that exceed the proportion of the contributions.

Even to the extent that benefits are proportionate to contributions, Social Security taxes are no more regressive than the fact that the poor man as well as the rich man must pay 15 cents for a postage stamp. No more regressive than the fact that a person who deposited $5,000 in a Postal Savings Account could later withdraw $5,000 plus interest on $5,000, while a person who deposited $500 could only withdraw $500 plus interest on $500. So much for that!

Alternative to Tenth Amendment procedure

Bear in mind, however, that the Tenth Amendment approach suggested above is proposed as the *simplest* way out of the present quandary. It is not the *only* way out. And if, despite the Supreme Court decisions and other arguments adduced above, the Congress or the courts should decide that foreign aid and "welfare" are not in contravention of the Tenth Amendment, regardless of the fact that the "general welfare" clause of the Constitution applies only to the taxing power and does not broaden the permissible range of activities delegated to the federal government, this does not in the slightest invalidate the basic thesis of this book—that the only way to stop inflation is for the government to stop borrowing and spending money in excess of its tax revenues or in excess of its current foreign exchange resources.

But if Congress does reject the Tenth Amendment procedures suggested above and in the following chapter, then indeed Congress must bite the bullet and have the courage to enact legislation eliminating all welfare and foreign-aid expenditures from the federal budget—a process that might prove as painful to a legislator as a surgical operation was to a soldier in the days when biting down on a lead bullet, and brandy, provided the only relief from pain available before the invention of anesthesia.

Reduction of government personnel

The same law that establishes the proposed investigatory agency and court should provide that all persons employed by the government in unconstitutional activities—including the entire personnel of agencies or departments whose total functions are ruled to be unconstitutional—shall be dismissed either immediately or within a six-month period of grace. For the fact that any person has fed at the government trough for one year or ten years gives no vested right to continued feeding at that trough for the rest of his working life when the activity in which he or she has been engaged is unconstitutional.

The personal hardship to which individuals in the bureaucracy might thus be put would be temporary at most, in view of the tremendous upsurge in industry, agriculture and commerce which would take place almost instantaneously, with jobs for everyone willing and able to work, as a predictable consequence of putting an instant stop to inflation—as has proved to be true in *every* country that has dared to take the steps necessary to that end.

And this job-creating renaissance in our economy would be accelerated and enhanced by the tax measures proposed in the two final sections of this chapter.

True, there would be some members of the bureaucracy, mostly political appointees, now enjoying salaries of $20,000 to $50,000 a year, who would be hard put to find such lucrative employment in the private sector, but there are few citizens who would shed tears over the plight of these privileged few. And there are some in government so incompetent, or so reluctant to engage in hard work, that they would be unable to find work to their liking in private employment. But these misfits would be comparatively few in number, and the National Federation of Federal Employees and other labor advocates in the bureaucracy could with ill grace complain of their dismissal unless they are willing to confess that bureaucrats are in general "unemployables" supported solely by the taxpayers' charity. And such, in my experience, is not generally the case.

The total number of federal civilian employees as of September 1979, including the Postal Service, is estimated at 2,454,000, a small fraction of the total work force of the nation, which is placed at around 104 million, so the problem of readjustment should not be insuperable.

The corporate income tax should be abolished

Aside from the elimination of all unconstitutional activities and expenditures of the government, all other outlays should be drastically cut and, in some cases eliminated. The cost of running the Internal Revenue Service could be cut to a quarter of the present figure if two much-needed improvements were made.

The income tax, personal and corporate, is the most costly part of our federal tax system to administer. And those two taxes, particularly the latter, constitute the greatest deterrent we now have to economic progress. *There should be no corporate income tax!*

This is something that the Treasury has never considered nor wanted to contemplate, because the corporate income tax yields some $60 billion out of total tax revenues of $402 billion (1978) and is budgeted to yield $71 billion in 1980 out of a total of $503 billion. And it is something that no Congress and no administration has ever dared sponsor for fear of outcries that the government is favoring big business.

The truth is quite the contrary. Elimination of the corporate income tax would favor labor, and the "little guy"—the average investor. Logically, there is no reason why J. P. Morgan & Company paid no taxes when it was a partnership, but as soon as it became a corporation, taking over the old Guaranty Trust Company and selling its stock to the general public, half its profits were paid out in taxes.

Why should the publicly owned Merrill Lynch, Pierce, Fenner & Smith, Inc.—one of the nation's largest corporations with assets of over $4 billion—pay income taxes when the old MLPF&S, a partnership, was tax-exempt? If Henry Ford had started his business as a partnership and procured his capital from limited partners instead of stockholders, the company would have been tax-free. Why should it pay millions of dollars in taxes today simply because it is a corporation with its stock owned by many thousands of investors?

The corporation is the democratic way of running a business. It is "people's capitalism" where everyone in the country can share in the profits of big business, simply by buying a share of stock. It is the American answer to Karl Marx. Everyone in this country who has a job, who is thrifty and saves for the future, can own his or her share in American industry and participate in the profits.

Some 35 million American citizens, not all of them wealthy, can point with pride to the Bell System and to hundreds of other American industries and say: "I own that company; all those high-power executives with their big salaries are working for me." AT&T alone has 2,939,000 stockholders and 61.5 percent of these own fewer than 100 shares apiece.

There is no reason in law or logic why those citizens should pay double taxes on their income, a tax on the profits of the corporation—*their corporation*—and a tax on the dividends they receive from it, particularly when the partners in the biggest, richest partnerships in the country—whose shares cannot be bought by the general public—pay only a single tax, a tax on their share of the partnership profits. And this is how it should be. There should be no double taxation of either partnerships or corporations, for they are merely channels through which the profits of the business flow through to the real owners—whether partners or shareholders.

The point where the tax should fall, logically and legally, is the point at which the investor acquires title to the profits—in the case of a partnership, when the profits are earned; in the case of corporation shareholders, when the dividends are declared. By this simple expedient, corporations would automatically be given every incentive for greater investment of their retained, untaxed earnings in the business, thus providing more jobs and increasing both production and man-hour productivity. Billions of dollars would thus be made available each year for reinvestment at the precise point where investment can be of greatest benefit to the national economy, thereby striking at the very roots of inflation and recession. *Think about it!*

There are other reasons why corporate shareholders should not be subjected to double taxation. Most of the salaries and wages paid in this country are paid by corporations. Most of the goods sold in this country are sold by corporations. If there were no corporate income tax, corporations could pay higher wages or sell at lower prices, or both. And competition would compel them to do so.

Let's take a look at the 1978 earnings figures for the three largest corporations in the country:

Millions of Dollars

	Number of Employees	Number of Share- holders	Total Wage and Payroll Costs	Total Taxes Paid	U.S. Income Taxes	Net Earnings	Retained Earnings	Dividends
AT&T	984,000	2,939,000	23,587	7,276	3,494	5,273	2,072	3,201
Exxon	129,000	695,000	3,405	17,353	1,100	2,760	1,298	1,472
GM	839,000	1,268,000	17,196	5,336	2,259	3,508	1,783	1,725
	1,952,000	4,902,000	44,188	29,965	6,853	11,541	5,153	6,398

First note that the wages of capital—the dividends without which there would be no investment capital, no corporation, and no wages or taxes paid—are not much greater than the retained earnings which the shareholders have permitted the companies to keep and plow back into the business in order to provide funds for expansion and hence for more wage and tax payments. As a matter of fact, the 500 corporations that Standard & Poor's uses in computing its stock market index showed an average dividend payout of $4.67 in 1977 out of earnings per share of $10.89, meaning $6.22 of retained earnings plowed back into the business. For 1978 it is estimated that dividends averaged $5 out of $11.80 in earnings.

Note, too, that the three companies listed above pay out more than four times as much in taxes as they do in dividends; that in the case of General Motors income taxes alone are greater than dividends. And in this respect General Motors is more typical of the generality of industrial corporations in the United States than are AT&T or Exxon. The figures for all corporations in 1977 were $71.8 billion in income taxes, $43.7 billion in dividends, and in 1978 $83.9 billion in income taxes, $49.3 billion in dividends.

Elimination of the corporate income tax would certainly mean some $84 billion (the amount the United States collected from that tax in 1978) to be distributed to the public in the form of wages, or lower prices, or plowed back into the business, or—to a much lesser extent because of competition—in higher dividends. And almost certainly in all four directions, which would mean the greatest boost to economic activity and prosperity that this country has ever had.

And, incidentally, note, too, that the wages of labor in the three largest corporations in the United States are more than six times the wages paid to the stockholders. And, even in Exxon, with its relatively small labor force (in comparison with AT&T and GM), and its vast investment behind each employee ($322,000 in total assets, $157,000 in shareholders' equity), wage payments were more than double the amount of the dividends. For all corporations, payroll costs in 1977 totaled $1,232 billion, or 28.2 times dividends, and in 1978 $1,301 billion, or 26.4 times dividends.

Still another reason for doing away with the corporate income tax is that it would eliminate at a stroke the major loopholes in the present tax laws—the controversial depletion allowances, the special exemptions and deductions lobbied through Congress, sometimes in return for political contributions. Above all, it would eliminate the extravagance and the swollen expense accounts that add so much to the cost of American merchandise.

No longer would business management tolerate theater, nightclub and yachting parties on a Lucullan scale, costly office furnishings, incestuous expense-account entertainment of one business executive by another on a reciprocal basis, while they smilingly sneer off the expense: "The government pays half the tab, you know."

And thus elimination of the corporate income tax would go far toward restoring or establishing higher standards of honesty in business, and hence in government. Furthermore, it would directly reduce inflation and provide a push to the economy so instantaneous and powerful that it would more than offset any temporary depressing influence that might result from a 50 percent cut in government expenditures and in the payrolls of the federal bureaucracy. *It is a means to the "miracle" of instant monetary stabilization without shock.*

This is a proposal whose adoption would not only decimate the ranks of employees at the Internal Revenue Service and Department of Justice, but would throw out of work thousands of tax accountants and tax lawyers, tremendously reduce the paper work of big and small business—and shock into horrified disbelief my former colleagues at Harvard Law School, where I was once a senior editor of their *World Tax Series.* So you may expect to hear the outraged outcries of all these estimable people. But we should try it; we'll like it. *Think about it.*

Our major competitors in world trade—Canada, the United Kingdom, France, Germany, Japan and Belgium—have realized the burden of this double taxation on their industries and its consequent handicap to their export trade, and they have abandoned the corporate income tax as an economic absurdity—something that tax experts have been trying to tell the world for years. I have been preaching the gospel for over twenty years, but "the poor man's wisdom *is* despised, and his words are not heard."—Ecclesiastes 9:16. Recently the European Economic Community (the Common Market) has asked all its members to follow the French, German, and Belgian examples.

And two years ago at their annual meeting, the left-wing Americans for Democratic Action called for abolition of the corporate income tax, a move undoubtedly influenced by their realization that elimination of the tax would mean higher wages, lower prices and increased investment in plant. And probably because they know that many of their members are shareholders, either directly or through pension systems, in the biggest corporations of the country. Pension funds already hold *majority ownership* in most of the top thousand corporations in the United States, which is one reason why the American corporation is "people's capitalism" and our answer to Karl Marx. *Think about it.*

And think what it would mean to public utility rates. Today when one of the State public service commissions, or the FCC, finds that a telephone or other utility company is entitled to earn $10 million more in net income, it must grant the company rate increases that will produce $20 million more in revenues, because half of the increase will be eaten up by the corporate income tax. If that tax were abolished, the rate increase allowed by the commission would be half as much. *Think about it.*

Reform of the personal income tax
The revenue lost by eliminating the corporate income tax could be made up—*if and to the extent it might be needed with a reduced budget*—by a simple change in the personal income tax that would do away with all the rest of the much-debated loopholes—and throw out of business practically all the rest of the tax lawyers, tax experts, tax accountants, and IRS auditors.

We should do away with *all* deductions, *all* exemptions—the tax-free interest on state and municipal bonds, the deductions for medical expenses, theft and casualty losses, even the personal exemptions and the exemptions for dependents. Everything except the deduction for charitable and philanthropic donations—because, if we do away with government welfare and government subsidies to the colleges, we must provide every incentive for private charity.

Why should we subsidize overpopulation by granting $1,000 deductions for dependents? Shouldn't everyone have brought home to him or her that everything the government spends comes out of our own pockets or purses, whether we earn $2,000 or $200,000 a year?

And there should be no special treatment for long-term capital gains. Why should the income from capital pay a lower tax than the income from labor? (There are plenty of reasons; I plead guilty to momentary but explicatory demagoguery. Capital gain generally represents a profit made over a long period of time, and it is confiscatory to tax it at the full rate when the apparent "profit" may really represent nothing but the debasement of the dollar over that period.)

So the income tax should be paid on total income of all kinds from all sources, with perhaps a minimum taxable income of $500, not that in principle there should be *any* exemption, but that the cost of collecting the tax on lesser amounts would prove exorbitant.

Wow! Higher taxes, you say. No! Definitely not! Because the tax should be at a lower rate, at a much lower rate, say on a sliding scale of from 1 percent to a maximum of 25 percent or less *on total income,* and not on an income scaled down with exceptions, deductions and loopholes. The 25 percent maximum should answer the complaints of the long-term capital gain beneficiaries, and would also take care of the constitutional amendment, now pending state ratification, that would limit the income tax to 25 percent.

The rates should be graduated so that they bring in the same $298 billion or so of revenue budgeted for personal and corporate income taxes combined in 1980—or, rather, to bring in the substantially diminished revenue that would be required if our federal expenditures were cut in half as they should be.

The "miracle of stabilization" in the U.S.A.

There could be no surer way of putting an *immediate* stop to the present inflationary process and the present recession than the combination of these measures. In fact, there may well be no other feasible means of ending the present disastrous trend. And there could be no greater stimulus to the prosperity and well-being of our nation than the enactment of these proposals. We would witness *immediately* the "miracle of stabilization"—and a resurgence of optimism, of business activity, of jobs, of prosperity without parallel in the history of this country.

This is not an idle promise. The "miracle" of *immediate* monetary stabilization and economic recovery has taken place in *every* country that has had the courage to put an end to runaway government spending. And the result cannot be achieved by presidential conferences with panels of businessmen, economists or labor leaders, nor by presidential pronouncements and pious, patriotic, political proclamations—by jawbone and wishbone. And no austerity or sacrifice or bullet-biting is needed, *except on the part of those feeding at the government trough.*

16. How to Stabilize

The way to stabilize is to stabilize.

Edwin Walter Kemmerer (1934)

The late Professor Kemmerer, the most successful monetary stabilizer in history, with a record of licking inflation in five countries of South America, knew that the cancer of inflation cannot be licked by a gradual piecemeal paring away of the malignant growth when what is needed is a radical surgical operation. Gerald Ford, when he was minority leader of the House, quoted Eisenhower as saying that "a war of gradualism cannot be won." And what proved so sadly true of Vietnam is no less true of the war against inflation.

Suppose, then, that the Congress and the new administration come to a realization of the seriousness of our present predicament and recognize that headlong inflation has never been licked in any country of the world by attempting to taper off inflationary pressures over a period of years. And that they agree that something must be done about it—*immediately.*

A joint board on national economic policy
And suppose they should decide that, instead of the President having his Council of Economic Advisers, and Congress its Joint Economic Committee, as at present—which can only prolong the confrontation—they agree to cooperate in a united attack on the problem.

For economists with radically opposing points of view can no more reach agreement on a middle way than can one group of engineers, dedicated to building a tunnel under New York Harbor, reach a compromise agreement with another group of engineers who advocate a bridge over the harbor instead. What middle way would they come up with—an underwater bridge? Or a tunnel suspended in midair?

And it is no more possible for a workable compromise to be

214

reached between Keynesian economists, advocating more and more expenditure by bigger and bigger government, and classical economists who believe, with Thoreau, that that government is best which governs least. So, suppose the President and the leaders of both parties in Congress, laying aside political differences in the national interest, decide to form a single Joint Board on National Economic Policy.

Say a board consisting of two representatives and two senators designated by the majority and minority leadership, with one or at the most two members of the President's Cabinet, most probably the Secretary of the Treasury and—because of the international implications of economic policy—the Secretary of State or Commerce. The chairman of the Federal Reserve Board should also be a member.

The board should be chaired by the President himself, as only the President can throw the full weight of executive authority behind the decisions of the board. And without that authority, the board would become merely an advisory body and not one for decision and action which is essential to the accomplishment of the task of monetary stabilization—i.e., stopping inflation and stabilizing the value of the dollar.

The overbalance in favor of the President's political party should not be significant, as all board decisions should be by consensus, as in a Quaker meeting house, if they are to win the necessary support of Congress. To ensure this support, it might be desirable to have the Speaker of the House and president pro tem of the Senate, plus the House and Senate minority leaders, kept fully *au courant* of the board's activities, under the same assurances of the strictest confidentiality that would be given by all members of the board.

But this is a matter for political judgment as to which I am not competent to advise. Similarly, I refrain from expressing an opinion as to whether the investigatory agency referred to in the previous chapter should be wholly separate from the board—say as an Agency for the Investigation of Constitutional Limitations—or whether it should serve under the board as its research agency or department. To simplify this exposition, I shall assume that the latter is the case.

The board members would not necessarily be economists. Some might be, some not. Because their function would be to *decide* on policy, on policies that can and should be supported by both the legislative and executive branches of government. And economists are not usually by nature or training equipped to make decisions; their business should be to advise, not to decide. And where they attempt to do both, the consequences may be disastrous.

Policy decisions should be made by *politicians,* using that term in its true sense—"one versed ... in the art of government; one practically engaged in the business of the state; a statesman." This is the definition, going back to the year 1589, according to the Oxford English Dictionary.

The administrator of the Agency for the Investigation of Constitutional Limitations would attend all meetings of the board and present his reports, possibly as secretary general of the board, but not as a voting member, inasmuch as he should not be a politician but apolitical and, above all, not a figurehead appointed for his prestige, but a knowledgeable expert. He would have under him a permanent staff of economists and statisticians as well as the lawyers and accountants who would, of course, constitute the corps of investigators for the performance of the functions described in the previous chapter and implicit in the name of the agency.

Whether or not the enabling act establishing the board, the agency, and the special Court of Appeals would authorize the administrator of the agency to act independently in abolishing governmental agencies and functions found to be in violation of the Tenth Amendment or other provisions of the Constitution—which would relieve the board members of many politically ticklish decisions—or whether the administrator would merely report to the board, which would then have the responsibility of promulgating or not the administrator's set of findings, is likewise a policy decision that must be left to wiser minds. But, in either event, it would seem to me appropriate for the enabling legislation to empower either the board or the administrator to abolish all unconstitutional agencies and activities of the government without further embarrassing Congress by the necessity of a decision in each case.

In the course of the administrator's investigations, however, he would supposedly unearth many phases of government action which, while not unconstitutional, are manifestly incompatible with the balancing of the budget and stabilization of the currency. Such as the matter of excessive government pensions, the corporation income tax, etc., the investigation of which would be the reason for his staff of statisticians, accountants and economists. And on these matters, he should report to the board, which would then, after due consideration, make its recommendations to Congress in the form suggested below. It is assumed for the purpose of this exposition that Congress could scarcely delegate to the board in advance the power to legislate on such matters, as this would presumably be held to be "delegation run riot," as in the case of Roosevelt's NRA.

In no case should any member of the board have his or her own staff economist or consultant, nor refer matters to an outside consultant, which would be fatally divisive. Instead, the board as a whole would have its own unified staff, appointed by the administrator of the agency, with all staff members working for a common purpose.

By the same token, no board member and no member of the agency staff should be chosen by or regarded as representing regional interests, or the interests of agriculture or labor or business or banking, nor racial minorities or sex or any other special or fractional interest. The problem is a national one, and can only be solved by people who have the national interest alone in mind.

Moratorium on spending

The law creating the board would define its powers and those of the appellate court and the Agency for the Investigation of Constitutional Limitations, at the same time establishing a six-month moratorium on all economic legislation and on all bills calling for the expenditure of monies unless approved by the board. It would be hoped that the board and agency could complete their main task within a three-month period, leaving only odds and ends to tidy up within the six-month deadline. Congress should likewise declare a six-month freeze on all new indebtedness of the federal government and of all agencies, except for the refunding of existing debt. And a six-month freeze on all increases in wages, salaries and dividends.

But *not* on interest rates or prices. Because, with the government and federal agencies removed from the borrowing market, interest rates of all kinds, whether on government or corporate bonds, home or business mortgages, or bank loans, would *immediately* start to drop, eventually reaching half to one third of the present levels. Making it possible for business to put out new stock and bond issues far in excess of 1977's $50 billion level, thus giving momentum to a drive for increased productivity which is the *sine qua non* of economic recovery. And making it possible for residential and commercial builders to borrow at reasonable interest rates, which would more than compensate for the temporary moratorium on borrowing by Fannie Mae and the other alphabetized government lending agencies.

And, provided that the dollar is stabilized at an appropriate level (see below), prices would either stabilize or start to decline because business and the general public would know at long last that effective action would soon be taken by the joint board to put a stop to the inflationary pressures. This has happened in every country that has dared to face and overcome a rampant inflation. (See Chapter 7.) So prices should definitely *not* be frozen.

Furthermore, even though this would mean a six-month moratorium on all spending and borrowing *legislation,* it would not bar immediate action by the executive branch to cut down on all domestic spending and drastically reduce overseas expenditures by all departments of the government. This would mean curbing foreign economic and military aid, cutting the nonessential expenditures in support of the half million American soldiers on foreign soil, and reducing the vastly overgrown embassy staffs in some 140 countries of the world, which could easily improve our balance of payments position—the drain on our gold and foreign exchange reserves—by $3 billion or more. *Immediately!*

And, finally, the law creating the joint board should permit the executive to defer for not over six months any items of expenditure by the government or federal agencies that, in the judgment of the joint board, can be postponed without detriment to the national economy. This power not to be subject to the anti-impoundment legislation.

A monetary stabilization program

Suppose that such a Joint Board on National Economic Policy were in fact created. How would it then commence its task of stabilizing the dollar, of putting an end to the present uninterrupted rise of prices?

Well, the board would have to procure the enactment of all or most of the measures set forth in the preceding chapter—a drastic remedy, but presumably the members would have agreed that surgery was required, not just a placebo. And presumably the status of the eight persons comprising the board—political figures of national stature and not just a council of economists known only to their fellows in university circles— would suffice to carry the weight of public opinion behind their decisions and, in the face of the worst crisis this nation has faced since 1932, the support of a majority in both Houses of Congress.

How these *politicians* on such a board would go about obtaining the support of the public and of Congress is not for me to suggest—I am not about to teach my grandmother to knit!

The "single package" and the "closed session"

One thing is paramount: *There should be no piecemeal enactment of anti-inflationary or economic recovery legislation.* The President, with the advice of the board, can take certain interim steps to relieve inflation, as has been indicated. But *Congress* should not be asked to pass any single anti-inflationary or antirecessionary bill except as a part of a complete indivisible stabilization and recovery package drawn up by the board. And this package of bills should be presented for congressional approval at the same time as the board—or the administrator of the Agency for the Investigation of Constitutional Limitations—promulgates the decision for the simultaneous abolition of all government agencies and activities determined to be in contravention of the Tenth Amendment or other provision of the Constitution.

In the first place, because no single measure or series of isolated measures can have any significant effect in stemming inflationary pressures and might even add to the nation's economic problems. And, in the second place, because any such measures, including particularly the abolition of unconstitutional agencies and activities, are bound to hurt someone, and the lobbies for the group or groups whose ox is gored would raise such unholy hell that the public, the press and the Congress would conclude—and quite rightly—that the board was bungling its job and creating chaos where previously there was only crisis.

Instead, a complete package of *all* the legislation required in a stabilization and recovery program should be prepared by the board *in closed sessions* and, when completed, presented to the Congress—and to the press and public—for enactment *en bloc.* A solution to the problem of "stagflation," not a stopgap—a surgical operation on the cancer of inflation and not a series of successive, ineffective and disagreeable drugs.

Closed sessions of both the board and the agency—with the agency administrator reporting to the board at all times—would be no more undemocratic than are the closed sessions of the justices of the Supreme Court, so long as the decisions of the agency are subject to judicial appeal, and so long as the bills drafted by the board are presented to Congress for public discussion and enactment. No more undemocratic than were the closed and super-secret meetings so effectively engineered by President Carter at Camp David where he managed to reconcile the otherwise irreconcilable views of such doughty antagonists as Menachem Begin and Anwar Sadat.

Our Constitution would never have been enacted if the delegates to the Constitutional Convention had not been sworn to absolute secrecy, so that no member felt constrained, as a matter of self-respect, to support to the bitter end some measure he had advocated in the course of public debate, and so that the various measures and compromises finally agreed upon would not have been torn apart and destroyed by partisan attacks in the thirteen states, either during the course of the debates in Convention or in the subsequent process of ratification. And not a single delegate to the Convention ever violated his oath, not even those delegates who refused to assent to the compromises reached in the final document.

At the close of the Convention, Benjamin Franklin, the venerable and venerated sage of the assembly, was called upon to address the presiding officer, George Washington, and his fellow delegates, which he did in these words:

> *I agree to this Constitution, with all its faults, if they are such. . . . The opinions I have had of its errors I sacrifice to the public good. I have never whispered a syllable of them abroad. Within these walls*

they were born, and here they shall die. If every one of us, in returning to our constituents, were to report the objections he has had to it, and endeavor to gain partisans in support of them, we might prevent its being generally received, and thereby lose all the salutary effects and great advantages resulting naturally in our favor among foreign nations, as well as among ourselves, from our real or apparent unanimity. . . . I hope, therefore, that for our own sakes, as a part of the people, and for the sake of posterity, we shall act heartily and unanimously in recommending this Constitution . . . wherever our influence may extend, and turn our future thoughts and endeavors to the means of having it well administered.

The meaning of floating rates

To go back to the Joint Board on National Economic Policy and the procedures that it would follow to ensure its success, how exactly would such a board go about stabilizing the dollar? Would they follow Professor Kemmerer's dictum that "the way to stabilize is to stabilize"? And hence fix the value of the dollar once and for all at so many grams of pure gold, making it once again the universal standard of value in international transactions? Or would they opt for floating rates?

Floating rates, it must be explained, have sometimes been used as a temporary expedient when a nation is uncertain what rate it should establish and can maintain. In Bolivia my own predilection was to follow Kemmerer's advice. I would indeed have liked to say that 5,000 bolivianos—or 6,000 or 8,000—were equal to one dollar. And the dollar then had a fixed gold equivalent.

I knew what rate we should establish—the price of tin and the wages demanded by the miners told me that. But neither I nor Dr. Costanzo and his colleagues whom the IMF had sent down to help me had the faintest idea what rate we could successfully maintain. Economically, it made no difference, at least in theory. But politically the establishment of a rate of exchange—and hence of wages and prices—that would be accepted by the public with a minimum amount of grumbling was of paramount importance.

The proper way to arrive at a viable rate of exchange—or a proper gold content of the unit of currency—is to make a thorough survey of the "parity rate of exchange," i.e., that rate of exchange which, if fixed, would place the country's price level at a parity with the rest of the world, in other words, a rate that would be *neutral* so far as encouraging or discouraging imports, exports, investments and the invisible components of the country's balance of payments. Neutral—because otherwise there would be the danger of starting a war of competitive devaluation, not in the case of

Bolivia, to be sure, but certainly in the case of a major trading nation such as the United States.

Conservatively, the expert stabilizer would take a pessimistic view of future world commodity demand and prices, make due allowance for factors unknown or imponderable—particularly the potential long and short-term movements of capital. And he would then fix the new value of the currency on the low side to discourage unnecessary imports or the further flight of capital, and conversely encourage the return of flight capital and investments from abroad—and, above all, to avoid the necessity of a second stabilization move at a later date which might shake public confidence beyond repair.

In Bolivia I had very much in mind the experience of Belgium in the mid-1930s, when they attempted to stabilize the franc at one rate, found they couldn't hold the line and were later forced to stabilize again at a less advantageous rate than they might have used the first time around.

With the experience the world has had since then, such floundering around would be the mark of the amateur, of persons whose memories do not extend back far enough, or embrace a sufficiently wide horizon, to read the lessons of history. Because those who don't read history are forced to repeat it.

An even worse folly is to announce a rate of exchange without having simultaneously taken those measures that are absolutely indispensable to maintain it. A viable rate of exchange cannot be fixed by fiat alone, no matter how determined the jut of the President's jaw when he makes the stabilization announcement.

The Nixon Administration was guilty of both errors when it raised the dollar price of gold in April 1971 and then had to raise it again in May 1972. And on neither occasion had it taken the steps that were essential to putting an immediate stop to the drain of foreign aid and continuing military outlays in Indonesia. Although it is true that the second devaluation was widely credited with having improved the American balance of payments in the latter half of 1973, this claim must be tempered by the fact that the position was reversed immediately in the first half of 1974, and that the only reason for the improved balance at the end of 1973 was the grain deal with Russia.

But in Bolivia it was impossible to determine what rate of exchange should be used. Statistics simply were not available, or were grossly unreliable. So we had no choice—the boliviano had to "find its own level." And what we did in Bolivia will help explain the mystery of "floating rates."

On the first day, we fixed the rate of exchange tentatively at 7,750 bolivianos to the dollar, but at the same time announced that it was a floating rate and that it would fluctuate up or down according to demand and supply, so the public would not later think we had blundered. Not pride—but to retain public confidence.

Each morning an exchange committee met at the Central Bank to determine the rate of exchange for the day's trading, being guided by the demand for bolivianos and the demand for dollars on the previous day— for the Central Bank stood ready to buy or sell as many dollars and as many bolivianos as the public wanted. If the boliviano were made too cheap, it would be inflationary, and if the dollar were made too cheap, it would encourage the flight of capital and our stabilization fund might be frittered away. From time to time, the committee did the unexpected in order to keep speculators constantly off balance and thus discourage speculation. And it worked splendidly for many months, becoming un-glued some fifteen months after I left Bolivia, when the Bolivian Gov-ernment had departed from the stabilization program just once too often; it was stuck together again with the help of an emergency crew from the IMF, and stabilized at the fixed rate of 11,000 bolivianos (or 11 new pesos) to the dollar, where it remained until, four revolutions later, it became unstuck again in the fall of 1972, and has since been held at 20 pesos to the dollar, despite the recent seventh military takeover.

The floating mark

That, briefly, is what a "floating" rate means and how it works, as in the case of Germany, where they revalued the mark in October 1969 to save the dollar from disaster. And then, in May 1971, they decided to "float" the mark temporarily to save their fellow members of the European Eco-nomic Community (the Common Market) from trouble, until they could determine what rate might best suit the interests of the EEC as a whole.

Neither of these actions nor the subsequent revaluations of the mark were a sign of "floundering around." They were taken because the continuing weakness of the dollar was endangering the stability of the whole world, and because Germany was doing its best to avoid worldwide disaster. Thus Germany revalued the mark upward again in December 1971, and yet again in June 1973 and October 1978, in spite of the fact that each upward revaluation made it more difficult for Germany to compete in the world market.

For one of the facts of life in international trade is that, if the mark goes up—if it takes more dollars and more pounds to buy 100 marks— then exports of German automobiles and other manufactured goods will drop. And so will tourist travel in Germany and other invisible exports. While, conversely, imports will increase—Germans can buy foreign goods more cheaply. So each German revaluation has hurt the German economy, but Germany was willing to make the sacrifice in the interest of world economic stability, knowing that a crash in the United States would carry down the whole world in its wake.

But can we then be indignant because the German Finance Minister at the international monetary conference in Nairobi in September 1973 was blunt enough to say that the main source of international inflation was the deficit in the United States balance of payments? Or because the European and Japanese representatives at that conference demanded full convertibility of dollars and gold? When it is clear that it is our own mismanagement of our financial affairs that, more than anything else, has upset the monetary balance of the world and produced the current worldwide inflation.

The permanent float

One more comment before we leave the subject of floating rates. There are some economists, particularly in the United States and England, who are such diehard antagonists of the gold standard that their pronouncements remind one of William Jennings Bryan:

> *If they dare to come out in the open field and defend the gold standard as a good thing, we will fight them to the uttermost... we will answer their demand for a gold standard by saying to them: You shall not press down upon the brow of labor this crown of thorns, you shall not crucify mankind upon a cross of gold.*

These latter-day boy orators from the river Platte violently attacked the pleas of French Finance Minister Valéry Giscard d'Estaing (now President of France) and West German Finance Minister Helmut Schmidt (now Chancellor) to do away with floating exchange rates, and characterized French and German insistence upon a worldwide return to the gold standard at the Nairobi conference of the IMF as "unrealistic," "nostalgic" and "emotional."

The opponents of the gold standard insist that there is no viable alternative to a currency float or rates so flexible as to amount to a float—ignoring the fact that in those countries that have adopted a currency float as a way of life, it would be more appropriate to call it a "sink" rather than a "float," for their currencies have inevitably continued to sink lower and lower in a sea of uncertainty. This despite the buoyant hopes of the spend-thrift governments which do not *want* their spending proclivities hampered by a fixed gold standard.

The former Secretary of the Treasury, Dr. George P. Schultz, whom the historian of the International Monetary Fund characterized as "the principal architect of the managed floating rate regime," stated in

March 1974 that he regarded the introduction of a system of floating rates as his greatest achievement. But it will be noted that the advocates of floating rates are all theorists; those with practical experience in foreign exchange are all in favor of fixed rates.

And *in theory* I must admit that I can find no reason to reject the arguments for freely floating rates of exchange so convincingly adumbrated by Professor Samuelson in his standard text on economics and by dozens of other academic economists before and since. But *in practice* floating rates have proved to be an unmitigated evil for reasons that it would take too long to enumerate and substantiate.

The chaos in international foreign exchange rates, and in international commodity prices, consequent upon floating or flexible—i.e., unstable—currencies, was responsible for the $40 million failure of the Union Bank of California branch in Switzerland, the $450 million collapse of the Bankhaus I.D. Herstatt of Cologne and three smaller German banks, the $37 million failure of the Franklin National Bank, the $50 million loss of Union Bank of Switzerland, the $40 million loss of the Bank of Brussels, the $75 million loss incurred by Lloyd's Bank, one of England's four largest banking institutions and the $6 billion loss of the Deutsche Bundesbank.

With floating and unstable currencies, banks and business corporations are *compelled* to hedge—to buy or sell raw materials and foreign exchange in advance—in order to avoid losses arising from future market fluctuations. Formerly, under a worldwide gold standard, fluctuations in foreign exchange rates were limited within the "gold points" to about one half of 1 percent on either side of par, while fluctuations in commodity prices were governed by supply and demand and were not wholly beyond the limits of prudent prognostication. And arbitrage operations in foreign exchange or commodity futures gave banks and businesses the protection they needed—not speculation, but insurance.

But with the no-limit risks imposed by floating currencies, there is no safe way to hedge these multimillion-dollar bank and business operations. A wrong guess can be fatal to the best-laid plans and there is always the temptation on the part of management to establish a good record by attempting to outguess the market. Or even to attempt to conceal previous losses in commodities or foreign exchange by buying futures in excess of prudent hedging requirements. I can cite one such case dating as far back as my experience as a banker in 1920–23!

It can be safely predicted that a continuance of the present international floating foreign exchange regime—the biggest "permanent floating crap game in the world"—will mean losses and bank failures in this country and abroad far greater than any that have taken place thus far in the present world crisis.

And you will remember that it was the failure of the Austrian Kredit Anstalt that triggered the worldwide crisis of 1931.

Moreover, contrary to the assertions of the advocates of permanently floating currencies, there *is* a viable alternative. The gold standard is *not* obsolete. West Germany, France, Japan—the three countries of the world whose economic progress over the past two decades has been most remarkable, with unemployment practically nil, balanced budgets and favorable balances of payments (except for the year of the petroleum crisis)—are all stout advocates of the gold standard. And Switzerland, with no voice at Nairobi, is and has been for over a century so staunch an adherent to the gold standard that its currency is the soundest in all the world and its banks a haven for flight capital from every country where a system of floating fiat currency prevails—including the United States, the United Kingdom, and the ninety-four other backward nations in the IMF.

France's temporary defection from the gold standard in January 1974 came as a consequence of the extreme pressure on its balance of payments and gold reserves resulting from the worldwide energy crisis and sharply higher petroleum prices. However, Giscard d'Estaing then announced that the franc would be allowed to float for only a six-month period—to sink would be a more apt description—following which a new fixed gold equivalent would be established.

Although the six months' grace expired, and it was not until January 1975 that France returned to a fixed gold equivalent for the franc, there was never any reason to doubt the sincerity of that pledge, considering France's historic and dedicated commitment to the gold standard—e.g., following Franklin Roosevelt's devaluation of the dollar, France continued to honor the gold clause on its national and municipal dollar bonds by paying them off at the rate of francs 25.52 to the dollar, equivalent at the time to approximately $1,690 for each $1,000 bond. While, at the same time, the United States Government voluntarily increased its Canal Zone annuity payments by approximately the same percentage, thus tacitly admitting that it had defrauded all its other creditors, domestic and foreign.

Stabilization policy for the United States
There is one other reason sometimes advanced for adopting a floating currency, aside from uncertainty as to just what rate is viable, and that is that some people believe that a floating rate helps to frustrate speculation which might jeopardize the early difficult stages of monetary stabilization.

I do not share that belief. In my experience, a floating, uncertain rate encourages speculation, while a fixed rate deters it, provided that the fixed rate is a proper one and the government has taken those measures necessary to maintain it. Not just a blustering declaration of its determination, or the threat of dire punishment for violators of the law, but the actual elimination of those conditions that made for instability in the first place.

Now, to get back to the United States, would our hypothetical Joint Board on National Economic Policy decide to revalue the dollar once and for all, or would it opt for a floating dollar? It would be hoped that they would adopt the first alternative.

In this country, provided the measures advocated in Chapter 14 are enacted, there should be little problem in determining the parity rate of exchange. Our statistics are copious, and as reliable as those of any country of the world. The Joint Board might well ask the Fed, the IMF and their own staff of agency economists to make separate estimates of the parity rate—for consideration not decision—and then make their own final decision on the conservative or pessimistic side.

The level arrived at would probably be somewhere between the present official rate of $42.2222 an ounce and the topmost world-market gold price of $282 an ounce. The rate chosen would depend upon how much longer this government continues its present policies of deficit spending at home and abroad.

It would, of course, be less humiliating to settle on a rate as close to $42.2222 as possible, meaning the least possible devaluation of the dollar. But humiliation and pride are factors that must not be allowed to enter into the equation, as we know from the sad example of England when she tried in vain to reestablish the historic $4.8665 value for the pound. The $42.2222 level would also be the most desirable from the viewpoint of inflation; in fact, at that rate, prices would start to tumble almost immediately because such a rate would mean the *revaluation* of the dollar to the levels of six or seven years ago. And therein lies the danger. Deflation of prices would be a boon to the aged and retired, but it would wreak havoc with the economy in general and almost inevitably lead to unemployment and another crisis that would prove even harder to arrest than the present one.

Stabilization at a value of $282 an ounce for gold, on the other hand, would mean *devaluation* of the dollar to less than one-tenth the pre-Roosevelt level, and almost certainly to a continuation of the present rise in prices, although at an attentuated rate and for a limited period. Politically, such an extreme devaluation would be easy to maintain because, although it would work an injustice to the elderly, the retired and investors in bonds and mortgages, it would have an overexpansionary effect on production, employment and the economy in general. But, as it would not put an immediate stop to inflation, it could be politically counterproductive.

And, even more important, it would mean such an excessive devaluation of the dollar that it would almost certainly result in a competitive devaluation of sterling, marks, francs, yen and other currencies that could lead to bitter confrontation and economic warfare.

The ideal, then, would be a dollar stabilized perhaps at a gold value of somewhere between $100 and $150 an ounce—or say a foreign exchange value which makes the dollar equivalent to 2 German marks or to 2 Swiss francs or 200 Japanese yen—arrived at in informal consultation between representatives of the joint board and the central banks or Finance Ministries of England, France, Germany, Japan and Switzerland. Stabilization accomplished in that manner would have a salutary effect on all the world's currencies and, in the United States, would result in the instantaneous "miracle" of stabilization, with ultimate price trends and the extent of long-term economic progress dependent largely upon how well the Joint Board on National Economic Policy accomplishes its task.

Above all, the establishment of a gold or foreign exchange value for the dollar must not be a matter of feeding statistics into a computer and coming out with a mathematically exact answer, for there are unknown and imponderable factors in the world economy that cannot be computerized and cannot be ignored. Wisdom dictates the use of the most thorough statistical analysis possible as a starting point, but the ultimate decision must be based on policy, judgment and experience.

The stabilization of the dollar

If and when the United States decides to fix a permanent and sustainable gold value for the dollar, it will call for the utmost prudence and tact on the part of the Secretaries of State and Treasury and the chairman of the Federal Reserve Board. For a dollar rate that is fixed unilaterally, and suddenly sprung upon a startled world, might have unfortunate repercussions in other nations and could lead to a series of competitive devaluations that might be as disastrous as the present uncertainties surrounding the dollar.

But the fact that the present inflation is worldwide, that prices for the internationally traded commodities are determined in world markets, and that these prices are fixed in gold equivalents, does not mean that the United States is powerless to stabilize the value of its own currency by unilateral action—by balancing its budget, returning to the gold standard and reducing government expenditures abroad to the point where gold and foreign exchange start flowing into this country again instead of away from it. In fact, such action would be certain to bring down the dollar price of gold and of other internationally traded commodities, *and would help to relieve the worldwide inflationary pressures for which the deficits in the American and British balances of payments have been primarily responsible.*

And to claim that the United States cannot be responsible for inflation because the phenomenon is worldwide is like Mrs. O'Leary claiming that her cow could not have been responsible for the Great Fire of 1871 because, not only her barn but all the other houses in Chicago were ablaze. (Mrs. O'Leary's cow may be apocryphal, but it's an apt story.)

Consequences of monetary stabilization here

If and when dollar stabilization in terms of gold—and eventually, it is hoped, in terms of the other major currencies—is brought about, one dividend that can be counted upon with a fixed rate of exchange, and which would not materialize with a floating rate, is a homeward flight of the $30 billion or so of American-owned flight capital abroad reported in the balance of payments as "errors and omissions," and perhaps some $10 to $15 billion of unremitted balances available to the multinational companies.

Such a return flight of capital, following a successful stabilization, is as certain as the homeward flight of the swallows of San Juan Capistrano. It has occurred in *every* country that has ever witnessed the "miracle of stabilization"—even for a brief while in Bolivia, where, Lord knows, there was precious little incentive for capital to return.

Our present ills arise from the fact that our government has become a warfare and welfare state (79 percent of its expenditures and over 90 percent of its indebtedness are attributable to those functions, including interest on indebtedness for past wars). And the fact that the present major business of the Federal Reserve System is to finance those functions (over 95 percent of its loans are to the federal government and agencies). The remedy therefore is to get the Fed back into its proper business of financing the banking system so that the banks in turn can finance the nation's agriculture, trade, industry and construction, and make the government one that meets Jefferson's ideal: "A wise and frugal government which shall restrain men from injuring one another [and] which shall leave them otherwise free to regulate their own pursuits." Not a panacea—a cure-all—but a sure and tested remedy for inflation.

A remedy that will ensure a new era of prosperity, a new era of cooperation between the President and the Congress, with no sacrifice of the independence of either branch of government.

Meanwhile, until a complete and indivisible stabilization package can be drawn up and enacted, any steps to ameliorate through welfare the situation of those most affected by inflation and recession can only aggravate the underlying causes of both, thus prolonging and intensifying the agony, and serving to discredit the administration in the minds of the public.

17. How Can You Protect Yourself ?

Put not your trust in money, but put your money in trust.
Oliver Wendell Holmes (1858)

Suppose the administration fails to follow Jefferson's precept, and that we drift even closer to the concept of a totalitarian welfare state. What can you, the individual reader, do to protect yourself from the consequences of continued and unbridled inflation? Not much, I'm afraid.

Should you borrow?

It is true that in the case of the first German inflation, the trillion to one affair, one man, Hugo Stinnes, did emerge from the holocaust the richest man in all Germany. He probably could not have foreseen the extremities to which the inflation was ultimately carried but, so long as the value of the mark continued to decline, he pursued a consistent policy of incurring more and more indebtedness on an ever-escalating scale, and his courage and foresight paid off to an extraordinary degree.

He had started out as the controlling shareholder of a small mining and shipping company in the Rhine-Ruhr Valley. As he saw the value of the mark decline—and this took vision, for most of his compatriots never thought of the mark as declining, but of prices as rising—he decided to have his companies buy out other companies that, like his own, were making millions in marks—and losing their shirts.

And to accomplish this, his companies borrowed from the banks as heavily as they could. He kept the process up, with either his original companies or his acquired companies buying up more and more of the mines and industries of the Rhine-Ruhr Valley, borrowing millions and then billions and trillions of marks from the banks which, by then, he also controlled.

At the end he found himself the owner of a substantial part of that normally prosperous region of Germany. His entire debt to the banks didn't amount to a row of beans—and a very small row at that. *A trillion to one!*

But not many people are in a position to emulate Herr Stinnes' accomplishment. Or would have the courage and ability to carry it through to a successful conclusion. Suppose you *did* borrow to the maximum possible extent, whether as an individual or as the owner of some corporate enterprise. And suppose that things did not go as you anticipated. What then? Could you pay your debts? Would you have the nerve to continue borrowing—the sky's the limit? I wouldn't, I know.

Of course, we can say as a general rule that, in times of inflation, one should borrow. In March 1933 I borrowed all I could on my insurance, invested it in the stock market on margin and did quite well. But interest rates today are so high. And is the stock market safe? Can we afford to take the chance? I can only warn that borrowing on stocks, bonds or commodities is risky, and best left to professionals. But, I might add, don't be in any hurry *to pay* off your mortgage. Some years hence, you can pay it off much cheaper—or for practically nothing.

Bonds, life insurance, savings accounts
Anyone can tell you that, in time of inflation, you should not buy bonds, preferred stock or life insurance, or put your money in a savings account. Your dollars will be worth less and less, you know. But suppose the inflation comes to an end? And interest rates are so high now that maybe putting our money out at interest, at least as a stopgap, could be the best investment we could possibly make, particularly in Treasury bills or Certificates of Deposit. And life insurance and savings accounts are essential.

Furthermore, there are some AAA and AA bonds selling at a substantial discount from par because they pay 3 to 8 percent interest on face value instead of today's higher rates. And, by buying at present discount prices, you can get 9 percent on your money, plus the possibility of capital gain. Interest rates cannot possibly remain forever at current levels. Or can they?

Not if the President and Congress balance the budget and the government stops borrowing. Then interest rates will drop and the bonds bought at a discount will give us substantial capital gains. We can be absolutely sure of that—*if!*

And certain other bonds are convertible into common stock at a fixed conversion rate—a two-way hedge. If the inflation continues, the common stock—provided your investment is well chosen—should go up in value, and your bonds will too because they are convertible. If, on the other hand, the inflation ends, then interest rates will drop and the bonds will rise in price on their own steam. And, as good times return with the end of inflation, both the stock and the bonds will go up. Meanwhile, you will be getting a better return on your convertibles than if you had put your money directly into stock—and safer, too. You can't lose. Or can you?

I may say that I have put some of my money into convertibles and, until recently, into high-return tax-exempt bonds? Tax-exempts? When I advocate doing away with tax exemptions. Yes—again a two-way hedge. What's good for the U.S.A. is good for G.J.E. And unless tax exemptions are ended, which I believe would be good for the U.S.A., I stood to get a good return on my money.

After the California tax "revolt," however, I disposed of my state and municipal bonds—not that I had qualms as to California's solvency, but that I feared the tax revolt might spread. And, in fact, it has spread: In the November 1978 referenda, voters in six states voted to limit state or local taxes, while in six other states voters placed a limit on state expenditures. If any one of the states or cities should default because of tax limitations, it could wreak havoc in the tax-exempt market. So I put the proceeds into AAA and AA bonds giving a yield of 9 percent or more. Which may or may not prove to have been a good idea, but at my time of life I invest for current income and safety.

For many investors, however, particularly those in the highest brackets and willing to run the double risk of a California-style tax rebellion and the populist demand to "close the loopholes," tax-exempt bonds do offer an amazingly high return. The "general obligations," pledging the "full faith and credit" of the state or municipality, not the more risky "revenue bonds" dependent on the revenues of some particular bridge, toll highway, etc. A 6 percent tax-exempt bond gives a net return equivalent to a taxable income of 12 percent to anyone in the 50 percent tax bracket, i.e., having a taxable income of $44,000–$52,000 on a joint return. For someone in the $100,000–$120,000 bracket, 6 percent tax-free is equivalent to a taxable return of 15.79 percent. And so on—your broker can provide a table showing the equivalents in your particular tax bracket. But I do not recommend state and municipal bonds for those in less than a $50,000 bracket; they are too hard to sell, meaning that they may have to be sold at two points or more below the current bid-and-asked prices, and should be bought only for long-term investment where there is no likelihood of "emergencies."

Foreign investments available in the United States
Early in 1972, worried about Nixon's economic policies, I purchased South African gold mining stocks as a hedge against dollar debasement. I

didn't send my money abroad, though, because you can buy on the New York Stock Exchange a wide variety of "American Depositary Receipts" covering German, Dutch, English and Japanese industrials and public utilities, South African gold mines, etc. These are receipts issued by New York banks for foreign stocks they hold in their possession for account of American investors. When you buy these, no money is sent abroad; there has never been any 16 percent surcharge on the foreign income; you are buying from another American investor and not sending a penny to the South African companies, if you have any qualms on the subject.

These stocks are then a hedge against future dollar debasement—if the rest of the world does not collapse with us. After all, it is a hedge—not a steel wire fence. And I must admit that I disposed of my gold mine shares in July 1974 at a substantial profit—precisely at the time that various brokers started recommending them to their clients. My fear was that their 100 percent rise in price had been exaggerated by speculation—the stocks were then selling at a higher price than the value of all their known gold reserves, yet unmined, at the then current price of gold. It is true that I again purchased these shares, as well as some Canadian gold mine shares, in December 1976, motivated by well-grounded fears of worse inflation in the United States.

The Democratic platform called for expenditures of $1.5 *trillion.* And, although political platforms are meant to run on, and not to build on, I was afraid that the pressure groups that had procured the President's election might compel him to fulfill at least a part of his promises.

At the same time, I added substantially to my holdings of bonds payable in Swiss francs that I had originally bought after President Nixon's first devaluation of the dollar. These bonds have done handsomely, not because the Swiss franc has appreciated in value, as most financial writers report, but because of the continued debasement of the dollar, particularly since January 1977.

Since then, the continued flow of flight capital into Switzerland, together with wise management of Swiss domestic affairs, has caused bond interest rates there to drop from close to 6 percent to less than 4 percent. So bond prices have risen in francs as well as in dollars, with the risk of certain bonds being called for redemption if selling above their call prices.

The bonds in question are the obligations of high-rated borrowers: Dupont, Dow, Sears, Philips, the World Bank, Oslo, Japan, etc. They are free of Swiss tax, but American citizens and residents must, of course, pay U.S. tax on income from them or from any other foreign investments.

But, in February 1978, the Swiss Government concluded that

their internal economy was threatened by the inward flow of flight capital, particularly from Italy, Latin America and the United States, and the Swiss banks and brokers were prohibited from accepting any additional investments in such bonds. The Swiss simply did not want any more dollars—and can you blame them? The embargo was lifted in January 1979, and the Swiss market is once again open to foreign investors.

Even prior to that, it was still possible—legally—to purchase and hold Swiss franc bonds outside of Switzerland, and banks and brokers in West Germany, the Netherlands or Belgium can handle these transactions, charging brokerage and custodial fees. But it would not normally be practical to make these arrangements for investments of less than $500,000, certainly not for less than $100,000. There are several brokerage houses and at least two New York trust companies that have a splendid record of investment in foreign currency securities for their clients and which can help you in such operations.

A word to the wise: Be sure before you act that you are dealing with an absolutely reliable firm and that you report your holdings on Treasury Form 90-22.1 and pay U.S. tax on all income and taxable gains. And don't let any smart consultant tell you how you can evade the U.S. tax. Tax avoidance is permissible; tax evasion is not.

In sum, the very highest grade bonds, payable in Swiss francs, are, in my opinion, not just "as good as gold," but better, for they provide a modest interest yield instead of calling for storage and insurance charges as in the case of hoarding actual gold. Not that the Swiss franc today is actually on the gold standard. No country is able to provide that security today, with the British pound and the American dollar—the two major currencies in international trade—so uncertain in their fluctuations. But the Swiss franc, like the German mark, does have an official gold equivalent and, of those two currencies, the Swiss franc has an unbeatable track record. On the other hand, Swiss francs have risen so high over the past two years in terms of other currencies that the German mark is probably a better investment medium at this time.

But remember that the United California Bank and their coinvestors—knowledgeable and honorable people by any criterion—lost $40 million in Switzerland of all places. In commodity speculation, however, not in Swiss franc securities.

Common stocks

Traditionally the conventional hedge against inflation is an investment in common stocks. And, of course, one is normally well advised to avoid public utilities, which always have difficulties—or at best a time lag—in getting rate increases commensurate with the increased cost of doing business. On the other hand, utility stocks and bonds have dropped to such low levels that selected purchases of AAA utilities might be advantageous. I have recently made investments in utility bonds, not stocks—operating companies, not holding companies.

In general, it is a truism that investments in mining companies whose assets consist largely of ore reserves afford a logical hedge against rising prices. More speculatively, mines that hitherto have been marginal or submarginal often prove profitable as metal prices rise, and the leverage in such stocks can be tremendous. But inflation has been so long-lasting that many of these stocks have risen sky-high and are no longer attractive. You must consult your broker for a selection of stocks in this and other industries that are likely to benefit from continued inflation.

The 1929 crash and the present dangers

Remember that the risk of loss is always as great as that of gain. There might even be a total collapse of the stock market such as occurred in 1929.

In 1929 the Achilles' heel of the market was the fact that most of the stocks actively traded on the New York and other stock exchanges were held on margin. In any well-established corporation, the majority of shareholders are long-term investors. They hold their stocks through thick and thin for the sake of the dividends, perhaps hoping for sufficient price appreciation over the long term to compensate for the gradual loss in the purchasing power of the dollar. These shares do not generally come on the market, save at long intervals of time.

For example, in the case of AT&T, the bluest of blue-chip securities, there are over 647 million shares outstanding, and on the average trading day in 1977 some 100,000 shares were bought and sold—less than one fortieth of 1 percent, say ⅛ percent in a week of trading. And even the most speculative stock of those traded on the Big Board will rarely have more than 2 percent of its shares traded in any one week, save under extraordinary circumstances. For example, in the most active trading month of 1978, 895 million shares changed hands on the New York Stock Exchange, out of 27 billion shares listed—3.3 percent, or 2.9 percent by value.

Yet it is that small minority of shares that is constantly bought and sold back and forth by the in-and-out speculators that makes the market, that sets the price for all the shares of the company whether held for speculation or investment. And the line between the two is by no means clear. In these days, any investment is a speculation.

Well, in 1929, practically every actively traded share—that small minority of the total outstanding shares of the listed companies—was held on margins ranging for the most part from 10 to 20 percent. For an investment of $1,000 one could buy $10,000 of stock, thus multiplying tenfold the potential profits. And from 1926 through most of 1929, there seemed to be no limit to the profit potentialities as thousands of people rushed into the market, sending stock prices to absurd levels, many times the level that could be justified by any conceivable dividend returns.

So, when the crash came, when it became clear that market prices bore no relationship to real values supportable by either assets or dividends, prices tumbled even more vertiginously than they had risen. Brokers frantically called for further deposits on margin accounts, and, when their customers could not supply additional margin, their stocks were dumped on a market where practically everyone wanted to sell and practically no one wanted to buy. *And the entire movement, up and down, was the consequence of sales and purchases of an infinitesimal percentage of the total outstanding shares of the companies involved.* The rest is history. And it was the undue expansion of credit—the margin account—that was chiefly responsible for the irrational rise of stock market prices and their equally irrational fall.

In 1979, margin accounts are restricted to a more sensible level—50 percent. But there are many who are worried by the $12 billion of borrowings against securities, and question the wisdom of even that more moderate incentive to speculation. And there are three other potential Achilles' heels in the stock market today that were not present in 1929, *and that might lead to a crash that could rival the 1929 disaster:*

1. The greater part of the actively traded shares—the shares that determine the market price for all shares whether traded or not—are held by institutional investors, including mutual funds, pension funds and trust accounts. These are not in-and-out traders but investors in the true sense of the word. Yet the size of these institutional investments is so great and their investments so concentrated among the blue-chip issues that when any one of these major investors decides to dispose of its holdings in any one particular issue, the sale is enough to shake the market. And the consequences tend to snowball. A sharp drop in any blue-chip stock weakens confidence in the market as a whole; investors in mutual funds start to panic and decide to cash in on their holdings; the funds are then forced to sell more of their investments to provide the cash for their investors; and this weakens the market still further. This state of affairs remains a sword of Damocles perilously suspended over the present market.

2. Over the past twenty years big business in the United States

has become increasingly concentrated in fewer and fewer corporations and this concentration has largely taken place in the form of conglomerates— vast enterprises whose activities are not confined to any one line of business or even to several related lines, but are spread out over an enormous spectrum of totally unrelated businesses covering practically the entire gamut of profit-making operations in this country and abroad. The danger is not bigness *per se,* for big enterprise is requisite for long-term planning and technological improvement, which are the bases of progress and prosperity in this country. Nor is the danger that of the "multinational corporation" *per se,* for in many cases international operations are the very essence of the enterprise, and the multinational company serves to bring progress and prosperity to every country where it is established, including the country of origin. But the modern conglomerate achieves its expansion, not so much by reason of inward growth, but by mergers which it accomplishes by trading its own stock for that of the companies it acquires—an endless pyramiding of values—and by accounting practices which, while not illicit, exaggerate the apparent earnings of the consolidated structure, thus pushing up the market price of stock in the conglomerate which in turn enables it to make continuing acquisitions on favorable terms. The danger is that, while these accounting subtleties work very well over a period of continuing expansion, and so long as there are accumulated capital gains which can be reported as income to produce an apparent constant rise in annual earnings, the process has not been tested over a period of severe adversity. And a crash in the case of any one of the major conglomerates could well trigger a disastrous reaction throughout the entire stock market. This is quite aside from the danger inherent in the difficulty of finding any one man capable of managing so diversified a range of enterprises as is comprised in the typical conglomerate. And retirement or death of the financial genius who formed or expanded the conglomerate might well mean the demise of the conglomerate itself.

3. The most perilous Achilles' heel in the present situation is the vanishing dollar *and the measures taken to counteract its effects without eliminating the cause.* Particularly the drastic increase in interest rates which is in part attributable to the Federal Reserve Board, but chiefly to the continuing sale of government bonds and notes to finance continuing deficits, and to the insatiable demand for working capital and credit which is an inescapable consequence of inflation. The solvency, and even the continued corporate existence, *of every public utility in the country* is gravely threatened by the increased cost of borrowed money, by the inflationary rise in operating and new plant costs, by the consequent

inadequacy of depreciation accruals and reserves, and by the politically motivated failure of state and federal public service commissions to grant timely and adequate rate relief. The bankruptcy of any major public utility—its failure to meet interest *or amortization* on its bonds—would send a shock wave throughout the investment community that might well rival in its consequences the 1929–32 crash, with a catastrophic repercussion on the entire economy of the country.

But if the further debasement of the dollar is avoided by timely adoption of the measures set forth in Chapters 15 and 16, then none of these perils presents any danger that cannot be met by market forces and by minor changes in our antitrust and securities and exchange regulations.

This recital of potential risks makes it clear that investment in common stocks may not prove a foolproof solution to one's private investment problems. On the other hand, if the dangers of the vanishing dollar are overcome, this may be the ideal time to initiate a long-term program of investment in common shares.

Consider that if the oil-producing Arab states were to invest in the New York Stock Exchange even a small fraction of their extraordinary revenues resulting from recent increases in the price of oil, it could mean the injection of billions of dollars a year of new money into the marketplace. In 1975 new foreign investments in the United States totaled $10.1 billion, in 1976 $31.8 billion, in 1977 $44.4 billion, and in 1978 $33.8 billion (est.). And this represents only what has been reported by the banks; it does not include real estate or direct investments and covers only a small part of the investment in securities.

Net new foreign investments in securities (stocks and bonds) amounted to $6.9 billion in 1977, $4.9 billion in 1978; of these amounts, $3.1 billion and $1.6 billion respectively represented purchases by the OPEC countries. With higher oil prices in 1979, this figure may increase enormously.

Even where the Arabs do not invest directly in American stocks and bonds, their investment in other countries, and in American real estate, Treasury bonds and other investment media should release a commensurate supply of other available capital which can then be expected to flow into American security markets. It is true that the Arab states are now engulfed in a wave of speculative expansion at home which has lifted their imports from $33 billion in 1974 to an estimated $99 billion in 1978, and hence decreased the available surpluses in current account in their balance of payments from $62 billion to an estimated $18 billion. But 1979 should show a different picture and, taking OPEC and other foreign investment together, some $10 to $15 billion a year may well flow into

American security markets, which could pave the way for the greatest bull market since 1933.

Warning: This is not a prediction, and most stock market analysts are forecasting a recession in 1979. But, for the long term and with the possibility of a substantial flow of foreign investment into this country, and bearing in mind the relatively high dividend returns and certainly the extremely high current interest rates, investors may wish to consider a long-term program of either direct investment in common stocks or convertible bonds, or in the mutual funds discussed in the following paragraphs.

Mutual funds

There are a number of "closed-end" funds traded on the New York Stock Exchange. Your broker can advise you which these are and which ones he recommends. The closed-end funds are bought and sold on the market at whatever price may be fixed by supply and demand, free of any loading charges—just your broker's normal commission.

The closed-end company has several advantages over the usual mutual fund: (1) Because it does not have to redeem its shares, it is not forced to keep a large amount of cash on hand, uninvested; (2) as it is never confronted with the problem of redemption of its own stock, it can invest in small but well-run companies whose stock may not be as quickly salable as that of the large corporations which, in general, pay lower dividends and are vulnerable to strong selling pressures whenever the demand for mutual fund redemptions exceeds the purchase of new stock in the mutual funds which are compelled to concentrate their investments in a limited range of large corporations for the sake of liquidity.

And these closed-end funds are now selling at substantial discounts from the aggregate market value of the securities which they hold in their portfolios. So you are not only buying securities at a bargain price— 15 to 35 percent less than you would pay if you were to buy the underlying stocks themselves—but the income on your investment will hence be commensurately higher than if you invested the same amount of money in the underlying stocks or in the usual mutual funds.

I have several of these closed-end funds in my portfolio, believing that the managers of these funds are better able than I to make a wise selection of stocks. Then, too, I have an instinctive, perhaps nonrational prejudice against buying mutual funds from the mutual fund promoters, the same as I have an instinct against buying real property from the development companies that send me all those attractive folders in the mail, sometimes addressed to me personally as "Resident." I may be missing some wonderful opportunities, but that is my way of looking at it.

Real estate

You can also hedge against inflation by buying real estate—a marvelous hedge if you happen to buy a property for $10,000 that you can later sell for $100,000. We are always hearing of the multimillionaires who made their fortunes in land—perhaps a farm inherited from Great-Great-Grand-pappy in the heart of New York City. And there are millions of us who hope that we, too, may hit the jackpot.

But the average net return on real estate *after taxes* is not as high as you might think—less than 5 percent over the years. *Average*, you know—not the big deal that people are willing to talk to you about. You could buy a clinker, you know. If you are a New Yorker, your mind may turn to the marvelous opportunities there have been in Manhattan real estate over the past thirty years or more—say on the East Side from Fiftieth Street to Seventieth and all the way over to the East River. But you may remember, too, the once proud properties on Riverside Drive and Central Park West and their now faded glories. And the shopping center of the city has moved uptown from Ninth Street to Fourteenth, then to Eighteenth and Twenty-third, then to Herald Square at Thirty-fourth, then up to Forty-second, and now to anywhere between Forty-eighth and Fifty-seventh streets on Fifth and Madison avenues.

And in each area that has been successively abandoned by the fine shops—say down at the old John Wanamaker store (formerly A. T. Stewart) on Ninth Street—real estate values are now either stagnant or actually lower than they were when those areas were in their heyday.

And, in Washington, real estate has been an even more precarious venture. Properties in Georgetown and the slums of Foggy Bottom have skyrocketed in value, while upper Sixteenth Street, once the *crème de la crème* of neighborhoods, is now a place where your neighbors may be hoods, and values have plummeted to a fraction of their former worth.

In 1973, Aluminum Company of America reported losses of $7.4 million in their real estate transactions, while International Telephone and Telegraph Corporation wrote off a loss of $35.4 million in such operations. In all, between 1968 and 1975, ITT lost $400 million in its Levitt & Sons real estate subsidiary.

While, in 1978, the nation's largest REIT (real estate investment trust), the Chase Manhattan Mortgage and Realty Trust, defaulted on $38 million of its notes and filed a petition in bankruptcy in February 1979. This was a highly responsible firm—no question of fly-by-night promoters—but it lost heavily in a rent complex in Puerto Rico, a shopping mall on Staten Island (New York City), and in Florida condominiums. And high interest rates—thank you, Federal Reserve and Uncle Sam—proved its downfall.

So unless you know that you are much smarter than the managements of ITT, Alcoa and Chase Manhattan, perhaps the only real property you should buy is a little plot about six foot by two, which will eventually come in handy.

That is said with tongue in cheek. The best investment one can make in times of inflation is in real estate, particularly in vacation, rural, urban, suburban or exurban property for one's own use and long-term enjoyment and profit. But, if you buy from a developer, no matter how enticing his brochures and free trips to Dreamland may be, the profits may be his, not yours.

And, if you have a really keen business sense and know the ropes, there are profits to be made in purchasing income-producing real estate with borrowed money. There are also those who have made fortunes in public housing; in fact, the facilities offered by the Department of Housing and Urban Development have been turned into a racket by certain investment and construction concerns, generally those with good political connections. And for those in the upper tax brackets, because of the peculiar acounting principles espoused by HUD and the IRS, even a loss in a public housing development can be turned into a tax-saving which may be double the amount of the "loss."

But the pitfalls of income-producing and public housing realty speculation are many, and the risks and headaches are commensurate with the possibilities of gain. Beware of those who tell you otherwise.

Miscellaneous investment shelters

The most widely touted hedge against inflation at the present time is gold, and there is no doubt that gold bars—not the tiny jewel-like slivers promoted by private mints and foreign exchange dealers, but real gold bars of approximately 12,500 grams weight (27.6 pounds)—are a solid hedge. And, to a certain extent, so are gold coins—to the extent that present prices represent true gold content or a true, permanent numismatic interest, and not just an inflated value, boosted by speculators, that may prove transitory. The gold Krugerrands can be purchased at only a moderate premium over the spot price of gold. Canada, too, is planning to mint $50 gold coins to be sold on their gold content basis. And, beginning in 1980, gold medallions, 900 fine, and weighing an ounce or half an ounce, are scheduled to be minted by the U. S. Treasury, honoring such personalities as Marian Anderson, Louis Armstrong, Willa Cather and Alexander Calder; these, too, are to be sold at only a modest premium and are hence a safe small-scale investment.

The same can hardly be said of the medallions that recent Treasury Secretaries, including William E. Simon and W. Michael Blumenthal, have had struck by the United States mint in their own honor. And beware of any private mint that advertises gold medals, ostensibly at bargain prices, but which turn out to be only ten-karat gold, in other words, less than 420 fine (i.e., 42 percent gold, 58 percent base metal).

Some experts prefer silver to gold as a hedge while, for my part, I consider that platinum is the most undervalued of all the precious metals in comparison with its long-term price and present uses. I used to import and sell platinum precipitates from Colombia some fifty years ago.

But if you buy and keep metal bars in your own vault, they will have to be resmelted and assayed when you want to sell them, as it is all too easy for crooks to smelt and adulterate a goldbrick, or hollow it out and fill it with lead, or play any of the other tricks that goldbrickers have been playing for centuries. And if you store them in a bank or other depository, or deal in warehouse certificates, you must pay a fee instead of getting interest on your investment.

It seems to me that the best way to invest in the precious metals is to deal in commodity futures and, if I had the gambling instinct, I would buy platinum futures today. But I shall confess that the only time I ever dealt in commodity futures—a short sale in sugar—I lost my shirt, and the only other time I was tempted to sell short, but fortunately refrained, was in coffee. Yet I was a coffee dealer and expert for years, and my family has been in the sugar business for over a century. So I could be wrong on platinum, too. (This was written on November 17, 1978, when platinum futures were quoted at $302 per ounce on a 50-ounce contract, and readers who are interested may check on whether I hit the nail on the head or vice versa; I do not care to stake my money or my reputation on the vagaries of the market.)

Which brings us to diamonds, which have certainly risen spectacularly over the past five years or more. So much so that Tiffany's has published advertisements warning that, in their opinion, diamonds are grossly overpriced as a result of speculation, and they are refusing to purchase any more. Which may merely mean that, while they undoubtedly do know diamonds, they do not know money and fail to realize that diamond prices have not really risen but that dollars are only worth a fraction of what they used to be worth. It also means that, if you buy diamonds from their old stock at prespeculative prices, Tiffany's is a reliable place to shop. The best investment I ever made was 1.37-karat diamond purchased over fifty years ago.

But remember that retail diamond prices are roughly double the wholesale price, and that you are looking for trouble if you think someone "can get it for you wholesale." You have only to walk down Forty-seventh Street between Fifth and Sixth avenues and watch the sharp-eyed dealers in New York's diamond center to know that no layman can hope to bargain successfully with those professsionals. Or with their counterparts anywhere else in the country. For investment, only the finest gems of at least one karat and over are appropriate, and anyone other than an expert who buys such gems from any but the most trustworthy jeweler or diamond broker is foolish. Quite aside from the fact that the wholesale price of diamonds is controlled by the most successful permanent monopoly in the world, which makes speculation doubly hazardous for the layman. Alternatively, one may purchase American Depositary Receipts for De Beers Consolidated Mines, Ltd., the worldwide diamond quasi-monopoly, but the risks are so difficult to appraise that this must be regarded as a speculation rather than as a hedge against inflation.

And the same risks are present in the case of works of art, antiques and so forth. Antiques are undoubtedly a good investment—they're not making them anymore. Although there are some fakes that have fooled even the most famous museums in the world. And art is a speculation. I can recall a Meissonier being auctioned off in Paris in 1931 or 1932 for $75 whereas, a decade earlier, Meissonier was one of the most highly regarded painters whose pictures hung in the Metropolitan, the Louvre, etc. And I have in front of me, as I write, a picture by a catalogued student of Corot which I bought for a pittance at the sale of the William Randolph Hearst collection, for which Hearst had paid thousands. At the other extreme, the *kitsch* of eighty years ago, late Victorian furniture and the simply awful, factory-produced sculptures, prints, shell-encrusted boxes, toys—the kind of things one used to throw rings at in the Coney Island amusement park—are now worth hundreds of dollars.

So, while antiques are a good investment, particularly good quality antique furniture, first editions, sixteenth- and seventeenth-century atlases, etc., the purchase of antiques or of art *as an investment* is highly speculative. The best rule is to buy what you like for the pleasure of owning it and, if your taste happens to be corroborated by the judgment of others, you will find you have made a good investment financially as well as in the satisfaction of ownership and daily contemplation. Modern furniture is just secondhand furniture the day after it is bought, while antique furniture may continue to appreciate in value.

But try not to buy anything while it is at the height of fashion, for fashions change. For example, Picasso died some two years ago, leaving an estate valued by dealers at more than $1 billion, and by the tax collector at $240 million. But the bulk of the estate consisted of 1,885 of his paintings, 3,222 of his ceramics, 1,200 sculptures, 7,000 drawings, and 30,000 engravings, etchings, lithographs and tapestries. Can anyone doubt that if this volume of art is ever placed on the market, particularly if public taste veers away from abstract art, his paintings, engravings, etc., will plummet in value as dramatically as they have risen over the past thirty years?

There is one further category of investment shelter that warrants a brief comment—Certificates of Deposit in Eurodollars, which can be purchased through one of the large banks or brokerage houses in New York. They come in short-term (one year or less) and medium-term (eighteen months to five years) maturities, and are chiefly traded and held in London. They pay interest rates, free of English taxes, that usually range from ⅛ to ½ percent higher than CD's of comparable quality in the United States. But although they can be bought in denominations as low as $25,000 for the short-term and $10,000 for the medium-term maturities, the normal trading amount is $1 million and multiples thereof. Which means that they are bought primarily by corporation treasurers looking for an outlet for temporarily idle funds.

How old are you?

To a large extent, your investment requirements depend upon your age. If you are well beyond middle age, perhaps retired, then income is probably your immediate need, and you may not have time or temperament to speculate in an inflation hedge. For anything you do with your money is speculation, whether you put it in the savings bank or try to hedge. And if you are old, perhaps the best investments, at least temporarily, are the ninety-day Treasury bills or Certificates of Deposit. Or, for the longer term, the various kinds of bonds I have mentioned—convertibles, tax-exempts, bonds selling below par.

Whereas if you are young or in your prime, and have a good many earning years ahead of you, the best advice I can give is to invest in mutual funds, real estate or convertible bonds, tend to your business and not worry. Your income will go up if the inflation continues. And worry won't stop the inflation. While, if everyone tends to his or her own business, it is the best way out of an economic slump.

Caveat emptor

But I must warn you, if you are thinking of taking my advice seriously, that the only time I have ever been emphatically correct in my analysis of economic trends was from March 1933 until well into Roosevelt's first term. And then I cashed in on most of my gains and invested "conservatively" in bonds. The conservative approach was a mistake; I should never have sold my common stocks.

And during that period, as manager of the international securities division of the largest investment advisory concern in the world, although I did pretty well for our clients as a whole, my outstanding successes were the result of luck—pure chance. Such as a fortuitous meeting with Hjalmar Horace Greeley Schacht, to whom I took an instant and—as it later proved—well-founded dislike. And learned, perhaps through a slip of a member of his staff, that Schacht intended as part of his German economic recovery program to have the German states and municipalities buy up their defaulted bonds bit by bit at bargain prices—20 cents to 40 cents on the dollar—instead of using the money to pay the interest that was due to the bondholders. So every time the bonds slumped—and I watched the market closely—I advised our clients to buy, and every time the bonds went up 15 or 20 points I advised them to sell.

And there were other instances where luck, not expertise, paid off well for our clientele. As I am no longer in the investment advisory business, my present lack of expertise is phenomenal. So if you rely on my investment hints—well, maybe you had better just toss a coin.

One good rule, however, is never to buy for investment anything that is being touted by a promoter—and that applies to stocks and mutual funds and real estate and commodity futures, as well as to the bright-minted gold and silver coins, medals and toy-size ingots so copiously advertised by private mints in recent years. For remember that the promoter is not burning with an altruistic desire to make you a wealthy man or woman, but is trying to make a tidy fortune for himself in an untidy world. And the owner of the mint is hoping that you'll be the lamb.

At every period in economic history that there has been a dramatic boom in prices, whether of Dutch tulip bulbs, Florida or other ocean-front real estate, gold, silver or commodity futures, there has been a promoter ready—after the bloom of the boom has faded—to exploit the suckers. So why succor the exploiters?

But, truly, for advice on what you should do to protect yourself against inflation, you should not consult me or even your most trusted banker or broker, but a shrewd and honest speculator such as Bernard Baruch. Wise, farseeing, this remarkable old man lived to be the trusted adviser of five presidents, the recipient of many confidences, yet he kept his secrets to himself. And though he went on and on for over ninety years, no one ever had occasion to refer to him as "the babbling Baruch." If you can find your own modern-day Baruch as an adviser, you are fortunate.

And perhaps the best way for you to beat inflation is to spend only the same amount of money on food that you spent in 1975. It not only will help you to lick inflation but will do wonders for your waistline.

18. The Impossible Dream

There is probably no defect in the world's economic
organization more serious than the fact that we use
as our unit of value, not a thing with a fixed value,
but a fixed weight of gold with a widely varying value.

Edwin Walter Kemmerer (1927)

In line with Professor Kemmerer's comment, there is indeed a potential
solution for the present problem, but it is a long-term solution and one that
must be preceded by the measures suggested in Chapters 15 and 16.

It is a solution that might perhaps not prevent, but would at least
make much less likely, a recurrence of the unfortunate events of the past—
the succession of wild booms and slumps that has marked the economic
progress of this nation and of other countries far less fortunate than our
own.

But it is a solution that, I must warn you, would shock practically
every banking friend that I have to the marrow of his bones, and would
make some of my economist friends think that I had taken leave of my
senses.*

So take it or leave it—it is a solution not likely to be adopted
unless the whole world is driven to it by an economic disaster of such
magnitude as we have fortunately never experienced. Or unless the central
banks and economists of the world are illumined by an angel of light
descended from heaven.

---

*A skeptical reader might wonder whether I could possibly have any economist
friends left after all my unkind comments on their views. The answer is that I
sincerely trust I do, for I have only the highest regard for them and for their
erudition in economic matters, save only with respect to what I regard as the
Keynesian aberration. And economists—the best of them, not the mediocrities
who are found in all professions—are like lawyers who may strive mightily in court
and then eat and drink as friends and colleagues.

246

Which is perhaps why this solution is advocated by me, not as an economist, but as a lawyer. For you have never heard of an economist or a central banker—or an accountant, for that matter—who was a saint. Yet I can name for you *twenty* lawyers who were saints, and *ten* more who were beatified although not canonized, including such well-known members of the saintly brotherhood and legal profession as St. Ambrose, St. Ives, St. John Capistrano and St. Thomas More.

So, from that beatific height, as a *brother-in-law* of those saintly eminences, I venture to propose—A STABLE DOLLAR!

The "Stable Dollar"

Such a proposal was first conceived by Naval Academy mathematician Simon Newcomb in 1879; enthusiastically advocated fifty-five years ago by Irving Fisher of Yale; recommended by E. W. Kemmerer of Princeton; then was taken up by Professors George Warren and Frank Pierson of Cornell and, under their influence, was converted into law by Franklin Delano Roosevelt.

Very few people understood then, or realize now, that this was the purpose of the amendment to the Agricultural Adjustment Act of 1933, drafted under Professor Warren's guidance, which gave the President the power, "By proclamation to fix the weight of the gold dollar . . . at such amounts as he finds necessary from his investigation *to stabilize domestic prices* or to protect the foreign commerce against the adverse effects of depreciated foreign currencies. . . . . "

And, in a radio address on May 7, 1933, President Roosevelt announced:

> The Administration has the definite objective of raising commodity prices to such an extent that those who have borrowed money will, on the average, be able to repay that money in the same kind of dollar which they borrowed. We do not seek to let them get such a cheap dollar that, in effect, they will be able to pay back a great deal less than they borrowed. In other words, we seek to correct a wrong and not to create another wrong in the opposite direction.

Later, on July 3, 1933, in a message to Cordell Hull at the World Economic Conference in London, the President stated:

> Let me be frank in saying that the United States seeks the kind of dollar which a generation hence will have the same purchasing and debt-paying power as the dollar we hope to attain in the near future. That objective means more to the good of other nations than a fixed ratio . . . in terms of the pound or franc.

And in a radio address to the nation on October 22, 1933, the President outlined at length his monetary policy, and emphasized:

> *When we have restored the price level, we shall seek to establish and maintain a dollar which will not change its purchasing and debt-paying power during the succeeding generation. . . .*
>
> *My aim in taking this step is to establish and maintain continuous control. This is a policy and not an expedient. It is not to be used merely to offset a temporary fall in prices. We are thus continuing to move toward a managed currency.*

And this aim, almost universally ignored in this country, was approved by such conservative journals in London as *The Statist* and the *Monthly Reviews* of Lloyd's Bank and the Midland Bank. And it was supported by two of the outstanding bankers of the world—Reginald McKenna, chairman of the Midland Bank, and Russell Leffingwell, a partner of J. P. Morgan & Company.

Success of the plan

Furthermore, the plan worked. Within six months, the 41 percent devaluation of the dollar brought farm and other basic commodity prices back from the catastrophically low levels of 1930–32 to more reasonable levels, where farmers could again make payments on their mortgages, and mining companies resume payment on their defaulted bonds.

We have never had such a surge of recovery in this country either before or since those halcyon days of the early New Deal. It worked magnificently, and for the reasons I have analyzed in Chapter 10, and more fully in the studies referred to in that chapter. And the explanation of its success—the mechanics of money and prices—shows that, by altering the gold value of the dollar up or down, week by week or month by month, the dollar price index for the major basic commodities can be altered at will—*or permanently stabilized.* And that other prices, and the cost of living, can be kept more stable than they have ever been before, because of the importance of these major basic commodities in the economy and in the price and living cost indexes.

But, after reaching his goal of boosting prices, the President abandoned the objective of a dollar of a permanently stable purchasing power, under the influence of his left-wing or "liberal" brain trust (Tugwell, Berle, Wallace, Hopkins) and of conservative bankers, but particularly under the advice of right-wingers such as Moley and Farley, the latter warning him of the difficulty of raising campaign funds if he persisted in "tinkering with the dollar." So, instead, he once again *stabilized* the gold content of the dollar, but at a 41 percent lower level. Thus putting us back on a fixed gold standard which, at so many times in our history, has led us up and down the roller coaster of inflation and slump, of boom and bust. But at least a fixed gold standard was better than no standard at all, as we have today with nothing but fiat money.

To cap it all, after having been elected following a campaign in which he warned us that too many liberal governments of the past had been wrecked on the shoals of unbalanced budgets and unsound finance, he embarked on the ill-fated National Recovery Act and a series of New Deal measures that over the course of years have brought our federal budget up from a little over $3 billion to its present dizzy $629 billion height. And that was the beginning of all our misery, as the young lady said in the song, after she had "jumped into bed just to keep that sailor warm."

My own monetary platform

What I am advocating, then, is a return to the announced goals and methods of Franklin Delano Roosevelt in order that this nation may at all times have a dollar of reasonably constant purchasing power.

It can be done, as has been proved. But it can only be done if we return to a gold standard, where anyone can freely buy, sell, hold, hoard, import or export gold at any time and with no restrictions. That would certainly pull the rug out from under the feet of the gold speculators of London, Zurich and other points.

But the price of gold in terms of dollars would be changed from week to week or month to month in order to keep the index of basic, internationally traded commodities stable. Because such commodities are the only ones that are directly responsive to monetary measures (see Chapter 10).

With a "stable dollar" thus defined in terms of the major primary products, consumer prices might fluctuate to some extent—there is no way in which money management can prevent that. But the fluctuations would be far less disruptive than at present. Food prices would be practically stable except for seasonal differences and the normal fluctuations attributable to good or poor crops for particular products. Prices for machine-manufactured goods would be reasonably stable, some prices going up and others down, depending upon whether or not innovation, invention and productivity in the particular industry outstrip labor's demands for higher wages. Prices for handcrafted goods would, in general, rise to the point where the domestic product would be increasingly replaced by imports.

And the cost of services would undoubtedly continue to rise until many of us are forced to dispense with such services. The average household would do without a butler, a cook, a waitress, a nanny, an upstairs and downstairs maid and a tweenie, and, in more elegant establishments . . . Well, you get the idea—most of us would cut our own hair, shine our own shoes, do the cooking, laundry and household chores, and, if we are lucky, we would have the help of a sleep-out or once-a-week maid.

But, all in all, the cost of living would remain reasonably stable, certainly much more stable than if the major basic commodities were allowed to fluctuate as they have always done in the past. Because these commodities enter into the production of practically all the goods in the general index as well as directly into the index itself.

With such a plan, an "incomes policy" would also be desirable and, even though it might take years or even decades to work out, with capital and labor lying down together like the lion and the lamb before the fall, it would be worth the effort.

But I do not deceive myself into believing that a stable currency will prove *politically* feasible—certainly not immediately. And I am not even sure that it would be *desirable* unless it could be worked out as part of an international monetary agreement so that the *international* index of prices for primary products could be managed by an international body, free from political interference. And, so far as I know, the International Monetary Fund is adamantly opposed to "tinkering with the dollar," as Roosevelt's enemies used to call it.

If, however, some future Governing Board of the IMF—or some smaller but more effective international agency set up to replace the present unwieldy 138-member hodgepodge—decides to establish a truly stable international monetary unit based on a world index of basic commodity prices, and wholly divorced from foreign aid or other political or eleemosynary purposes, then in that case the $200 billion or more of SDR-denominated international reserve assets could well be used to that end. But this does not seem to be in the cards at the present writing.

Regard this chapter, then, not as expounding something that I am seriously advocating at the present time, but as one additional insight into the role of money, thus bringing to its conclusion this discussion of inflation, money and prices. It is a possibility, not a probability.

But it is manifest that a dollar of reasonably constant purchasing power, year after year, would remove much of the pressure behind runaway wages and soaring government budgets to meet rising living costs. It would have manifold advantages over the present system, just as constant measures of weight and length and volume are infinitely to be preferred to the varying standards of the past.

But although a constant dollar would ensure the value of our savings and insurance and pensions and remove one cause of labor unrest, as well as promote the stability of all business and contractual relationships, it is no guaranty of the millennium. There might still be future Vietnams, and crime on the streets, and people who expect the government to save them from the consequences of their own improvidence.

19. Conclusions

Inflation is our domestic Public Enemy Number
One. A Government big enough to give you everything
you want is a Government big enough to take from
you everything you have.

Gerald E. Ford, Jr. (1974)

President Ford was so right—so categorically right—in what he said that it is hard to understand why his administration should have been so wrong—so categorically wrong—in its program for overcoming inflation and recession. Yet he allowed himself to be gulled and beguiled into taking the easy course of spending ourselves into bankruptcy against his deepest convictions as to what is right and what is wrong. The kindest thing that can be said of the Ford program was expressed by his friend, George Meany: "Weird!"

The 1974 anti-inflation program

The program proposed a $16 billion tax cut, a $52 billion deficit in the 1975–76 fiscal year, and $93 billion more of government and agency borrowing in 1975. It was a program that was a sure prescription for more inflation with further recession in its wake. A program that looked forward to six more years of 5½ percent or higher unemployment and 4 percent or more cumulative inflation!

Except that, of course, six-year projections of unemployment and inflation, and of gross national product, personal income and corporate profits, are utterly absurd—the most noisome garbage ever spewed out of the maw of a berserk computer.

Not that the proposals emanating from Congress were any less weird or would have proven any less disastrous in their consequences. Quite the contrary, for by the time Congress got through with the administration budget, the actual deficit was over $66 billion rather than $52 billion, plus at least double the $24 billion proposed for the nonbudgetary

252

agencies. And the inflation and consequent recession following the congressional amendments—Congress had no program of its own—proved even more disastrous and overwhelming than the presidential program.

So far as the Carter program during the first twenty-two months of his administration is concerned, the less said the better. But, if any attempt had been made to carry out the President's $1.5 trillion of campaign promises, this country would have had a far worse inflation than that of the Truman era depicted in Chart 4.

Yet, surprising as it may seem, none of our Presidents or Congresses are to be faulted for their preposterous proposals. For they are the victims of an almost unanimous consensus of the professional and therefore presumably "expert" economic opinion in this country, with the "liberal" economists on the Joint Economic Committee of Congress demanding even more spending and greater budget deficits than the more "conservative" economists of the Federal Reserve System and the President's Council of Economic Advisers.

Both sides have been befuddled and bedazzled by Keynesian economics and Phillips curves even though such theories have been wholly discredited by the actual course of events wherever they have been applied. And, even more alarmingly, both sets of advisers seem to be completely blind to the fact that—with our total abandonment of the gold standard and the government unbalancing our balance of payments to the tune of $21 to $25 billion a year and our gold and foreign exchange reserves at least $275 billion in the red, perhaps $800 billion—we are internationally bankrupt, with the dollar a paper fiat currency no sounder than the French *assignats* of 1789 or the German Reichsmarks of 1923 or the American Continentals of 1776.

One would have thought that a breakthrough might have been made under the previous administration, for never before or since in the history of this country has so able a body of economic advisers been assembled to counsel the President on the economic problems confronting the nation: the Secretary of the Treasury, William A. Simon, an exceptionally brilliant and successful financier; President Ford's closest personal adviser, L. William Seidman, a highly intelligent, prosperous and worldly-wise accountant; the chairman of the Council of Economic Advisers, Alan Greenspan, a practicing economic consultant and a star pupil of the late Willford I. King (who would certainly have objected vociferously to the present deficit financing and printing-press money); the esteemed chairman of the Fed, Dr. Arthur Burns, a former professor of economics; and, as a frequent outside consultant, Dr. Paul McCracken, former chairman of the Council of Economic Advisers and certainly one of the ablest of the eleven economists who have headed that body since its inception in 1946.

Yet these professors of economics and businessmen, for all their learning, were amateurs all, seemingly ignorant of the facts of international finance and of what has taken place in other nations of the world—in Latin America, in Germany, France, Brazil and other countries that have confronted or failed to confront the problems of inflation. Ignorant too of the methods used by Kemmerer, Schacht, Erhard, Rueff and others in conquering inflation "overnight" and bringing about the instantaneous "miracle of stabilization." Dr. Burns, indoctrinated as were the others in the fallacies of Keynesian economics and the Phillips curve—the false theory of the necessary "trade-off" between inflation and unemployment—was such a novice in the world of international finance that, as previously pointed out, he thought the current phenomenon of high unemployment coupled with high inflation was "unprecedented" and he coined or used a new term to describe it: "stagflation."

The ex-chairman of the Council of Economic Advisers, after his pet economic theories and his espoused program of gradual step-by-step recovery failed to work under President Nixon, blithely commented in the *Journal of the American Economic Association* that "it's back-to-the-drafting-board again." Certainly a merry way of looking at a multibillion-dollar disaster brought upon his fellow citizens, thanks in part to his economic advice.

So we are forced to conclude that all the weapons for combating inflation wielded by President Ford's prestigious body of economic counselors proved in the end to be as worthless as a bladeless knife without a handle.

It seems most strange that Congress and the administration—men of intelligence who would not dream of submitting to an appendectomy by a doctor who had never performed an operation—should have entrusted a much more delicate operation on the anatomy of the nation to doctors of economics who had never rescued a country from uncontrolled inflation nor succeeded in lifting it out of the depths of a depression, and were totally inexperienced in the experience of other nations of the world.

It is hoped that the present administration will be more successful. For although President Carter's team of economic consultants falls short of President Ford's in prestige, the President himself is a shrewd and successful businessman with a businessman's skepticism of government controls and intervention in the economy. And his newly appointed chairman of the Fed, likewise with a successful business background, may turn out to be a person of the same frame of mind. Unfortunately, even after two years in office, they are both too new on the job to have penetrated the mysteries of bikini accounting in budgets and the balance of payments, but, when and if they do, the President may reach the conclusion that the welfare advocate "is a liar and the truth is not in him," as I have heretofore pointed out. Thereupon abandoning all the ill-informed promises of the 1976 campaign, and setting forth to straighten out the nation's problems of inflation, stagnation and unemployment in the only way they can be straightened out, as shown by Kemmerer, Schacht et al.

For there can be no doubt that a President who has shown the courage, determination and persistence to convene and bring to a successful conclusion the Egyptian-Israeli conferences at Camp David and Washington, with the still-flickering hope of peace on earth to men of goodwill, will have the courage and determination to carry out the measures necessary to put an immediate stop to the continuing debasement of the dollar, even though it will mean the repudiation of all his campaign promises and of most of the economic measures thus far enacted under his administration. Provided, of course, that he is convinced that such action is both essential and inescapable if the general welfare of the nation is to be preserved.

Let's get the facts

Yet I repeat that neither the Congress nor the administration, past or present, is to be blamed for what has happened. *For they simply do not have the facts.* They have been self-deceived by the government's bikini accounting that seems to reveal everything but conceals the essential, as I have iterated throughout the book. And I am certain that if the members of Congress and the administration realized how *desperate* the situation really is, they would have the courage to do what is needed regardless of political expediency.

I have been using the term "bikini accounting." Some would call it—quite unfairly—"crooked accounting," for it is certainly misleading the public and the Congress to misstate the balance of payment figures by billions of dollars each year; to speak of budgets, deficits and debt ceilings and omit the expenditures of federal agencies, including the Postal System, as well as the losses of "government-sponsored" institutions and government guaranties; to conceal the desperate foreign exchange position of the dollar; and to cease publishing the budget accounts in the traditional way when the figures become too ghastly to admit. Or to change the statistical methods so that, for example, the GNP figures released in November 1977 and later showed a growth rate of 4.7 percent instead of the 3.8 percent that would have been shown by using the old method, and to report partial "producer prices" instead of the traditional all-commodity wholesale price index so as to minimize the actual rise in prices by 20 percentage points.

I am under no illusions that I myself have all the facts, for it is impossible for any one man, not now in the government, to ferret out the truth from reports whose prime purpose is seemingly to conceal it. But I have at least pointed out some of the more serious fields of falsehood, and the figures I have given are certainly more revealing than those the government has given to the press and public.

There can be no more urgent task for the President's advisers than to subject the present set of accounts to the most intensive audit and analysis possible—an audit that should not be made by unrepentent Keynesian economists or persons who believe that the bigger a government is and the more it spends, the better. Nor by bureaucrats or former heads of HEW or AID or some other alphabetized agency of government—persons who have a vested interest in defending their own actions and in denying that they have betrayed a public trust by squandering the taxpayers' money.

Immediate recovery is possible

This audit should be published, and all the facts made available to the administration, the Congress and the public so that the nation may be made aware of how desperate our situation is—internationally as well as domestically—and hence prepared to take the heroic measures that *must* be taken when the present deficit spending program fails, as it is bound to do.

And we can then embark on a true anti-inflationary and anti-recessionary program. A program not necessarily identical to that presented in Chapters 15 and 16, but embracing the two essentials of a genuine balance in government spending at home and abroad. A program such as those that have proved *instantaneously* effective—with no bullet-biting, austerity or sacrifices—*in every country* that has dared to face the problem squarely and courageously.

If it *must* be done, it *can* be done! Which is why I say, *Don't sell this country short!*

But how can I be so certain that such a program would be *immediately effective*—effective quickly enough so as to make all the emergency welfare schemes superfluous? When practical politicians, journalists and newscasters—the wisest of our leaders—keep on insisting that we must not expect any miracles, that it takes years to reverse an inflationary and recessionary trend. And when this popular wisdom has been parroted and pontificated so often that it seems to have the ring of truth.

It is not lack of wisdom in our leaders and their advisers that makes them skeptical of instant cures, but simply that their vision is not wide enough, and their memories do not go back far enough, to encompass at first hand the *"miracles"* that actually took place in Germany in 1923–24, and in five countries of South America between 1922 and 1928.

For so powerful is the prevailing cult of youth—a very fine cult, indeed, I must admit when I recall with delight those brilliant young graduate students whom I met at Harvard and Michigan—that people forget the importance of experience: "The devil knows more because he is old than because he is the devil!" as José Hernández writes in *La Vuelta de Martin Fierro ("El diablo sabe por diablo pero más sabe por viejo").*

As John Dickinson warned at the Constitutional Convention in 1787: "Experience must be our only guide, as reason may mislead us."

And experience in every one of the nine countries cited in Chapter 7 shows that if the government truly balances its budget and ceases to spend overseas in excess of the capabilities of the balance of payments, inflation and recession will stop *immediately*. Why should the United States prove an exception?

To the contrary, this country with its unrivaled resources would achieve the "miracle of stabilization" more certainly, more dramatically, than any other country in the world.

The Keynesian years

Less than a month after President Carter launched his wage and price program, a fortnight after he arranged to borrow $30 billion to save the dollar from going down the drain, his newly appointed anti-inflation administrator, Professor Alfred E. Kahn, declared that, if the "voluntary" plan fails to stop inflation, the only alternatives would be mandatory controls or a depression. And he added, quite correctly, "mandatory controls won't work."

This is the conventional wisdom of the times, that the only way to stop inflation is to have a depression, or a recession, or a "cooling down" of the economy—differences in terminology, pure semantics, as no two people are in agreement as to just how bad a slump must be to earn the most depressing nomenclature. This is the wisdom that is accepted by the majority of economics professors and has been embraced by the members of the Federal Reserve Board who are engaged in paving the way for depression and disaster with the highest discount rates since the Federal Reserve System was established.

It seems amazing that the persons who have guided, and are now guiding, our economic destiny should wear blinders that so completely obscure their peripheral vision that they fail to see that there is indeed a third and proven alternative—the alternative chosen by Kemmerer and Schacht long before the present crop of "experts" were old enough to remember, and by Erhard, Röpke, Rueff, Ikeda and others in this generation.

There is only one explanation that occurs to me to account for this incredible myopia in men of such indubitable intelligence—and I am thinking not only of President Carter's present advisers but of President Ford's closest counselor, one of the most intelligent men I have ever met, who exclaimed that "there would be rioting in the streets" if the government cut its welfare programs, and of President Nixon's chief economic adviser, who is beyond doubt one of the soundest, most practical economists in university circles today, but who had to "go back to the drafting board again" when all his pet nostrums ended in failure. And that explanation must be that these gentlemen have simply discarded, have refused even to consider the possibility, the *necessity* of the government reducing its expenditures at home and abroad, not by a mere 10 or 20 percent, but by at least 50 percent, so as to remove the government *and all its agencies* completely out of the money and capital markets, immediately and definitively.

And they must have discarded this approach, partly because they are too young to remember Schacht and Kemmerer, partly because they are too conditioned by years of indoctrination in Keynesian doctrine, but chiefly, it would seem, because they have regarded it as their duty not to propose any plan that, on purely pragmatic grounds, they regarded as impractical. And that should be a political judgment, a policy decision to be made by politicians, as I have said before, and not by economic advisers whose duty it is to advise what ought to be done, what *must* be done, leaving it to the President to decide whether it *can* be done, and *how* to do it.

The instantaneous "miracle of stabilization" is, as Dr. Röpke has said, "no miracle at all, if the essence of the [German] reform of 1948 is clearly understood. . . . The real miracle lay in the fact that . . . in a world still under the spell of inflationism and collectivism, it proved possible politically and socially to return to the economic reason of the market economy and to monetary discipline."

There can be no doubt that President Carter (and the same was true of his predecessor) is capable of engineering that miracle, and would be eager to do so if only his economic counselors had refrained from exercising a policy judgment and had advised him that the Schacht-Kemmerer approach *must* be followed and that it *will* work.

Let me quote here from Gerald Ford's Farewell Address, which, although written, was unfortunately never delivered:

> *Government has spent too much time and far too much money answering the demands of pressure groups, at the expense of the individual. In our complex and collectivized society, the individual—the forgotten American—has been shunted aside, his wants unmet, his goals unfulfilled. . . .*
>
> *If we are to avoid economic collapse, we must stop the runaway growth of government. We must stop living beyond our means, as too many of our political leaders irresponsibly give in to demands for more and more spending—without concern for the future. . . .*
>
> *It is time for the American people to look their government straight in the eye and say, "No more! We will make the decisions about our lives. You protect us from foreign aggressors and domestic criminals and give us a stable currency and courts of law, and we'll do the rest."*

If ever President Carter (or his successor in the Presidency) resolves to do what, in his innermost convictions, he knows must be done, putting aside the claudicating counsel of his economic advisers and embarking on a Kemmerer-Schacht-Erhard program of sound monetary, budgetary and free-market policy, this country will witness an immediate "miracle" of monetary stabilization and economic recovery dwarfing in magnitude the miracles that occurred in the eleven instances cited in this book.

And the American achievement will almost certainly be followed by England, thus paving the way for a renaissance of prosperity throughout the free world such as has not been witnessed by any generation now living.

And the past four decades of "inflationism and collectivism" will thereafter be known as the years of the Keynesian aberration, and economists will truly have to "go back to the drafting board" to relearn all that they have mislearned and mistaught over the past forty years.

No acceptable alternative

If we fail to put a stop to government spending, if Congress and the administration think they can disregard the constitutional limitations on federal power, and spend and spend, tax and tax, borrow and borrow for undertakings that are "reserved to the States respectively, or to the People," then we are surely on the long, slow road to national decay. We shall follow in the footsteps of England, which, since the inception of the dole and the national health insurance and other welfare schemes, has deteriorated into a fifth-rate power economically, after Russia, Germany, Japan and the United States, with the Arab states and China looming on the horizon. Yet England in its heyday was certainly one of the greatest civilizations the world has ever known, and is still preeminent in its system of law and institutions, its intellectual achievements, and in the charm of its cities and countryside, its literature and its people.

The Spenglerian decline of American civilization is just as inevitable if we fail to heed the warning given by England's experience and that of the inflation-ridden countries of South America, and if we fail to profit by the examples of Germany, Japan, Switzerland, France and other countries that realize the folly of expecting the government to give us everything we want—*a government big enough to take from us everything we have.*

And on this note, we conclude our study of *What's Behind Inflation and How to Beat It,* trusting that we have succeeded in our objective of explaining the subject with the clarity demanded by the precept of St. Augustine quoted in the opening chapter.

Index